NASTY WOMEN PROJECT

NASTY WOMEN PROJECT

Voices from the Resistance

Edited by ERIN PASSONS

gatekeeper press

Published by Gatekeeper Press
3971 Hoover Rd. Suite 77
Columbus, OH 43123-2839

www.GatekeeperPress.com

Logo and Cover Design: Caryn West
Statue of Liberty photo credit: Tom Reese / wowography.com,
Pink Hat photo credit: Lacey Monet Carroll
Editor photo credit: Tyler Kapper

ISBN: 9781619846456
ISBN: 9781619846463
eISBN: 9781619846470

Library of Congress Control Number: 2017933590

Printed in the United States of America

*For my children, London and Kaya, and the generations
of nasty women and bad hombres to come.*

*May your voices rise together,
May your voices be strong and clear,
May your voices be brave and truthful,
May your voices speak without fear.*

Contents

Introduction

Let's send one another friend requests to drown out the Trump supporters from our feed.

I FORGET THE LIBERAL women's group where the comment was posted, or who had posted it. I do remember commenting, *I'm in,* before refocusing my attention on Wolf Blitzer and the map of America, where blistery red dots like cold sores spread from coast to coast. After Trump won Florida, I gave up. I sent out one last tweet—*See if we warn you next time there's a hurricane, assholes!*—and marched off to bed.

The next morning, I shot an email to my work: *can't come in, jumping off the Congress bridge,* and spent the day sprawled out on the couch in my pajamas, sobbing into a bag of strawberry licorice, while furiously reading and commenting on social media posts written by my five hundred new friends. The posts ranged from the ultra-depressed to the inconsolably angry, but there were funny moments too. We refused to say his name, so we came up with nicknames. *Prima Donald. Twittler. The Angry Cheeto. Vanilla Isis.* The list went on.

The next morning, I begrudgingly returned to work, walking directly over to my friend Kerry the moment I arrived. The night of the election, we had texted back and forth, each text more solemn than the last, until both ends went silent. I hadn't heard from her since.

"I had dinner with a Trump supporter last night," Kerry said upon seeing me.

My mouth dropped to the floor. "You what?" I asked.

"I had dinner with a Trump supporter, and he explained why he voted for Trump. . . ."

Kerry went on, but I had stopped listening, my mind too busy imagining my gorgeous, intelligent friend (who happened to be African American) forced at gunpoint to share dinner with some outdated cowboy relic from *Hee-Haw*.

". . . and he said if I had expressed to him my concerns before the election, he wouldn't have voted for Trump. So that got me thinking—maybe the silver lining in all of this is that it opens a dialogue."

I snapped back to reality. "A what?"

Kerry nodded. "People of different races, religions, beliefs— we all have a common enemy now. We must unite, but before we unite, we have to educate ourselves on the plights of those most affected by Trump's administration, and turn their cause into our cause. The darkness inspired by Trump will only bring forth more light. That's the silver lining in this."

Outraged, I came home that night and logged onto social media. "Can you believe what my coworker said . . ."

I posted and waited for the confirmations to start pouring in. *The nerve of her! What was she thinking? There's no silver lining!*

Instead, the first comment I received was *she has a point.* Followed by *yeah, she's right.* Followed by dozens of other similar comments.

That's when I started hearing terms I'd never heard before: *white feminist, intersectional feminism, ableist, cissexism.*

I shut up and learned.

As the days wore on, my social media world expanded. Stories of discrimination flooded my wall. One friend had found a note on her car: *I hope your marriage is reversed and you both burn in hell.* Another friend who owned a health food store posted about an interracial couple walking in and asking if it was okay for them to shop there. Another friend posted about her coworker, a Vietnamese immigrant, crying in her arms, scared her two elementary-aged children would be sent back to a country they barely know.

I went to bed at night with their stories in my head—nightmares of deportations, angry graffiti scrawl, and restless mobs of white-hooded men marching the streets bearing iron crosses.

Then, on November 28, my fear reached a whole new high. *Politico* released an article: "GOP eyes best chance in years to defund Planned Parenthood." "With Trump in the White House next year, conservatives say it's just a matter of time before a defunding bill becomes law," the article read. "Eliminating Planned Parenthood's approximately $550 million in federal funding" means "low-income women in Medicaid wouldn't be able to go to Planned Parenthood for cancer screenings, contraception or other health services unrelated to abortion."

I posted a link to the article and added, almost as an afterthought, *We should put our stories in a book and donate the proceeds to Planned Parenthood.*

One friend responded immediately, *Great idea, but who has experience writing a book?*

I do, I thought.

And so the Nasty Women Project was born.

I called for submissions from women of all fifty states with all different backgrounds. Women of color. Women from the LBGTQ community. Single mothers and mothers of children with special needs. Domestic abuse survivors and survivors of sexual trauma. *Give me your courage, your strength, your paragraphs of truth yearning to be free.*

Submissions flooded my inbox from all over the country—many from California, Texas, and the battleground states. It was easier to find writers in some states than in others. Floridians, still bitter over my election night tweet, wanted an apology before agreeing to contribute (which I humbly gave). The Dakotas and Nebraska are still not counted for, but hey, if you're out there, we're already eyeing stories for volume 2. Join us!

With every story I had the privilege to read, my faith in the project grew. These women, for the most part, did not live public lives. They were women you met in grocery stores, at airports, in train stations, with whom you may exchange a moment of pleasant conversation before going about your day, never giving them a second thought. And yet, their lives held no shortage of tragedy and triumph. They were America's unsung heroes; as mothers, daughters, educators, scientists, artists, and companions, they were the invisible hands guiding our country into a better tomorrow.

The full potential impact of our project didn't hit me until a few days ago, when I received a card from one of the contributors. The card simply read *Thank you*, but that was enough. My knees buckled to the floor, tears flowing like a stream from a faucet. This contributor was from Ohio. She had been raped as a teenager, but had never told anyone because she didn't think they would listen. Thanks to our project, now they will.

That's what this book is really about: giving women the opportunity to share their voices, and by doing so, encouraging other women to do the same.

The stories of the Nasty Women Project deserve to be heard now more than ever. Storytelling leads to activism and unity, which are our best defenses against the oppressive, tyrannical agenda perpetuated by the Trump administration. When my friend told me that the darkness inspired by Trump's presidency would only bring forth more light, I didn't believe her at first, but now I do. I hope after reading our stories, you will believe too.

—Erin Passons
Austin, Texas
February 3, 2017

Content warning: this book contains accounts—at times, harrowing—of verbal, emotional, and sexual abuse and harassment; violence; sexism; sexual assault; racism; ableism; homophobia; and more, which may be triggering, obscene, or offensive for some readers.

United-States-based resources:

National Sexual Assault Hotline: 1(800) 656-4673

National Domestic Violence Hotline: 1(800) 799-7233

Trevor Project Lifeline: 1(866) 488-7386

Childhelp National Child Abuse Hotline: 1(800) 422-4453

National Suicide Prevention Lifeline: 1(800) 273-8255

Northeast

*If every life is a river, then it's little wonder that we do not
even notice the changes that occur until we are far out in
the darkest sea.*

—Alice Hoffman[1]

---

1   Hoffman, Alice. Incantation. New York: Little, Brown, 2006.

Afro Bo Peep, age 39
Educator, author, and part-time poet
Philadelphia, Pennsylvania

America: An Obituary

WHEN PRESIDENT OBAMA won, I took it very personally. The fact that this Black man was elected president, manifested such an exhilarating and incredible victory—it permeated to my very soul, and I felt such pride and joy for our country. What an amazing place you were, America: welcoming and full of hope. Here, it didn't matter what your religion or race, or color was, because everyone here had a shot at the American dream. Even though you had your problems, you were so progressive. You were so progressive that in my lifetime, in my 92-year-old grandmother's lifetime, in my 102-year-old great-aunt's lifetime, a Black man got to be president.

Today, my post-Election-Day feelings are very different. Hope has been replaced with hurt. Joy has been jilted. Pride is now pain. I didn't expect to take this election so personally. Yet, as I sit here writing, heartbroken, with tears streaming down my face, I am in mourning of the end of the hope and progress I felt eight short years ago when people unified and banded together to elect our departing president.

Today, on my third wedding anniversary, I am grieving. I grieve for suffragettes like Ida B. Wells, Alice Paul, Sojourner Truth, Elizabeth Cady Stanton, and Margaret Sanger—women who fought for women to be valued, respected, and counted in this country. Yesterday, November 8, 2016, America chose a man who probably knows little of their sacrifices and certainly in his actions and his comments, he doesn't respect women in this nation who represent the suffragette legacy. I grieve for Muslims, Hispanics, African Americans, the LGBTQ community, and people of color, because we learned yesterday just how much we don't matter. Around the world, people are either grieving with me or laughing at us today.

My dear America, how I loved you. How I had such high hopes for the inclusive, progressive nation you could be. I had no idea how much hate and discord you had in your heart. I had no idea *this* was what you wanted to be, but since a man was elected who "tells it like it is," I'm going to follow his example: Bigoted, racist, fear-mongering white America destroyed our country. Third-party-voters who couldn't put country before their personal hippie pride helped destroy our country. Complacent eligible voters who abstained from voting because "I don't like either candidate"—also provided a deadly assist. You are the collective of assassins responsible for slaughtering the America of hope and progress, but I take comfort in two things.

First, I take comfort in karma's sweet 'uppance of whatever happens next, whatever misery may come as a result of your being duped. Each of you shall feel whatever sizable portion you deserve.

Second, to those of us in mourning today—we will remember all the great things this country represents. We must hold on to our goodness and hope. We cannot live our lives in anger and fear. Now more than ever, we must unite, love, and protect one another in order to resurrect the sentiments that lifted America, lifted us all, those eight years ago.

"Beloved, let us love one another, for love is of God, and everyone who loves is born of God and knows God. . . . There is no fear in love; but perfect love casts out fear."—*1 John 4:7,18a*[2]

---

2   Scripture taken from the New King James Version˙. Copyright © 1982 by Thomas Nelson.

S.A. Williams, age 41
Librarian
Massachusetts

Rising

"As we go marching, marching, we're standing proud and tall. The rising of the women means the rising of us all."[3]

I DON SUFFRAGETTE WHITE.
Just like I have for each Laurel Parade. Just like Hillary at the convention and again in the last debate. For my alma mater Mount Holyoke College, the longest continuing women's college in the United States. For my fellow alumnae and all my fellow Seven Sisters graduates. For women rising.

For ten-year-old me, standing on a city street, red-faced from embarrassment and confusion as middle-aged men hurl catcalls at me.

A seed planted. My body is the enemy.

For eleven-year-old me, holding back tears and wishing the

---

3 James Oppenheim. "Bread and Roses." 1912. http://www.massaflcio.org/1912-bread-and-roses-strike

scratchy wool chair would open and swallow me whole as the principal tells my mother: "She can't come to school anymore unless she wears a bra. She's distracting the boys."

Roots stretch and grow deeper inside me. My breasts are the enemy.

For thirteen-year-old me, shaking with anger as my balding geometry teacher glares at me. "Are you cheating? How are you completing the assignments? You don't stay after class to ask for help like the other girls." I dropped from the advanced math track on his whim. I go from a girl who dreamed of being an aerospace engineer, to a girl who joked with all seriousness that "math is hard."

Roots twist deeper. I am limited by my gender.

For seventeen-year-old me, swallowing angry tears in the midst of a furious argument with another balding, mustached white man trying to dictate my future. I crunch the assigned reading in my shaking hand, an article titled "Dan Quayle was right." It argued that children raised by single moms were destined for failure. Joined by my fellow students, we argue that our lives are not limited by our absent fathers. The teacher laughs awkwardly and backs away from our arguments. "For God's sake, don't take it personally." The cardinal sin of women and oppressed people everywhere: taking their lives personally.

New roots sprout. My voice gives me strength.

For the same seventeen-year-old me, falling in love with an image of women together, learning and growing, surrounded by ivy-covered walls, on a glossy postcard. Ignoring the jeers of my mother's male colleague: "Why are you applying to all those Harvard pickup schools?"

For the same seventeen-year-old me, stumbling into a campaign headquarters in 1992. Hours perched in a metal folding chair. Licking envelopes. Watching the dial spin on the rotary phone, calling strangers, asking them to vote for two new women senators and a president with a wife who didn't just bake cookies. It was "The Year of the Woman."

New roots. Women together can do anything.

The 41-year-old me walks into the early voting polling place feeling like she has an army of women with her and that, united, they can do anything.

*   *   *

Election Day. I don the colors of the flag. An ivory blazer with blue and red piping. I pair it with jeans and a blue T-shirt. I adorn the lapel with various Hillary pins: *Pantsuits for President, Votes for Her,* and *Deal Us In.*

I ignore the niggling feeling tiptoeing up the back of my neck. Today will not be a bad day. I shake it off like an unwelcome spider.

I watch the map turn red, infected blood seeping across our nation. My cocktail sits half-finished in my glass, my stomach refusing to allow me refuge in alcohol. My wife has already gone to bed. She sensed the doom early on; my Pollyanna side got the better of me. I thought women could do anything. At two a.m., I bury myself under the covers. I feel the darkness clouding in, but a glimmer of hope lingers like the last burning ember of a fire. When my alarm goes off what seems like a few minutes later, I pick up my phone and read the word *conceded.* The ember dies.

*   *   *

I don black, shrouding myself from head to toe.

For the woman who spent her life racking up a list of qualifications that far exceeded any man, yet who still didn't win.

For a country that moved racism out from behind closed

doors, spoken about in hushed tones, and put it on display, spotlights shining, voices amplified, before a cheering crowd.

For 41-year-old me, precariously perched atop a house of cards made of hard-fought civil rights and government-funded income.

For my wife and the endless river of hospital visits and surgeries brought on by her chronic illness, and the insurance that keeps us afloat. For all the times I have had to use the word *wife* with a nurse or doctor, sometimes being forced to repeat it in response to their confused "who?"

For my job in a place that might cease to exist in this new regime. Over fifteen thousand people working to keep our air, water, and land clean, all declared the enemy.

*   *   *

I don defiance.

I shed my 41-year-old skin, outgrowing the confines of the good girl, the rule follower.

Each day, reality sets in a little deeper. Roots twist and stab. There is that much hate in America. Anger and sadness wash over me. Resolve floats on top of the waves, a life raft I cling to. Occasionally, a wave overtakes it. I come up sputtering, looking around, confused and misplaced. *Where am I? Is this my country? It feels familiar, but something just isn't right.* I take solace in the millions of life rafts floating around me, before another wave crashes.

I find out my job is gone via *The Washington Post*. Or probably gone. Most likely gone. No one seems to know. I pack two boxes haphazardly. Shoes, mugs, and postcards in a tangled heap. An umbrella that will be no match for the flash flood I'm expecting.

I'm too unimportant for anyone to tell me I can't talk or post, but the gag order feels like a strip of duct tape across my mouth. I find refuge in the Badlands National Park rogue tweets. We rise. We resist. The tweets disappear before my eyes. An iron curtain slamming down. Facts erased. Not government secrets. Not matters of national security. But basic high-school-science-level facts. Erased. This is my straw. It's paper thin, but on top of everything else, it's too much. My back snaps. I don't know how to bear the weight anymore.

I have trouble sitting still. A child bouncing in her seat, desperate for recess. My fingers itch. I start printing. Page after page of public documents that might soon disappear. It's not really an act of rebellion. They're public and could have been printed at any time. But each sheet of paper feels like a shot fired.

* * *

I don red.

Like the blood pumping through my veins. Like the fire burning inside me, at times a raging inferno, at times a single glowing ember. Always there smoldering beneath the surface, ready to be stoked by my resolve. I keep showing up, sitting at my desk, and wondering when the phone will ring to tell me to go home. I keep printing.

Melissa Lirtsman, age 34
Founder of I Hope You
New York, New York

I Hope You Fight

ON November 8, 2016, I voted for Hillary Clinton, my two-year-old daughter helping me fill in the circle on my ballot. We both wore pantsuits. I expected to feel some pride voting for a woman. I didn't expect to feel so intensely the incredible weight we women carry—those dark experiences of being objectified, silenced, and reduced. I didn't expect to spend the rest of the day holding back tears or feeling my heart beat so quickly.

I voted for Hillary Clinton because she's an incredible public servant who cares about people and policy.

But I also voted for my seven-year-old self, who would sit in the back of the car during road trips and imagine word-for-word speeches about littering and kindness that I'd give one day as president—but was told I might want to stick to being a teacher or something more realistic. I voted for my nine-year-old self who was told if math was hard, then maybe I should focus on writing instead—that I shouldn't climb so high, go so far.

I voted for every time a girl's dreams have been reduced by someone else's reality.

I voted for my thirteen-year-old self, who was taught abstinence and avoidance were the best ways to talk about sex—leaving an impressionable tween to become indoctrinated to the belief that a girl's sexual value was inherent to her worth.

I voted for every time a girl doesn't learn about self-worth from our society, let alone from those she loves the most.

I voted for my seventeen-year-old self, whose mother showed more concern with my loss of virginity than compassion for my heartache.

I voted for every time a girl is made to feel her whole worth is tied to purity.

I voted for my seventeen-year-old self, who went to an all-girl sleepover but woke up with a boy and a condom wrapper next to me. I voted for being told by my girlfriend that it isn't rape because I'd been drinking and kissed him before I'd passed out.

I voted for every girl who doesn't know that such a thing is rape.

I voted for my eighteen-year-old self, for when my boyfriend broke up with me after I told him I'd been held down and raped until I almost vomited—because he felt he'd been cheated on. I voted for my fragile self, who mustered up enough courage to drive to the doctor to get a pregnancy and STD test, but instead of being offered a rape kit, was given advice about decision-making and not putting myself into dangerous situations.

I voted for every time a girl isn't empowered to make decisions for herself.

I voted for my entire life of being catcalled, stared at, followed, and touched without my permission.

I voted for every girl who grows up hearing the phrase "boys will be boys."

I voted for my 24-year-old post-graduate self, whose résumé was good enough to be brought in to interview for a director position but who was offered a position two levels down because of my age. And for my 27-year-old self, who was told that the only way I could get a raise or a promotion was by having a man ask for me—that young women didn't need promoting since they'd be getting married soon enough.

I voted for every girl who accepts less than she's worth.

I voted for my thirty-year-old self, who was admitted to the hospital at thirty-seven weeks pregnant with a condition that could affect either my life or our baby's and had to have very real conversations with my doctor and my husband about what we'd want and what I'd want if I wasn't able to make a decision for myself.

I voted for every woman who all too sadly understands the weight of that decision and the sacredness of its being between her, her doctor, and her partner.

I voted for my 31-year-old self, who finally learned what a vulva was so that I could teach my daughter the right terms.

I voted for every girl who is unaware of the power of her own body.

I voted for my 32-year-old self, who between finances, pregnancy complications, and a downsized company, became a stay-at-home parent at what was almost the pinnacle of my career. And for my 34-year-old self, who is trying to get back to work after taking time off for kids—and realizing the way out is much easier than the way in.

I voted for every woman who has to leave a baby too soon, who has to downgrade her career, or who is made to feel invisible in her role as a mother.

I voted for my 34-year-old self, who is raising two incredible children with compassion, respect, and thoughtfulness for the type of generation I hope they will be.

I voted for a bright future.

*   *   *

Just after midnight, I text my parents who live in Florida: *Please tell me you didn't help elect him.*

No reply.

The next morning, New York City wakes up with a wet, gray yawn. The air is thick with mist. The city moves at a slower, muffled pace. New Yorkers rarely make eye contact; today isn't much different, except when eyes meet, they lock for a moment in shared grief. Everyone's shoulders bend forward, the world weighing heavier on them than it did yesterday.

The sidewalks and the coffee shops are quiet. Even the subway paces through its underground veins in somber silence. My husband tells me: "The city hasn't been this quiet since 9/11."

The kids are up, and I dry my tears, change diapers, make eggs. My daughter's not obsessed with *Frozen*. Her closet is full of pictures of the Obamas and Adele and Hillary. She tells everyone Malia and Sasha have two dogs. She zooms around the house playing Superhero Hillary Clinton. She insists that maybe President Obama will come to her house to play guitar with her. Or perhaps she'll go to his. She's two-and-a-half and knows only possibility.

I don't want to tell her. It's not that I think she'll understand, but I haven't said the words out loud yet. I finally tell her simply that Hillary didn't win the vote, but maybe one day a woman will. She doesn't say anything for a moment and then simply asks, "Maybe Michelle Obama?"

She gives me my first smile of the day. "Maybe. Or maybe you."

I hope.

Other parents have older kids and harder conversations. They are writing letters, left at the breakfast table as they leave for work. They're different and the same: "Dear Child, We did not win the election, but we will not lose our values. We will still be loving, kind, inclusive. We will not be bullies or be full of hate. I hope you know your future's still bright. I hope you know I will fight for you and others. I hope you know that you can, despite this, achieve everything you want."

We all hope.

I go to my friend's house to watch Hillary concede. Before I leave the house, I put on a black blazer. It seems appropriate. I forget my umbrella, and the sky finally opens, cleansing the ground as she begins her speech.

Hillary hopes we continue to fight for what's right. She hopes our little girls know they are powerful, valuable, deserving.

She also hopes.

I go to bed that night, my head spinning words around and around. *Loss* and *promise. Fear* and *action. Love* and *strength.*

But mostly hope.

The next day, I buy a domain and start building a website. I gather all of the loose fragments of hope that have begun floating around the Internet: boycott spreadsheets and call sheets with names of Members of Congress, at-risk nonprofits, and organizations helping women run for office. I organize them for other women to be able to find. I want to help pay for the education of girls who are pursuing paths in public service and advocacy. A girlfriend designs T-shirts for me to sell so that I can start a scholarship fund. I start talking to the women in my life: neighbors, business owners, friends, and strangers. A sisterhood emerges as we talk about things we've never discussed before: politics, sexual assault, the environment, racial injustice, mass incarceration, and our hopes for our children. And how hopeful we would be about the bright blue and inclusive map if only Millennials had voted.

There's so much hope. But we must fight for it.

I've been too polite, too quiet. Too collaborative, too conciliatory, too apologetic. Too safe, too unaware. I've lived much of my life fighting a quiet battle inside my own heart, protecting others from my pain. That stops now.

I made one mistake in my thinking on Election Day: A brighter future isn't something you vote for. It's something you make.

I hope you help me tear down any damn thing that covers that light.

I hope you fight.

Dr. Christy M. Rehm, age 43
College professor and public school teacher
Dover, Pennsylvania

Why I Care

Lately, I've been deliberating about dreams deferred.
My personal D-Day, Tuesday, November 8, 2016.
Dream deferred day; day of dreaded despotism and
division; day of derailed diversity . . .

"**B**E A PRODUCTIVE member of society" is the mantra I've chanted and sung to my four children since their births. I've never espoused the thoughtless adoption of the be-all-you-can-be mentality. I want people to be self-actualized in the best interest of all humanity. Becoming a parent at seventeen made me value and desire civic engagement and service.

Dutifully voting since eighteen, children in tow, I have modeled civic responsibility. Demonstrating democracy in action, I have been elected to borough council and school board. Developing a spirit of service, I have danced, walked, and marched for countless organizations and served on church council. Defending sound science education, through the federal lawsuit Kitzmiller, et al v. Dover 2005, I have embodied activism. Displaying kindness, love, and compassion to all others, I have nurtured an unyielding respect for all humanity.

"Don't be such a sore loser, you crybaby libtard."
I've been mocked.
"Why do you care so much? It's only an election."
I've been questioned.

Throughout the turbulent 2016 presidential election, my husband and I escorted our children to political rallies to educate them on the issues, expose them to differing points of view, and allow them to formulate their own opinions. At the Donald Trump rally, the supporters were mostly Caucasian, chanting "Trump, Trump, Trump," fists raised in disgruntled defiance. Clad in an array of *Hillary for Prison* and *Trump that Bitch* T-shirts, they defensively shouted, "Get a job!" "Get off welfare!" "Go back where you came from!" and various racial slurs and curses. The most disturbing of those shouting disparaging comments were parents with their children emulating their disgusting language, behaviors, and gestures.

My six-foot-six-inch husband joined the protest, tearing off his dress shirt to reveal a handmade *No H8* undershirt and waving an *I Love My Muslim Neighbor* poster. I was left to defend my children in the defiant crowd. As nighttime fell, crowds of delusional supporters were turned away at the door, the police failed to separate the supporters from the protestors, and my children's faces flashed fear. We were accosted by a visibly drunk group of men who reeked of hard liquor. As I calmly stated my reasons for attending, one of the men admitted, "I'm a felon and can't vote, but screw that criminal bitch." I didn't point out the irony in his words.

Conversely, the Hillary Clinton rally we attended had a different vibe. Supporters lightheartedly shared stories, registered to volunteer, purchased merchandise with uplifting messages of equality, and ignored the handful of protesters waving Confederate flags.

Inside, the diverse crowd listened intently and cheered the positive messages. They waved posters with unifying messages, such as *VOTE, Students for Hillary, Steel Workers for Hillary, Hispanics for Hillary,* and *Republicans for Hillary.* Leaving the event, my twelve-year-old son beamed with pride as he purchased a blue Hillary Clinton T-shirt and hat, and as we walked to the car, he proudly donned his new attire.

"Pantsuits can't protect you," I've been harassed.
I've witnessed the divisiveness.

A few days after the rally, my son wore his T-shirt to our local market. A man in his late fifties approached and growled, "That better say Hillary for prison." Continuing his assault of curses until my husband approached, he became unhinged and screamed, "Trump can't be bought!" "He'll lock her up!" and "You're not American if you vote for her!" My husband diplomatically explained that citizens are expected to vote based upon their individual convictions, not ordered to vote a particular way based upon the norms or beliefs of those around them. The man continued to rage and stormed off in a huff yelling we were all going to hell.

Although I have always been a registered Republican, I vote based on the issues and deplore partisan politics. Additionally, I had volunteered as a local organizer and opened my home as the local campaign headquarters for the Obama campaign. Given my nonpartisan views and political experience, I was compelled to work for the local Clinton campaign. I worked all spare evenings and weekends phonebanking, pounding the pavement canvassing different neighborhoods, and recruiting volunteers. Working on this campaign was similar to my previous campaign efforts; I met many patriotic hard-working, tax-paying Americans who care about justice, equality, and social programs over personal and financial gains.

People also slammed doors, threatened violence, and screamed insults. Some men refused to allow their wives to speak and shouted that their wives knew "the right way" to vote. Some women whispered through locked screen doors that they would be voting for Hillary and covertly gestured their support. This election was more visceral; more focused on disparaging and destroying the candidate, not the ideas; and more distanced from facts and reality than any election I have seen. It felt like I had entered a political time warp, helpless to progress.

"Partisanship is not peaceful," I've discovered.
I've dealt with the differences and the disputes.

Enduring political conflict within a family is deflating. A number of my loved ones pledged their allegiance to Trump, while I worked diligently for the Clinton campaign. These relatives relentlessly shared fake news articles, slandered Clinton, posted detestable images of the Obamas, and spouted their racial and Christian superiority on social media platforms.

These family members were raised in York, Pennsylvania, an area inundated with race riots in the 1960s and 1970s, when white supremacists were also police officers, church leaders, and elected officials. I was raised on their racial slurs and watched them disown their children who engaged in biracial relationships or gave birth to biracial children. Yet, they insisted, "This is not about race," through coded comments about "clean(ing) up America" and Bible verses.

Election Day was brutal. After canvassing for thirteen hours, I was exhausted but forced myself to attend the nearby celebration. There were brief moments of merriment and accomplishment as local Democrats won their races. However, as the presidential returns came in, we sat in disbelief watching blue and swing states turn red. I had no tears. I was numb!

"Safety pins won't save you," I've been attacked.
I've deflected the disgusting deplorables.

The day after the election I wanted to pull the covers over my head and stay in bed. Working in a school district with a greatly divided political climate, I knew there would be turmoil and triumphing I did not want to face. Instead, I responsibly went to work. I could not have predicted the ugliness I witnessed that day. Teachers and students were welcomed to campus by Trump supporters and their Confederate-flag-wielding trucks. Female students cried after hearing "Now maybe you women will remember your place." Throughout the day, Trump-supporting students harassed Hispanic students in the hallways, shouting, "Next year, you'll be back in Mexico!" and waving goodbye. Some teachers cried, while other teachers strutted in the hallways wearing their Trump insignia. It turns out that I was needed by my marginalized colleagues and students, and that is a role I will always fulfill. Education has rescued me from poverty and racism, and I will always work to protect the education system. After the political dust has settled, I vow to be there to pick up the pieces brick by brick, idea by idea.

I care to defeat:
Democratic death by despicable despots,
Dishonorable desire to debunk datum and destroy decency,
Diligent and devout dogmas that dissolve diversity.

I've had a few months to come to terms with the election results. An enormous amount of work is needed to maintain the freedoms we are guaranteed by our Constitution. I have decided to do the following: change my political affiliation to Democrat; continue my involvement in local politics; volunteer for diverse causes; read about culture and globalism; reach out to those who are marginalized; donate money to targeted organizations; be vigilant about what is occurring on all political spectra; write and sing some political songs with my bands, Violets Lost and MisAmerica; tell my story; and resist. I might even go to work for a civil rights organization or earn a spot on *The 101 Most Dangerous Academics in America* list one of these days.

On Tuesday, November 8, 2016, a dream was deferred.
Wednesday, November 9, 2016, and every day thereafter
have become my personal days of decision, determination,
defense, defiance, and demonstration.
We have a dream to deliver!
Why don't you care?

Christine Dilkes Cook, age 49
Tutor
Washington, New Jersey

Generations of Pain

FOUR GENERATIONS OF strong women, many generations of pain carried in our bodies

Grandmother, mother, daughter, granddaughter

Each wears the pain of those who came before them, like ill-fitting skin

with battle scars she proudly displays, but secretly wishes would

disappear.

We persevere.

Aware of the spirits and stories and struggles that move us forward, always forward, mostly forward

Through intimidation, despite violence, past invisibility

Fearlessly carrying the pain

For all women.

Sarah Satterlee, age 31
Registered nurse
East Providence, Rhode Island

Too White to See
What Was Coming

OUR STATE MOTTO here in Rhode Island is one small four-letter word: *Hope.* I always loved this about us. The word *Hope* is emblazoned on our flag. It's the namesake of streets, schools, businesses in Providence and elsewhere throughout the state. Everywhere you look, there it is, staring you in the face: *Hope.* It's unavoidable, relentless, encouraging, and inspiring. After all, we are a state founded on religious freedom. Roger Williams was expelled from the Massachusetts Bay Colony in the seventeenth century, and he laid down his roots here. We became the first in the nation to say that freedom of religion should be the law of the land. This fact makes a history buff like me, a lifelong proud Rhode Islander, radiate with pride. However, we had slaves here, let's not forget the entire name of our state that still remains: *The State of Rhode Island and Providence Plantations.*

In the same way I had managed to overlook the truth of my

state's history in the rosy optimism of my worldview, I never really had cause to notice my whiteness. I didn't have any impetus to until November 8, 2016, happened. I thought that I understood privilege; I'd studied it in college and pushed against injustice where I saw it. I volunteered for organizations like Planned Parenthood, argued in the face of conservatives who rolled their eyes at Black Lives Matter, and marveled in my gorgeous awakening. But my whiteness, up until that day in November, had allowed me to believe we were ultimately moving forward. Yes, people of color were being shot in the street, conservative lawmakers were trying to push anti-LGBTQ legislation in other states and on the national level, but we were waking up. We had a black president and the recognition of same-sex marriage, and my little activist heart, in all of its whiteness, just believed that things always get better. Because in whiteland, that's the way it goes. The bad guy will always lose. But then we elected the bad guy, and everything I've ever believed to be fundamentally true was incinerated and pissed on.

That night, my "girl gang," and many groups like us, crowded in front of the television in our *Nasty Woman* T-shirts. We taped Hillary signs to the wall and tucked the champagne away in the refrigerator, we posed with a smiling cardboard cutout of Joe Biden, and we told our children we'd deliver the "good news" in the morning. My daughter begged me to wake her up when Hillary gave her acceptance speech. I promised I would. In the oblivious calm of my whiteness, I really believed Hillary's historic win would happen. Our election party that had seemed so exciting and hopeful now seems to me utterly ridiculous.

In the disappointment and blinding rage immediately following the election, I, like many others, took to social media to vent my frustrations. Clearly, there I would find camaraderie and outrage that matched mine, and for the most part, I did. However, I also was jolted into understanding my whiteness in a whole new way when conservative-leaning friends began to say things in response to my deluge of angry posts. They said things things like "I'm proud to be white," "Quit your whining," "You're starting a race war," and "Black Lives Matter is a terrorist organization, you know."

In my little blue state, the one with the *Hope* motto, you might think liberal values are the norm, but this is not so. Like many other places in America, the urban concentrations of cities in Rhode Island vote overwhelmingly for democratic candidates, but in the rural areas, like where I grew up near the beaches in the southwestern part of the state, conservative values and Republican votes reign supreme. I'd been hiding away in blissful serenity, just outside Providence with my ultra-left college-educated community who read *The New Yorker* and ate arugula without apologizing.

But we liberals had been living in disregard of our national truth: Hillary Clinton would lose because she was a woman and because people were okay with racism. These statements are "controversial" only in that those angered by them can't accept them, can't move beyond their immediate defensiveness in order to dissect the glowing parcels of truth inside. We will never move forward as long as people cannot face these two fundamental facts of our national identity. In the quiet of my whiteness, I did not know such ugliness existed. I believed that we would collectively hold hands and walk toward a better future. I know now that things are never that easy.

Since I can't spend the next four years sitting in my bathtub with a box of wine listening to Bob Dylan's "Blowing in the Wind" while intermittently shouting lines from Lincoln's first inaugural address to cardboard Joe and sobbing and apologizing to the ghost of Roger Williams, I have to take action. Well-meaning friends have said, "You can't do anything about it, so just hope for the best." Well, I'm going to damn well try to do something about it. Maybe I can't build a time machine and teach people to be intelligent thinkers and escape this whole Trump disaster, but I can donate to Planned Parenthood. I can actually listen to people of color instead of pretending I know everything. I can write, and I can call out racist, sexist, homophobic language when I hear it. I can read the histories of black Americans who died in riots like Hard Scrabble in Providence, instead of beaming with pride every time I regale friends with the stories of my progressive state's founding. I can vote. All of my activist activities that I used to do, now have a newer and more serious meaning, an urgency; there is no time to waste. Most importantly, I can teach my daughter to be a loving human being and to understand inequality and to never accept it, to always fight for what's right.

For example, I stood in line for a whole day once to meet Hillary Clinton at a book signing. When it was my turn to shake her hand, I excitedly told her how inspirational she was, to me and to my daughter. A few months later, she came back to Rhode Island to speak. This time I brought my daughter, and we stood in front listening. I really believed that nothing could stop this lifelong champion of the people. I had hope.

I was too white to see what was coming, and America's problems are bigger than I ever understood. But what I will not let happen is apathy (and extended bathtub time). That day when my daughter and I looked up at Hillary—a successful, relentless advocate of human rights, the *good guy* (despite the claims of conspiracy theory YouTube videos and the harsh dismissal by a jaded electorate)—I was hopeful. But I know now we cannot afford to separate *Hope* from *Action*. For meaningful change to occur, we need to hold onto both—the belief that things can better, and the understanding that they never will unless we get moving. So let's get to it!

Amy Erickson, age 33
Special education teacher;
currently, a stay-at-home mom
Small town, Pennsylvania

No Line in the Sand

AFTER THIRTEEN YEARS of Catholic school, it's safe to say I've read the Gospels. As far as I see it, Jesus, a Middle Eastern refugee born to a young mother, hung out with a hodgepodge of twelve groupies (not all of them on the up and up), was pretty tight with a prostitute, cured those with socially ostracizing diseases, routinely fed the poor, argued with Jewish fundamentalists, and even got pretty pissy with some townsfolk who thought they could run amok in His Father's temple. Nowhere in my reading do I recall Jesus's using His clout to pontificate on how great He was, how elite His followers were, and how everyone else was less of a person because they weren't white heterosexual conservative men.

It was and is impossible for me to understand what would ever draw someone to support a man who, for me, so obviously epitomizes vile hatred of others. Even more difficult was watching loved ones cast their votes for Donald Trump based on their "Christian values."

* * *

I was a Bernie Sanders supporter. I wore the T-shirt, hung the sign, and made the donations. My now ten-month-old daughter wore a *Babies for Bernie* shirt to the polls when we voted in April. We watched every debate with fervor; we were "feeling the Bern."

When the primaries occurred, I watched the Democratic elite's candidate climb in numbers. I celebrated every state that turned in Sanders's favor, but in my heart I knew the establishment would prevail. My husband had seen it coming, but my belief in the cause blinded me.

I hadn't paid much attention to Hillary Clinton or her proposed policies. Too caught up in the whirlwind of grassroots politics, I didn't bother investigating the partisan opposition. Donald Trump had been shoving his political discourse down our throats at every turn, so I knew I needed to prepare for the final showdown and read up on Hillary.

I began the self-education process. I perused her platform and researched her political past. As an educator, I found Hillary's devotion to children encouraging. When her husband was governor of Arkansas, she was the state's first governor's spouse to keep her job, which I readily admired. The more I learned, the more I valued and admired her.

The Democratic National Convention sealed the deal for me. Hillary Clinton entered the stage on a bore of the crowd's zeal. The undertow of chants pulled her to the microphone, and she accepted the Democratic presidential candidate nomination. In her speech, she addressed Bernie Sanders's supporters, telling us, "I want you to know, I've heard you." My support for Hillary was affirmed. I respected her acknowledgment of his advocates and her movement not to leave us behind or up for grabs.

* * *

There was a time when the Trump campaign was comical. For months, I laughed with the rest of the world at his tiny hands and ginormous ego. From his deranged primary debates to parading his one-time Republican opponents onstage as robotic groupies, Trump's campaign seemed to be an extension of his reality show. But my laughter at the comedy turned to fear as his numbers climbed in the polls and his outlandish rhetoric was taken to heart by supporters.

When the *Access Hollywood* video was released, I was gobsmacked. My cousin texted, asking if I had heard the latest Trump news, and I remember writing back: *wtf did he do this time?* Little did I know, the best candidate the Republicans could come up with was caught speaking of women as objects; we were the Leia to his Jabba the Hutt. His crass nature and flippant remarks should have been enough to enrage the masses. I thought that this, *this* would surely be the thing to arouse my "all lives matter" family and friends from their white-privileged slumber. If the racist, xenophobic rhetoric didn't open their eyes and change their hearts, then undoubtedly this misogynistic tone would do the trick. *This has to be the moment when America wakes up,* I thought. This has to be the line in the sand. But that moment never came. No amount of misogyny, racism, homophobia, xenophobia, or bigotry could convince America that Donald Trump was and continues to be the embodiment of everything immoral and unjust.

*   *   *

Every year in Catholic school, we read and discussed the Sermon on the Mount and its expression of the central tenets of Christianity. In the sermon, Jesus, as the model of our faith, taught His followers how to love one another, regardless of race or gender. How, then, can those who claim to be Christians support someone who continuously declares his disdain for marginalized groups of people? By aligning yourself with Donald Trump, you can no longer invoke your Christianity.

I've heard so many people, particularly people of faith, say they could look past his wrongdoings. When they're pressed further, the reply is always some variation of "He doesn't mean what he says," "It's just to get a rise out of people," or "It's all for show." When you turn a blind eye and a deaf ear and say nothing, you are in fact saying *everything*. You are telling others you approve of immorality and injustice. You are telling them you support the marginalization and vilification of those who are different from you. You are telling them that fear reigns supreme and that you will tolerate nefarious behavior. As President John F. Kennedy said in a speech: "The hottest places in hell are reserved for those who, in times of great moral crises, maintain their neutrality."

For those of you who identify as Christian, challenge yourself to read the Beatitudes and ponder, *Was aligning Christianity with the Republican party really what Jesus talked about?* I'm not being facetious. I'm also not suggesting Jesus was a Democrat. What I am suggesting is that you mull this over: *What social causes on the Republican platform align with Jesus's message?* If pro-life and heterosexual marriage are the only two matters you deem worthy of your attention, then you are sorely mistaken and are selling short your worth.

To those in my life who voted for Donald Trump, my message to you is this: I still and always will love you. Your decisions do not affect the unconditional nature of my care for you. Part of loving others is challenging them to be the best forms of themselves. Those who truly love us should shake our complacency. I challenge you to read this message, my story, with an open heart and an open mind. Do not close yourself off with defensiveness and explanations. I beg of you: hear the words that are on this page, read the words of the Gospels, and allow Jesus's examples be your moral compass.

* * *

Right after the election, I received a *Love Trumps Hate* pin in the mail. I had forgotten I had ordered it, and after all that had happened with the election, the fates seemed to be mocking me. I threw the pin in my purse with the intention of hanging it from my car's sunshade. A few weeks later, I reached into my bag and flinched in pain as something stabbed my middle finger. I pulled out the pin and grinned. The fates again intervened, this time as the literal pinch I needed to remember I am not alone. Thousands of us are banded together for life with a common cause of proving that misogyny, racism, homophobia, and xenophobia do not win. Like the civil rights and women's rights activists before us, we will not allow hate to silence our collective voice. We will teach our daughters they are strong, and we will lead by example. They will grow up to demand respect and equality. Love does and forever will trump hate. We nasty women will see to it.

Carmen Hernandez, age 35
Lawyer
Fairfax, Virginia

Juan Hernandez, age 35
Senior IT consultant
Fairfax, Virginia

People of Change

CARMEN: I'VE BEEN living in Virginia for the past four and a half years. Before that, I lived in Puerto Rico, where I was born and raised. My upbringing was very political. My parents and my grandmother were involved in local politics, and I was raised to understand the importance of voting. For us Puerto Ricans, politics is almost like a sport. We get invested in the campaigns, which have a party atmosphere, with loud music and a lot of revelry. My love for politics was so great that I earned my bachelor's degree in political science. During this time, my true awakening as a liberal occurred.

Juan: I've been living in Virginia since 2007. As it did for Carmen, growing up in Puerto Rico taught me the importance of participating in the electoral process from an early age. But as with so many others, I limited myself to voting and social media activism.

Carmen: I read Hillary Clinton's autobiography, *Living History,* and I was fascinated by Clinton's strong character, drive, and intelligence, so I was excited to be able to vote for her in the 2008 primaries. She won in Puerto Rico by a huge margin because we all love the Clintons like one of our own.

When President Obama named her as secretary of state, I was thrilled. I saw the move as a gesture of unity after a historic primary and an even more historic election. It was wonderful to see this smart and capable woman manage her role with aplomb. She did so much good for our country.

And then I moved stateside. Talk about a culture clash! I wasn't used to seeing overt signs of racism, but now I saw license plates with the *Don't tread on me* slogan and snake, commonly associated with the Tea Party, and cars (mostly pickup trucks) with the Confederate flag. While I can pass as a white American, I identify as 100% Hispanic/Latina, because that's who I am. My name is Hispanic, and I know I have a slight Hispanic accent when I speak English. Never before was I asked what language I was speaking until I came to Virginia. The only time that question was actually funny was when a girl commented she thought my best friend and I were speaking Elvish (as in *The Lord of the Rings* Elvish).

When Hillary published her book *Hard Choices*, my husband gave it to me for my birthday. Reading it, I got the feeling she was going to get into the election fray sooner or later, and I was thrilled when she did. However, when Bernie Sanders threw his hat in the ring, I felt conflicted. While I admire Hillary Clinton, I also like Bernie Sanders, and I identified very much with his values and his ideas. As the campaigns heated up, I allied myself with Bernie. Yes, I "felt the Bern"! I voted for him on Super Tuesday, even though I knew he wouldn't win Virginia. Many of us wanted to send the message that we supported his ideas and that the party should take note of those ideas. When it was clear the nomination was going to be Hillary's, I made peace with that fact and supported her.

Juan: While I was also quick to "feel the Bern," I was more realistic about his chances. I watched the preamble to the Iowa caucuses with great anticipation and anxiety, knowing that if he pulled off an upset there, he might just get the nomination. The resulting tie was a downer for me, because I knew his political momentum going forward would be dulled. I would have preferred Bernie Sanders to be the candidate, but I was also content with Hillary Clinton. I knew she had the experience and was absolutely qualified to be president.

Carmen: I also paid close attention to the GOP side. To me, Trump was not to be taken seriously. I thought he would rise quickly and burn out even faster until he dropped out—as usually happens in the primary season. But he defied everything. His message baffled me, and the moment he called Mexicans *rapists*, I was done with him. The more things he said, the worse I felt about him. How can this guy be permitted to run? How can anyone take him seriously? Why was the media giving him any sort of time?

I read about the Republican National Convention (RNC) with a lot of trepidation. The messages they espoused were horrible. I watched the Democratic National Convention (DNC) with hope. It was more uplifting. I loved that Bernie Sanders wanted to create unity, despite the sore feelings still around. I didn't blame Hillary for those. Like Bernie, I was with her, and some points of his platform were added to the official platform of the Democratic Party.

To me, Trump is a con man. He said a lot of outrageous things so that his followers would eat it them up, but I also took him at face value. I was disturbed he said so many horrible things about Hispanics, made fun of people who are disabled, trashed the media, and messed with a gold star family. The pussy-grabbing scandal was disgusting. It's shocking that his own party did not kick him out at that point.

Juan: On the one hand, I was not too surprised when Trump eventually won the GOP nomination. The GOP had been pushing the same sickening ideology and the same dog whistles down their supporters' throats for decades, especially during President Obama's two terms. So to me it made perfect sense that when one demagogue tossed away the dog whistle and brought in a bullhorn, the crazies flocked to him. I also thought he was probably the only candidate Secretary Clinton *could* beat; her qualifications aside, I thought she had such clear campaign baggage and vulnerabilities as a candidate that any other Republican would have beaten her handily. On the other hand, I was aghast this guy could gain the support he had after the primaries were over. How could he be garnering 42% support in the polls, given what he'd said? Every day, for months, I checked the polling aggregators, seeing Hillary Clinton's support wax and wane as the days went by and each new poll came in. By the time the RNC and the polls showed essentially a tied race, I was in a constant state of anxiety until the DNC and her poll numbers climbed again. When the *Access Hollywood* video turned up, I thought Trump was finished. That didn't stop me from worrying every day and checking the polls constantly, but I was definitely feeling calmer.

Carmen: Trump's last debate with Hillary Clinton was the one I remember the most, because of his claim that women could abort their pregnancies at nine months and his comments about "bad hombres" and "nasty woman." How could anyone back this person?

I wanted to feel hopeful about the election. I saw Hillary had great numbers in the polls, but they were too close for me. My husband is more into analyzing the polls, and he was studying them almost obsessively. He didn't feel comfortable with the numbers, especially when Trump seemed to bounce back after each scandal. To me, the extreme difference between the two candidates was appalling. We had a very intelligent, capable, and experienced politician, who knew about law and understood government. On the other hand, we had a guy who had the same experience in government as any other regular citizen (read: *none*), except that he was a loud, rich populist. The choice was clearer than glass; at least, that's where my logic took me.

In the days before the election, I was hopeful. I saw social media bursting with the hashtag #ImWithHer and videos of people excited about her. One campaign ad got to me: it was set to Katy Perry's "Roar," and the video showed reasons why we were voting for her—*respect, community,* and *fairness*—with images of people and the planet. I teared up and felt chills whenever I saw that video! At the same time, I didn't see many Clinton–Kaine signs or stickers, but I did see several Trump–Pence lawn signs and bumper stickers. I started to become anxious. *What if?*

On the day of the election, we were off early to vote. The line was fast, and we were able to cast our votes quickly. I had my two-year-old daughter on my lap when I filled in the bubble next to Hillary Clinton and Tim Kaine. I proudly wore my *I voted* sticker all day long, and my daughter wore one that said *Future voter.*

My husband was anxious all day long, and I started to feel my own anxiety in the evening. We were watching CNN, and Wolf Blitzer was driving me crazy because he interrupted John King, as he tried to explain the numbers. Friends from Florida kept saying, "Wait a bit longer! We're still missing some counties!" Meanwhile, the counties kept coming up red. I cursed Florida.

Virginia was starting to report too, and the state's map showed all red. But I kept saying, "Wait for northern Virginia, because we always take longer, but we pull through." In that sense, I was right, and that was a relief. Still, the numbers rolled in, and it started to look grim. With dismay, I posted the Electoral College map on social media. I could not believe the tide was red. Around 2:00 a.m., the defeat was clear. Never before had I felt an election loss as terribly as this one. *How could this happen?* I felt I couldn't love a country that turned its back on my gender, hated people of my ethnicity, and was so willing to deny rights for some just to feel righteous.

The next day, the sky was dark with gray clouds, and the air was heavy. It felt strange and still, like the world couldn't believe what had just happened. The day looked exactly how I felt.

Juan: When it was evident the "blue wall" had not just crumbled but collapsed, I was in utter shock. In hindsight, I didn't break down right away because when I saw Carmen do so, I swallowed my feelings and comforted her as best I could. I hugged her hard, kissed her gently, and let her cry as much as she needed, numb to what I felt and to the reality dawning on us. The results defied logic and every prognostication. *How did this happen?*

Carmen: I had to swallow the bitter pill and fight back. I started looking for places to volunteer. We, as a family, donated to Planned Parenthood. I also searched ways to volunteer at the American Civil Liberties Union (ACLU) in Virginia, preferably as a legal observer. I refused to take these election results meekly. While Trump might have won, Although Trump won, I am determined to fight for the rights of women and minorities. We wrote a note of friendship and solidarity to our Middle Eastern neighbors. We chose to take up some causes and be involved.

Juan: At first I wanted to understand why this had happened. I struck up a conversation with an acquaintance, a fervent

Catholic veteran who voted Republican since he's a single-issue voter. I asked him what made him vote Trump despite everything the candidate had said. We had an open and honest, though careful, conversation, where I found he was no fan of Trump but saw Clinton as a threat to the nation. Afterward, I jumped into "how do I fight this?" mode. I googled to find anything I could do, choosing climate change to devote my energy to. Soon I found an organization that pushed for bipartisan legislation as a first step to mitigate the climate crisis.

As time went on, I accepted that Trump would be president and chose not to cling to the hope of a recount or an Electoral College revolt, because I felt clinging to that hope would prevent me from getting off my seat and taking action. When not working with the climate organization, my plan is to encourage people I know to also take action however they can.

Carmen: For some time, I couldn't watch the news or even late-night comedy shows. I needed some time to digest the news, so I dove into reading. One book I read was about Eleanor Roosevelt and her cousin. Eleanor was an amazing woman, and her determination to work with certain causes really inspired me.

Juan: Carmen and I believe that people deserve the government they choose, and we apply that to Puerto Rico and the United States, regardless of who is in power. Why Trump has risen to power has no simple answer, although historic precedent exists. However, things don't have to be the same as with past populist leaders. We, as citizens, have a duty to make ourselves heard, and we have to make changes occur. We need to choose to be people of change.

Elizabeth Tambascio, age 38
Artist
Boston, Massachusetts

We the People

F RIDAY SHARE IS a weekly meeting at my children's school where students ranging from three to fifteen years old take turns presenting what they have learned or created. The whole school community is invited, and I like to go when I can.

It's a beautiful thing to watch the children support one another and it's particularly touching to see the older kids encouraging the youngest in their learning. Likewise, I love to watch the younger children observe their older counterparts demonstrate a robot they built, display a hand-drawn map of our community, share an ink drawing of a dragonfly, or sing a Native American folk song they have been practicing. Admittedly, I'm a softie, but I often find my eyes filling white sitting in the back rows of this public school auditorium.

This gathering is special because it gives the children opportunities to acknowledge and validate the hard work other students have put in, introduces them to new topics, and encourages them to seek out knowledge. It's a time to listen quietly, project their own voices, and to build community.

I'm the youngest of seven children and my family engaged in our own nightly community-building around the dinner table. Hearing what was going on in one another's lives, and expressing gratitude for the food on our plates, as well as for the hands that made it, were constants. When any disputes arose among us, my mother demanded we respect one another and work out any differences we had. When we were born, we were entered into a contract to stick together, no matter what life threw at us.

Throughout our lives, there have been stresses and strains. My siblings and I have had minor and major disagreements, but push our way through them. We have survived through illness, financial troubles, divorce, and death, and have held together.

The empathy and sense of shared responsibility practiced with my family have benefited me far beyond home, both at work and in other relationships. In turn, I feel strongly that my own kids should stick together, respect one another and work it out when needed. When they were born, they were automatically entered into the same contract as my siblings. I hope they will develop those same skills we did to help them make their way through the world.

*   *   *

The week before the 2016 presidential election, I attended Friday Share and the children's presentations reflected the occasion. One class presented the Preamble to the Constitution in song form: "We the People of the United States. . . ." Others shared drawings or reports. The whole school participated in political learning.

Even though we live in the bluest neighborhood of one of the bluest cities in one of the bluest states in the country, the kids were allowed to reach their own conclusions. Leading up to the election, students read about political office, held mock elections, and talked about whose voice matters in our world.

When I asked, "So whose does?" my five-year-old daughter responded, "Everyone's."

The school is a polling station so the next week I worked at their Election Day bake sale. Those of us at the table were all female—a mixed group in terms of age, orientation, and background but, on this day, uniform in our wishes about the election's outcome.

The room vibrated with a distinct, almost tangible energy. Excitement with a splash of nerves. A man gave us twenty dollars for a cookie and told us to keep the change. Two men, a couple, asked us to take their photo in front of the polling sign. They held matching travel mugs with a photo of the two of them. Finally, in the same city after years of dating long distance, it was their first time voting together. Parents brought their children to vote. A friend showed up to cast her vote wearing a cat shirt that read *Today the pussy bites back.*

Some expressed concern while others encouraged them to relax, all the while aware there was a possibility . . . But no.

I thought of Friday Share the week before and the students singing, "We the people . . ." All would be fine. History would be made.

*   *   *

The next morning, I felt the same thick, hard pressure in my throat that had been there for the past twelve hours—as if the concrete blocks in the pit of my stomach had scraped my throat while I attempted to swallow them down the night before. I accompanied my children to their classes, and as I was leaving, a mom I didn't know well called me over to a group standing in the hallway. She gave me a hug as we all kind of stood there looking for . . . something. I fought tears until I couldn't.

I thought of my children a few rooms away, and bit my lower lip hard. I knew things would be different and we, too, would have to be different. When that mom called me over, she gave me a glimpse of hope and I felt for those who didn't have a mom in the hallway to comfort them.

That day, and several times since, I've wondered if the electoral outcome is exactly what we needed. It's not. Clearly, it's not. But at the very least, it's what we should have expected. Our social and political constructs were built exactly for this, and we've allowed those constructs to remain in place.

I think about our society that elevates the rich and regularly gives passes to the most wealthy men for all manner of unfavorable actions. This is the success that we strive for so giving pass and supporting a man from this group makes sense.

I think about how we deliberately draw inequitable electoral boundaries and allow systems to remain that are designed to quiet black and brown voices. We shuffle generations of families through pipelines, from poverty to school to prison, and then hit repeat. Should we really be surprised that some people don't engage politically or exercise their right to vote, when they are reminded on a daily basis that their voices are not respected?

We turn the other way when neighbors or family members make derogatory statements about people of other backgrounds, faiths, orientations, or genders. We're emotionally exhausted by our day and what we have seen on the news that night, and we don't want to ruin dinner. After so much practice, looking the other way way for a politician isn't so hard.

I watch as we saddle women with unattainable expectations and offer them disparate rewards for their work. We demand that women perform this precarious tightrope act while others rattle the ropes. We are resigned to see one another knocked down—so why does it continually surprise anyone when women vote against their own interests?

We don't educate our children about the earth and how it sustains us, and how we mistreat it; about the people who live here, about their own history and your history and mine. Not all of our children are all taught to raise up their peers when they seek out and attempt to spread knowledge. I'm not surprised when, in turn, we elect leaders who don't understand the very basics themselves.

I wonder why we are surprised when leaders are elected who support conversion therapy or white supremacy or have their hands in oil or on women's bodies when big money and big politics and big egos are so often aligned. Clearly, an entire campaign can be successfully run by placing blame and fear on all manners of others. This is not new. The wealthiest in this world continually give us reason to fight each other so that our attention is not drawn to them.

We've lived with these and many more systems and structures that brought us to the day when over sixty million Americans thought voting for Trump was a good idea. So I don't want to talk about that day anymore. I don't need to be reminded about the popular vote or for "I'm With Her" to be our battle cry and I don't want to hear any more speculation about other strategies that may have worked. I want to talk about what really got us here and how we move forward.

We, the people, need to show our personal humanity and reclaim our collective humanity. We must face our national issues head on. We need to examine our own actions and claim our part in supporting the systems that led us here. We can't look away when they make us squirm with unease. We must dismantle these broken systems that favor the very few.

We should be empowered by our choice to sometimes step aside and be silent and be thoughtful and powerful when it's our turn to speak. Listen and share so that our personal knowledge can be collective knowledge. We can't be passive when any person's liberty is threatened. We must stand as individuals united in fact and compassion-based solidarity. We must practice kindness, love, and empathy daily.

We must make taking responsibility for our actions and responsibility for one another parts of our fight.

As Americans, and as humans, we have been entered into a contract to take care of each other. As my 77-year-old mother would say, like it or not, we're in this together. And, as my young daughter will tell you, everyone's voice matters.

Erika Haynes, age 46
Community educator
Willimantic, CT

Always an Activist

I HAVE ALWAYS BEEN an activist. In high school, my activism was about recovering the remains of the Vietnam War POWs and volunteering at an eldercare home. In college, I joined Amnesty International. As a mom, I have been active with International Justice Mission, fighting human trafficking and slavery, and Blessings in a Backpack, feeding children on the weekends. But during this election, I neither felt passionately about Hillary nor took the threat of Trump seriously. That all changed November 10, 2016. (November 9 was simply a day of recovering, getting my bearings in a new Trump world, and grieving for what could have been.)

On November 10, I changed my focus. I vowed to no longer stay silent. I am outspoken, both on social media and in real life. I found friends on liberal groups online. On Friday, November 12, my daughter and I went to our first post-Trump community action event, discussing "What Next?" I booked an Airbnb for the Women's March on Washington, and my daughter and I will be traveling for the event on January 21, 2017.

It's funny, this new world of action for me. *Action*, to me, requires stepping outside my comfort zone, doing what is right even when it isn't necessarily easy. Action is finding time during the day to make a phone call to an elected official; sharing political posts online while my daughter is in dance class; dragging myself to an action planning meeting when I would rather stay at home in my sweats, watching an episode of "American Housewife."

My husband is not an activist. When I began signing up for events and taking action, he told me he didn't understand the point. What happened cannot be undone, in his opinion. He might be right, and we might not be able to undo it. He and I are, however, accountable to our children; we must explain to our son and daughters how we let a Trump presidency, and the subsequent fear, happen.

Recently, my husband has changed his perspective, and we have an agreement: I will attend meetings and protests, wave my signs both virtually and in real life, and push all of us to do better for our children. He will do the unseen work in making this happen, staying home and watching our kids, and maybe even making a sign or two.

My life has changed forever because of this election. I lost friends: both (1) people I thought I knew but then learned that we do not share the same values or priorities and (2) people I was very close to who felt they had no choice but to retreat into their families in order to keep them safe. I made friends: my online family grew from three hundred to nineteen hundred, and during this process, I learned the importance of trusting others in order to come together for the greater good. I hold myself to a higher standard, one of honesty, accountability, and recognition, that says or do nothing is tacit assent. Truly, though, my heart is broken, and, no matter how I assemble the pieces, there will always be scars.

Jennifer Roth, age 47
Stay-at-home mom
Oradell, New Jersey

Born a Democrat

M Y GIRLFRIENDS AND I spent the summer of 2016 talking about the upcoming election. We talked over glasses of wine and cups of coffee. We talked about Donald Trump and about how a reality-TV personality with questionable success as a businessman could even be considered as a candidate for president of the United States. We talked about who the people were who supported him, even after the scandalous reports surfaced. We talked about Hillary Clinton and about how we thought she deserved to be the first woman president of the United States. We questioned the weight people placed on Hillary's emails and on Benghazi.

We dissected everything and everyone.

We were consumed.

We had been excited to see President Obama being sworn in as the first black president, and we were more than ready for the woman president—in our minds, no one was more qualified than Hillary Rodham Clinton.

In one of our chat sessions, my friend Alison told us how her eleven-year-old son had asked her if he was born a Democrat. She went on to tell us how she had explained to him that no one was *born a Democrat*—it was a choice, based on your beliefs and values.

I nodded as she told the story. No one knew this more than I.

*   *   *

My dad is a Republican.

I am not.

In 1976, I was in elementary school, and Jimmy Carter was running against Gerald Ford. I don't really recall what I heard in school or on TV; I just knew somehow that I was aligned with Jimmy Carter.

I remember a conversation with my dad. "You will vote for Jimmy Carter, right?" I asked.

"No," he said. "I'm a Republican. I would never vote for Jimmy Carter."

In 1980, Jimmy Carter was running against Ronald Reagan. My dad packed my brother and me into his black '70s Dodge Polara and drove us to the local fire station, which was being used as a polling place. We sat in the car while he went inside. When he came out, I asked if he had voted for Jimmy Carter.

"No," he said, "I'm a Republican. I would never vote for Jimmy Carter."

*   *   *

I believe my dad's strong affiliation with the Republican party came from serving in the army as a military police officer. He was conservative, but the mild-mannered and nonconfrontational type. My dad's brother was a different story. Uncle Stanley, who has never been married and never had a girlfriend as long as I've known him, was a die-hard pro-lifer and would fight tooth and nail with anyone who opposed his point of view. Forget the fact that he was legally deaf, lived below the poverty line in South Philadelphia's low-income housing, and would benefit a thousand times more than my family would with a Democrat in office. All that mattered to Uncle Stanley was that we did away with a woman's right to choose. The only trips I had ever known my uncle to take—aside from trips to visit us—were to Washington, DC, for pro-life rallies.

My brother also is a Republican. Our holiday dinners have always looked the same. The women in the kitchen, and my dad, uncle, and brother, content as clams, chilling on the couch watching Fox News—the one news channel that supported their narrow-minded beliefs.

Until last summer, my mother, now seventy-five, had never made a peep about politics. But one morning in July, she called me just as I was fixing my first pot of coffee. After a few minutes of idle conversation, she started ranting about how much she detested Donald Trump. She could not stand the look of him, his voice, or anything that came out of his mouth. The floodgates had opened.

After our conversation, I immediately called two of my friends who lived in New Jersey and were going to Pennsylvania each weekend to register voters.

A week later, my mom was a registered voter.

*   *   *

My husband and I have been married for thirteen years. We're politically aligned.

After Trump's nomination, my husband joked that he was going to vote for him.

"If you vote for Trump, I'll divorce you!" I threatened.

My husband chuckled. "Oh, really? Then I'll vote for him twice!"

"Then I'll divorce you twice!"

*   *   *

On the night of the election, I decided to have a small party with my like-minded friends. I cooked Mexican food to honor all the hard-working Mexicans whom Donald Trump wanted to deport. Each guest was given a metallic patriotic necklace to wear and had to enter through the silver fringed door curtains into the party room. A large banner with flags stretched from one side of the room to the other. Half a dozen patriotic Stars and Stripes fans dangled from the ceiling.

Election night seemed to never end. We switched from channel to channel. At one point, my mom meekly asked, "Do you think Hillary will really win?"

A chorus of voices answered her: "Absolutely!"

This exchange, as simple as it was, touched me. My mother grew up in a time when having a woman president was not even a possibility. I grew up in a generation where women could achieve whatever they set their minds to, and so would my daughter. That night, three generations of women were watching history unfold. It didn't cross my mind that Donald Trump could possibly win.

The hours grew later. I settled into the couch and waited. My daughter crawled into my lap and fell asleep.

Around midnight, they made the announcement: Hillary Clinton had conceded.

I cried myself to sleep, and I cried when I woke up the next morning, only a few hours later.

My daughter ran around the corner, her eyes lit up. I waited, knowing the question behind her smile. "Did Hillary win?"

*   *   *

One of the most difficult things for me, after the election, was looking at everyone and wondering if they voted for Clinton or

Trump. The 2016 election was not simply a matter of someone's political opinions' being different from mine; it was a matter of a loved one's support of a candidate with such hate-fueled rubbish.

After I voted on the day of the election, I went to my weekly tennis lesson shared with another student, a fifty-something white female. Our coach was a fifty-something white male. I didn't know them well and was too scared to ask whom they had voted for (I had already paid for the lessons, after all).

Midway through the lesson, I heard some talk across the court about Hillary and Donald. I placed my hands over my ears and yelled, "I don't want to know who you voted for because I like you, and if I know who you voted for, I might not be able to talk to you guys again!"

My coach looked at me for a moment before admitting: "I voted for Hillary."

The other student cleared her throat and said, "Really, Jennifer? I voted for Hillary. Trump wants to press a button to end the world."

Maybe so, I thought. *But he hasn't yet.*

Jennifer Dunn, age 37
Special education teacher
Cambridge, Massachusetts

The Night That Decency Died

I HANDED MY ID to the poll volunteer and watched as she ran her finger down the list of names. I smiled at all the *D*s her finger passed by on its way to my name.

Inside the polling booth, I told myself to mark the ballot clearly. *No dimpled chads.* I put my left finger on the bubble next to Hillary Rodham Clinton's name and colored that baby in with the precision of a neurosurgeon. I was claiming my place in history that morning. Meticulousness and a three-point check system were in order; I wasn't about to let a sloppy ballot put me on the wrong side of this story.

I handed my ballot to the poll worker and watched it glide into the machine. "Has it been busy?" I asked him.

"A steady flow," he replied. "A third of Massachusetts has already voted."

"Good," I said. *Thank God*, I thought. High voter turnout was usually a good sign for Democrats.

*   *   *

I sent my sister a message sometime around three in the afternoon on Election Day, asking her if she was excited. I had been shimmying all day, just as Hillary did during the first debate—breaking into random happy dances, pumping my arms in the air as I chanted to myself in the middle of the kitchen. "Hillary! Hillary! Hillary!"

My sister texted back saying she was nervous, not excited. The pit-in-your-stomach kind of nervous. *About what?* I wondered. There was no way that a country that voted for Obama twice, against good candidates, would ever vote for someone like Donald Trump. No way. I had total trust in the decency of my country.

* * *

On the night of the election, I put my three-year-old daughter to bed early and let my nine-year-old son stay up with us.

The early states went red, as they always do. I didn't panic. But then Florida went red too, and the stress started to build. "It's early," my husband said. "Don't worry." Still, my shirt felt tighter on my skin. My cheeks were hot. And I felt an incessant need to stand up, sit down, and stand back up again.

My son started to do the math. "If we get California, that's the most."

"We will definitely get California," I said.

"Texas is big too," my son said. "If we get that one, I think we will win."

"We won't get Texas," I told him. "Most of the people down there are Republicans."

"Why?"

"I don't know. Because their parents were? Some aren't— but most are, and they really like their guns, and meat, and big SUVs down there, and they think Hillary Clinton and people like us want to take those things away from them. And Hillary sent work emails from her phone, so they want her to be put in jail."

"Huh?"

"I can't explain it any better than that," I said. "It doesn't make sense to me, either."

"Okay. Mommy, are you scared?" he asked.

I was definitely scared. I was definitely angry, but I kept watching as, state by state, decency faded from the map.

My feet had definitely stopped dancing.

*   *   *

On the way to my kids' school the next morning, a man in a red hat stood on the street, holding a Trump sign. I'd seen him before, with *Impeach Obama and Clinton* signs, and had passed by peacefully. *If he doesn't understand that the secretary of state can't be impeached, then I shouldn't give him a hard time,* I had thought to myself, and let it go.

But the world was different now. I was different now. I saw the red hat first and steadied the wheel with my left hand. As I got closer, I stuck up my right hand and flipped him the bird.

"Uh, Mommy?" my son said. "I think what you just did is all of the swears."

"Listen," I said, looking at him through my rearview mirror, "you and your sister are half black, your favorite aunt is gay, and we have lots of Muslim and Latino friends who we love very much. There is nothing wrong with what I just did."

As the hours passed, hope faded further. As the days progressed, the KKK threw a party on a bridge in North Carolina; a Saudi student was beaten to death in Wisconsin; a woman in New York had her hijab ripped off her head and was told to hang herself with it. Protesters took to the streets. Trump supporters called them *crybabies* and *sore losers.* The news of these events was a lot to handle. It was enough to make me want to throw my hands up in the air and just give up.

But I can't. I have two children, and sometimes when I take them upstairs to bed after a long day, I catch the shadows of their silhouettes on the wall out of the corner of my eye—with their little Afros and footy pajamas—and the amount of love I feel for them nearly squeezes the breath out of my body.

So I will never give up—my children are worth fighting for.

Someone recently asked me why I was so angry over the election. As I looked into his eyes, I steadied myself and prepared to defend my point of view. But then, from out of nowhere, my voice answered, "*Why aren't you* angry about it?" Something in the way I said it, the way I emphasized the words *why aren't you*, made him apologize. And it occurred to me then that I don't need to defend my anger. There is a right kind of anger—an anger that should be embraced rather than avoided or swept away—and this is it. It is the anger over the death of decency in 2016 that will produce generations of new advocates in 2017 and the years that follow. Marches, books, boycotts, petitions, phone calls, and letters to Congress: all are born from the right kind of anger.

So let the voices sound. Let them emerge from every corner of this country, joining in unison; let the voices hum, grow louder and stronger together, and push us through this nonsense to a nation where decency lives once again.

Jocelyn Desmarais Goldblatt, age 42
Consultant
New Hampshire

Roar: Thawing

WHEN DID I lose my voice?

It died with *him* two generations ago. Hanging in the yard, in the freezing cold New Hampshire winter. He didn't die there though. According to the newspaper article my mother found a few years ago, my great-grandfather died sometime later of pneumonia in the hospital. The article also said that the baby was with Edith when she found him. The baby was my grandmother; Edith was her mother.

He did it because of money. Deep into the Great Depression, a promise of money fell through. He couldn't take the failure any longer. He left her alone with five children. Today I can look at the town records to see *wood and food* was given to *the town poor*—the handwritten words next to the name of my maternal great-grandmother are both sad and comforting. They indicate that the family was warm and fed and not entirely alone.

I grew up hearing stories about the orphanage and the day the state came to take all the children away. Edith had dressed them all up in nice clothes, fixed their hair, and washed their faces; she hugged and kissed them all goodbye. The stories— even the funny ones about playing tricks on the nuns—always made me feel sorry for my grandmother. When you feel sorry for someone, they can get away with a lot.

My voice stayed buried in my grandmother's pain and confusing behaviors, and my purpose became finding a way out of the cycle of unhealthy, toxic thinking for myself and for others. I made my way out of the shadow of hiding truth: "Don't tell nobody, or they'll take you away." I fought my way out of distrusting my own eyes, ears, and feelings. I defied my way out of crazy opinions about "other" people. I meditated, practiced, and loved my way into safe and warm surroundings.

I didn't grow up in New Hampshire. I did not know until recently that this is the very town where Edith kissed her babies goodbye. Fate and energy brought us to this place a few years ago. Ironically, the move provided us with a better financial situation than where we were. I'm convinced there is meaning in the way the details of my life have come together. If I am patient, my voice will be heard. I already hear my voice in the echoes of the women who have taken to the streets to say, "No more!" I hear my voice in the countless stories of survivors who, like me, are triggered so deeply by Trump's mannerisms and behaviors.

When Obama took office, I believed with all of my heart we were on our way to a great awakening that would finally heal all the hurts, the brokenness, the pain. Things would finally fall into their proper order. Leaders would take responsibility for their impact on citizens. No one would ever again hang himself, abandoning his family because of money. No mother would be left without means to provide for her children without a man. People would be recognized for their intrinsic value as opposed to their market value. Families in their various forms would be cherished and supported rather than forced to serve an economic structure that does not serve them.

I believed all of this right up until two in the morning on November 9, 2016. I woke my husband up and said, "We have a President-Elect Trump."

He laughed.

When I didn't laugh back, he said, "Wait, are you serious?"

"Very serious."

At first I was resolute—I would fight. I would make phone calls, write letters, and march. Maybe I would go to law school.

I have to admit that this election and its aftermath have shaken me to the core, and the voice I felt warming and thawing, froze once again. I retreated into a safe world where I could impact the things in my immediate sphere. I cleaned and did repairs, clearly a symbolic gesture to prepare for what's to come. I know I'm warming up for a long four years. May the warm breath of truth blanket the ears of those who have refused to hear.

My faith in a healthy future rests on my deep belief in democracy and humanity. I know that the lucid participation of citizens relies on everyday actions as much as in large demonstrations. I will be kind every chance I get and I will tell a loving and resolute truth whenever my voice is needed.

Jaclyn Schildkraut, age 36
Assistant professor of criminal justice
Syracuse, New York

A Lesson Beyond the Books

A S A FEMALE professor, I often find myself surrounded not only by bureaucracy but also by patriarchy. Since I began working in academia, I had nearly resigned myself to always making less than my male colleagues. Despite this frustration, I continued to put my head down and work hard, believing that if I could prove myself, the quality of my work would matter more than my gender. Accordingly, before the Fall 2016 semester, I had never considered myself a feminist.

Something about this election triggered a change in me, however, and feminism quickly established itself in my everyday responsibilities of teaching. I was determined to help my students understand how women and people of color are treated in and by our criminal justice system. I was also determined to show how these disparities bled out into all aspects of our lives.

During the Fall 2016 semester, I taught two sections of my university's American Criminal Courts class. In a broad sense, the course is an introduction to the criminal justice system and related laws. The second half of the term is always my favorite because we delve deep into case law to understand how the courts have interpreted and redefined the Fourth, Fifth, Sixth, and Eighth Amendments through their decisions.

Each student was provided a pocket version of the US Constitution. At the beginning of each section, we would go over the related amendment as it was written, and the students could then annotate their copies of the Constitution. As we progressed, just how patriarchal is the language of this longstanding symbol of our country quickly became more apparent to me than ever before. Each and every amendment uses the words *him* or *his*.

Thinking back, I am not sure why I was so surprised, given that the framers of our Constitution often are referred to as the "Founding Fathers." Still, given the political climate at the time—the fact that Hillary Clinton was constantly diminished for being a woman, for wearing a pantsuit, and for not smiling enough—I found myself all the more aware of how this language might be perceived or what impact it might have, particularly among my female students. To compensate, each time an amendment used the word *his*, I would read it as "his or her."

This practice led to a poignant moment in one of the sections about one week after the election and the heartbreaking loss that accompanied it. We began our discussion of the Sixth Amendment as we had done before—by reading and analyzing the text. Like before, I made sure to emphasize the *his and her* in the language—it seemed more important than ever now, in my mind. I will never forget what ensued.

One of my female students who was sitting toward the back of the room tentatively raised her hand. When I called on her, she asked in a nervous tone if I thought that our country would ever revise the language of the Constitution to represent both men and women. I remember pausing, gathering my thoughts, and drawing a deep breath. "I would like to believe we would," I told her. Then I had to break the harsh reality: "If it does happen, it likely won't for some time. While as a country we have made great strides, there is still a glass ceiling that needs to be broken. We were not even able to elect a female president because of the patriarchal beliefs that are so ingrained in our nation."

I will never forget the disappointment on her face. I will never forget the disappointment I felt having to tell this to her, and how I wished our country was better so that I did not have to. I also never will forget what happened next.

The room was silent, as if in the midst of the aftermath of a bomb blast. Many students sat there, looking as if they were really trying to process what I had just said. Then one of my other students—a white male—raised his hand. I nodded, giving him the floor to speak. He said, "I believe when the framers of the Constitution wrote the document, they just used *his* to mean everyone. They really meant everyone was included." A collective gasp echoed when he was done speaking, and all eyes turned to me to see how I would respond.

Feeling myself being pulled between sadness, shock, anger, and disbelief, I quickly regained my composure and then proceeded to spend the next thirty minutes explaining why that was not what was meant and that the use of masculine pronouns was absolutely intended. I explained that women have always been viewed as lesser than men, and that view is why any specific mention of women was omitted from the Constitution. I highlighted that until 1919, white women did not have the right to vote for their Commander in Chief; black women did not have the same power until 1965. I pointed out that until 1974, women could not get a credit card without their husband's signature (single women, be damned—no credit for you!). Then I reminded them that in 2016, women still make less than men, are still pigeonholed into "gender-appropriate positions" (e.g., women as teachers but not as principals), and are devalued for doing the exact same things that men do and that a woman was not able to be elected president, despite being vastly more qualified than the male candidate.

At the end of my discussion, I chose to end class. I did not want to have the points I had raised get lost amid a continued lesson about the right to an attorney and a jury of one's peers. As I finished, several students clapped, which I was not expecting. On their way out, some of my female students came up and thanked me—a small gesture for being the voice they needed. It was then that I realized what an absolutely awesome responsibility being an educator truly is. Teaching is not just about facts and tables—it is about participating in and conveying the bigger picture of what it means to be a citizen of this country. As I left the classroom, I smiled to myself, for Hillary Clinton was the one who inspired me to be a feminist and to be the voice others needed. After all, *her* voice had been the one I needed.

Kimber Dion, age 39
Filmmaker, mommy, and graduate student
Small town in New England

Firestarter

"The great challenge of this gathering is to give voice to women everywhere whose experiences go unnoticed, whose words go unheard"

—*Hillary Clinton*[4]

NOVEMBER 8, 2016. Election Day. *The* day. My blazer hung on a hot pink hanger, waiting to be proudly worn. That day I set my alarm way too early in anticipation of voting. My four children and I stood in line together for an hour amongst Trump supporters in small-town America. I wept as I dropped my ballot in the box and proudly sported my *I Voted* sticker. Walking back to the car, my youngest son asked if Trump had a chance. I immediately shot back: "Of course not, honey; America is smarter than that." Who knew that

---

4 Clinton, Hillary. Speech, United Nations Fourth World Congress on Women, Beijing, September 5, 1995.

hours later I would eat those words as the numbers started to come in?

My daughters were especially excited about a woman president and had been so inspired by hearing Hillary speak. My sons were disgusted hearing Trump speak and disrespect women. At school they were among a small handful of students who were pro-Hillary and daily had to hear awful things about minorities, gay rights, and women's bodies. The day after the election, boys ran through the hallways of my daughter's high school chanting, "Grab 'em by the pussy!" Others were telling kids to "go back to where they came from" and saying that soon Trump would be deporting them.

*   *   *

About a month before the election, a friend asked what the big deal was with Trump's remarks about grabbing women and doing what he wanted, that it was nothing more than "locker room talk." In response, I headed to social media and posted publicly about my sexual assault.

When I was in high school, I was assaulted by my then boyfriend. We had dated only a few months and had agreed to not have sex. One afternoon, he decided he would take what he wanted by force. I eventually told my close friends and my mother. My parents called the police, and when I was interviewed by the assistant district attorney, the first question he asked was how many sexual partners I'd had. He wanted to know what was I wearing at the time of the assault. I was humiliated and ashamed, and the person who was supposed to be on my side and walk me through this process was essentially blaming me for being raped.

There was a girl inside of me who wanted to be strong and change the world, but I slowly shrunk away and hid my heart far, far away. I pushed down the memory of the assault and decided to pretend what happened wasn't a big deal. I started wearing big baggy clothes, dyed my hair dark colors, stopped wearing makeup, and threw out all my tight jeans and lace bras. I hid my face and my heart, hid that I was a woman. Being a woman meant being hurt.

It took a decade to come to terms with being assaulted and to openly talk about it. Negative voices told me that the assault was not a big deal, my fault, or just sex and that nobody would want to be with me. Now that they considered me to be dirty used goods, their words—that I didn't have the right to say no and shouldn't have been alone with him—rang in my head. After all this time, I still catch myself speaking these negative things to myself. When I hear Trump talk to women like they are nothing but blow-job machines, my stomach drops. I feel sick in the pit of my being, my soul aches, my guard goes up, and I feel like I'm back on that couch in the summer of 1994. I want to stand up for myself, my body, and my rights.

To stand up boldly for other women's rights to their bodies, especially for my beautiful daughters, is important to me because I do not ever want them to feel like they are just a body for a man to take and do what he wants. I want them to own their sexuality and be confident in their skin, knowing that they can say no or yes and that their choices will be perfectly okay and respected 110%. I want my sons to know that a woman has the right to say yes or no and that they must absolutely respect and honor women's boundaries, and vice versa. With his atrocious behavior toward women, the idea of having Trump at the helm of our country terrifies me to my core. How many men will think they have "permission" to take what they want and feel no regard for that person? How many women will be even more terrified to come forward if they have been raped? How many young girls will hide their secrets and feel shame and not share their pain?

I cried myself to sleep the night of the election, praying there would be different news when I awoke in the morning. I was in shock; I felt dumbfounded. How did so many Americans turn a blind eye and a deaf ear to his bullying? How did so many women turn their backs on other women and vote for him?

While I grapple with discouragement and fear, I remember Hillary's talking about our rights and continued awareness that we are stronger together. We must fight, not only for ourselves but also for our daughters, nieces, granddaughters, and the generations to come. We must not be silent; we must share our stories; we must hold one another up; and we must take the hand of the woman next to us and say, "Get up; let's keep fighting! We are brave, bold, and worth it." We *are* worth it. We will stand back up, channeling our rage, fears, and our wailing. And we will change the world. We will always be *stronger together.*

(daughter)
Coco Grace Kelly Dion, age 10
5th-grade student
Small town in New England

Madame Prez

O N ELECTION DAY, I was so excited! I was excited for Hillary and for girls all over our country. Hillary fights for girls' rights and better education for us and for us to make choices about our bodies. When Donald won the election, I was mad and wondered why people voted for him. He is a bully and says bad things about women. If he went to my school, he would get expelled for being a mean bully. I felt so sad that my friends and grandparents voted for him. Donald Trump doesn't care about my voice, but Hillary does. She encourages me to stay in school, get good grades, be kind to everyone, stand up against bullies, and be a role model to other girls. I am proud to tell everyone that I look up to her and she is my hero. In my school, I was voted class president. One day I want to go to Brown University and be the real president of the United States. My friends tell me I'm bossy enough to be president, but my mom says that I am *leadership material.*

Melissa Paciulli, age 44
Mother, daughter, engineer, and PhD candidate
Amherst, Massachusetts

In My Grandfather's Name

WHEN MY GRANDFATHER died a few years back, I was heartbroken. I was his first grandchild, and we had a special bond. I looked to him when I needed guidance and support, and he was always there with encouragement and love. He was the one I called to take a look at my first house before I signed on the line.

When I graduated from high school in 1990, he was there with a special gift for me. He was so proud to give me $2,000 he had saved for me beginning the day I was born. This was an unwritten contract for me to attend college. His expectation was that I would be a first-generation college graduate. Education was extremely important to him; it was everything he dreamed of for me. His heart was filled with hope and pride for me that day, and I will never forget.

Looking back, I would never have had the heart to tell him I had the best summer of my life on that money—I just wasn't ready. I left the East Coast, made my way across the country at nineteen, and married in Vegas. After exhausting my options without an education, I returned home and attended school while I was eight months pregnant with my daughter. My grandfather remained supportive because he knew I had a strength that I did not know I had. He saw potential in me. He was my biggest fan when it came to my education.

Over the years, I have dedicated my academic achievements to my grandfather. This year, I will proudly complete my doctor of philosophy in engineering. It has not been an easy path for me as a single parent and a woman in a STEM field, forging my own path and breaking down barriers one by one. This journey has required a level of commitment and fortitude I never dreamed I had. It has required building an inner strength that has gotten only stronger.

When my grandfather passed away, I was honored to take his ashes across the pond to Normandy. I spoke in front of many of his dear friends about how much I respected him for his sacrifice in WWII on D-Day and about how much he loved his country and theirs. His sacrifice impacted not only his life but also his children's and grandchildren's lives—mine. He had been a force that shaped me into the woman I am, and I was so proud to honor him that day. I scattered his ashes in the water on Omaha Beach with a sense of pride and connection that was magical.

When we went through his life possessions, my mother came across my "file" in his paperwork. There was a picture of me at a young age in pigtails, a copy of the diploma from my undergraduate degree, and a picture of Hillary Clinton. I smiled so much that day at how my grandfather had thought of me and Hillary Clinton together, that he thought I could even contend with a woman of that magnitude. I laughed and cried. My grandfather—my biggest fan.

And then the election of 2016. I was elated. I was proud. I was walking on a cloud. I was about to help elect the first women president, and nothing could bring my mood down. I felt connected to this election with a newfound sense of purpose of action and progress. My candidate was qualified and brilliant and had spent her life building her résumé to the level of competency required for her dream job.

After each debate, I waited to see what *Saturday Night Live* was going to highlight and then had a great laugh. I knew my grandfather was smiling down. There was no doubt in my mind that Hillary would not win. She was *it*. She was breaking that glass ceiling.

The morning of the election, I put on my Wonder Woman sneakers, my pantsuit, and my pearls. I took pictures going into vote; I took selfies of my smiling face coming out. *This* was history happening, and I felt it. I felt a connection to the strong women in America, to the woman that was about to make history as our first female president. Nothing could go wrong. When I arrived home, I put my Hillary shirt on, opened some wine, and got ready to watch the results come in. I smiled all day. My grandfather was smiling down.

I could not believe the results as they rolled in. I felt betrayal, but this was a feeling I was familiar with. The feeling of being misunderstood. The knowledge that you are qualified, but you are a woman. You are the better candidate, but you have a resting bitch face. The feeling of being proud of your work, but scaling it back so that you are not aggressive. The feeling of "almost."

I have experienced many hurdles in my non-traditional life. This is not an easy path—to forge new ground. It is often painful, confusing, difficult, and full of disparaging remarks from doubters, but I have a strength in me that has been nurtured and can be seen by others, even when I cannot see it myself. We must join our individual strengths together.

When I initially joined my community—the women who were organizing a demonstration, the women who were ignited to run for office, the young international students who volunteered with me to tutor young girls in STEM—I felt solace. But now I had a new feeling. I felt change, I felt strength, and I felt action. I knew this feeling. This feeling was connection. Not individual connection but the type of connection that takes movement and collection of individual strength, building something unbreakable. We are stronger together, truly.

My grandfather is smiling again.

Sarah Mullen, age 30
Secretary, Veterans Affairs
Smyrna, Delaware

Born This Way

I HAD SUSPECTED FROM the age of three that my son was gay. So did the rest of our family. Shane never came out to us; he never had to. Gay was never a choice for him. He was genuinely born that way.

* * *

Shane was a pleasant, easy-going baby. He loved to be held. I would spend hours rocking him and talking to him. His cousin, Cole, was only six weeks older than him, and seemed to be developing motor skills faster than Shane. But when I voiced my concerns to the pediatrician, he advised us not to compare one child's developmental milestones to another's.

As time went by, Shane's growth continued to be slightly delayed. Our family doctor recommended having tubes put in his ears, in addition to testing for any developmental delays. We immediately set about getting these things done.

Weeks later, the results of the evaluation came back: Shane

needed speech therapy and therapy for gross and fine motor skills.

Shortly after his third birthday, when Shane had completed his at-home therapy, he started the *Early Choices* program through our school district and began to flourish. His first progress report read, "Shane is the most caring child in our class. If another student shows any signs of distress, he will stop what he is doing and go comfort that child, asking them if they are ok, well after the event. He also really loves the dress up area."

At home, Shane lined up all of his toys by type. Trucks with other trucks, stuffed animals together. He created patterns out of blocks, and could often be found wearing his shirt on his head, the neck band around his hairline, and the length of the shirt cascading down his back like long hair.

One day, Shane stopped playing with his trucks, and started showing more interest in his sister's toys. As a parent, when your child makes a choice that breaks the rules, you rush to correct them. *No, Shane, boys don't play with dolls. Boys don't marry other boys.* I felt like all I was doing was telling him no.

I spent the next year trying to break Shane of his "girlie" behavior, but it was hard—especially when we were out in public. We'd be at the park and I would have to wrangle dolls away from him, praying no one would notice the boy in the football shirt carrying a Barbie Doll™.

Close to Shane's fifth birthday, I read an article written by the mother of a boy who wore princess dresses to daycare. I'd suspected other parents were going through the same situation as Shane and I—that I wasn't the only parent who had a child who was slightly off-center. So I made the decision to back off as much as possible.

Keeping with my new philosophy, I vowed to protect Shane as much as possible from the kids who might make fun of his choice in toys. But as it turned out, it wasn't the kids who were mean—it was their parents. Adults would approach me during class parties and ask if I knew my son was playing at the kitchen set with the girls. I overheard parents say, "Poor Shane plays with girl toys because his teenage mother doesn't care enough to correct him." My son would come home from school in tears because his friends were told by their parents not to play with him.

As Shane grew older, I let him make more of his own decisions. I stopped trying to control the items he chose and found pleasure in. I started buying him dolls, and allowed him to watch the programs he found entertaining. He started to open up more at home. He would occasionally slip and say things like, *When I grow up and have a husband* or *When I get a boyfriend* . . . Sometimes I still corrected him, because in my heart, I wasn't quite ready to accept the truth.

You see, when you bring your mushy ball of human home from the hospital, you are absorbed in helping them meet their milestones. You focus on walking, talking, potty-training, alphabet recital, counting to one-hundred, writing their name, learning to read, graduating high school. You wonder whether they will become a doctor, or a lawyer, or a cop. You don't think about them taking a path that is foreign to you.

But time has brought acceptance: I have now accepted that Shane will never bring home a girlfriend home. I will never watch him walk down the aisle with a blushing bride, never watch his wife grow heavy with my grandbaby.

But you know what? I no longer care about any of that. My son will change the world—maybe not for the masses, but definitely for his friends and family. I know this because he has already changed the world for me, and very much for the better.

*   *   *

After the inauguration, Shane came home from school and asked me if I agreed with gay conversion therapy. I was so taken aback. It had *never* crossed my mind to think that my son has a disease that needs to be shocked out of him. Donald Trump has given us a vice president who feels that gay people can and should be electrocuted into submission. The idea that all the progress the LGBTQ community has made could be rolled back, leaving my son with less footing than the generation before him, is very unsettling.

As a parent, my number one job is to protect my child. I will go to the ends of the world to ensure, support, and protect Shane's basic human rights. I will sit in the front row with tears in my eyes as he marries the man who fills every dark space in his heart with light and love. I will open my heart and home to that man, and love him even if his family cannot. I won't change the verbiage of my story when I speak about my son and his future husband. I will advocate for him and the millions of others like him, and will fight with my last breath for him to be equal in the eyes of the government.

America—often called the land of milk and honey—tends to be sweeter, more generous, to those who don't rock the boat. My hope for Shane is that he knocks the boat over.

Selena R. Bira, age 48
Call center supervisor
Winthrop, Maine

War Cry

WHEN I WAS a girl, I spent a great deal of time with my mother's best friend, Vikki. Vikki had always been my role model, the kind of woman I wanted to become. She was smart, strong-willed, and brave—everything a girl would envy in the '60s. And she did it all: work, run a home, raise her children, and continue her own journey in writing, all while looking like she stepped out of *Harper's Bazaar*. Because of her, I believed I could have it all too.

Vikki became my voice. When I was fifteen, she discovered I was being physically assaulted in my home by my stepfather. When the police and child protective services removed me from my home, they asked whom they should call for me. I gave them Vikki's number. She raced to the police station and hugged me tightly the minute she saw me. "I'm so sorry. You're safe now and always will be from this day forward," she said. Before she had arrived, I'd been thinking about my mother and how devastated she would be when she learned of what happened. But the moment Vicki's arms wrapped around me, all those thoughts vanished. It was the first time I felt protected. The hurt and profound shame that had clouded my existence were being replaced by Vikki's quiet steadfastness. I could breathe in her bravery and use it to bolster my own resolve to survive.

When the court threatened a few days later to place me back in the house where I'd lived with my stepfather, Vikki held me as I cried and begged to stay with her. My hands were shaking, my mind racing with fear, face flushed and covered in salty tears. "Even if I have to sell everything I own and take you far from here, you will never have to live with your stepfather again, I promise you!" she said. I believed her.

Vikki kept her promise, which ultimately caused a decade-long chasm in her longtime friendship with my mother. My mother felt betrayed, but years later, she would tell me of her self-hate for not seeing the abuse occurring right in front of her.

* * *

I, like so many women, felt the urgency and importance of the 2016 presidential election. After all, Hillary Clinton had spent her career challenging the roles and rules of what woman could or should be. Brazen and unafraid, she stood her ground, no matter the opposition or judgment that might follow—that kind of bravery reminded me of Vikki.

As a married lesbian with a younger daughter to protect, the possibility of Donald Trump's presidency left me feeling like I was ten again, alone and unprotected in the dark.

Two months later, I still don't know how this happened. I do know that, lately, I have been thinking a lot about what Vikki once taught me—nothing can be gained from letting our lives be ruled by fear. We must stay strong and refuse to be complicit.

As I write this, I'm fueled by my desire to make a change. I can feel my pulse quicken, my rising excitement—maybe it's a war cry for me to love my body, to love other women, to reach out in love to the new neighbors from a land far away. I make a resolution: I will not hide my love or gender to make others comfortable. I will rise up each day with a purpose and know that my marriage to my wife—who is judged daily because of her masculine clothing—matters. That our daughter matters. I will not permit anyone to steal my joy of the world.

*   *   *

I saw Vikki over the holidays this year. Her laugh remains a soothing lullaby to my tired mind. She is retired and busier than ever, but times are hard for her financially. Her retirement savings barely gets her by. Throughout her career, she was never rewarded with the same pay as the men in her office. She stayed at the same position year after year, while less qualified male coworkers received promotion after promotion. Therefore, she has to live very frugally, planning months in advance for costs such as replacing parts on her camera and changing the tires on her car.

Vicki and I didn't discuss this election, but we shared our uncertainty for the world's future. Vicki reached out and patted my hand. "But I still have hope," she said.

So do I.

Anonymous, age 46
Former director in IP Services industry; activist
Pittsburgh, Pennsylvania

On Predators

I KNOW A PREDATOR when I see one.
I know a predator when I see one because I had to study one in order to survive my childhood. Years of sexual, physical, and emotional abuse changed me. It would take decades for me to fully understand the impacts and ramifications of those changes.

Just before my fortieth birthday, I was forced to confront the darkness in my childhood. Within days of learning that a trusted loved one was in close contact with the predator from my life, I was frozen. The simple act of functioning was no longer an option. When my husband told me it was time to go to the hospital, all I could do was nod my head in agreement as tears streamed down my face. Within hours, I found myself sitting in the waiting room of a psychiatric facility wondering how I got there. I felt humiliated and could not recognize this person who was being admitted to a hospital program for mental health reasons. I didn't think I belonged there. By having a good marriage, being a good parent and exhibiting a diligent drive in my career, I could pretend that I was ok. I could pretend I didn't feel broken every day of my life. I could offer others grace and acceptance regarding trauma and the ensuing stigma of a mental health disorder, but I had none for myself. For weeks, I attended a daily program meant to combat the suicidal ideation I was experiencing. I signed the informal contract not to harm myself, took the medication, participated in the discussions and the many forms of artistic therapy, told numerous medical professionals painful details about my past, and humbled myself in ways I couldn't have understood without the experience of true desperation. The work was grueling, as it forced me to confront some cold hard truths about myself and see who I was in the past and who I had become as an adult. My surface reflection was polished, considerate of others, and determined for success. My deeper self-view was distorted, shattered and withholding. I denied the intensity and depth of my pain, until it consumed every ounce of strength I possessed, leaving me raw and isolated, afraid to be touched. I was overwhelmed with a constant barrage of shame, guilt, and anger until numbness set in and I could no longer feel anything—not even hope.

It was weeks before I felt the stirring of emotions. It was brief, but it was enough to allow me to see a possible new path—the beginning of a new worldview, understanding of my past, and anticipation for my future. This path included investing my energy toward introspection, growth, and healing. It also included the knowledge and acceptance of my new diagnosis of PTSD. It is a mental health diagnosis that finally explained the physical responses I felt throughout my body. It is my brain's response to perceived danger. As my body responds to dangers no longer present, I have rapid speech, a racing heart rate, an inability to still my body or manage my thoughts and a weight on my chest that feels like impending death. On rare occasion, I freeze and temporarily shut down. I denied the root cause of these responses, these triggering events, for decades. It would take years for me to begin unraveling the abuse and the ongoing effects of the abuse. Only then could I emerge from behind the shadow of denial.

I learned about doublespeak in therapy. Identifying it and decoding it is a skill I carry with me from my youth as doublespeak is inherent in every family where there is abuse. It also plays a prominent role in politics. The 2016 election was riddled with doublespeak and this was my wheelhouse. I was determined to learn from the familiar discomfort I experienced when I paid attention to the words and actions of Donald J. Trump. I began to follow his campaign closely and research his past. It did not take long to identify a pattern as I observed Trump say one thing in a speech; contradict himself on social media; laugh it off with a reporter; deny it in a debate; and then use public humiliation to shame everyone involved, labeling them enemies. I even began to expect the outrage from his supporters toward anyone who would dare hold his feet to the flame of human decency. Yet, even with all I learned, I did not predict the outcome of this election.

I was convinced this would be a landslide turnout for Clinton. I spent enough time engaged in political conversations online to know her statement about deplorables was not only true but underestimated. Even knowing this, I was optimistic. For me, November 8 2016, could not arrive fast enough. I was with my husband and my daughter at our close friends' home when I felt *it*. The first prickle of awareness regarding Clinton's defeat felt like a cold glass of water spreading through my body. My thoughts started racing, my cheeks flushed, and my adrenaline pumped in a familiar way that overloads my senses. I recognized the feelings I know too well: the onset of the physical symptoms of PTSD. I was entirely aware of why I felt physically chilled, with a leaden stomach and a hollowed sense of sound and environment. I knew everything was too intense; my brain was saying *enough*. I had to run, to leave, to get out before my newly exposed wounds became visible.

Arriving at home didn't help. My usual safe places no longer felt as secure or had that grounding effect I needed. My usual comforts felt hollow. The betrayal I felt six years ago was back. This time it was in the form of over sixty million Americans' voting for a predator and expecting me to call him Mr. President. I barely slept the night of the election. I stared at the ceiling in the dark and again let the tears fall down my face. I got up and paced around my silent house. There was no escaping what would come next for me. This part of awareness is acutely painful because I knew the nightmares would return and I was facing grey days with terrifying nights. I am aware of the reasons I didn't sleep that night or the many nights since. I know why I suddenly felt unsafe within the same surroundings I've lived in for years. I understand, more than most, why people suddenly felt outraged and were responding in defensive ways to loved ones or friends, simply because they voted for Trump. People I've loved most of my life cannot see a predator when they are right in front of them. But I can—and so can millions of other people.

Men and women both know the feeling of trauma, usually the result of a predator like Trump. He is entirely known to me—there is no question in my mind. The nausea I experience when I write his name, look at his face, or see and hear his cold, calculated words is based on knowledge and personal experience. I know for certain that we elected a predator to be our president. His need to control others is his main driver, and it is unrelenting. I know predatory behavior when I see it. When my life depended on it most, I learned. I spent a decade learning a predator's nuances, patterns of behavior, and body language. I spent a decade studying a predators' speech patterns and reactions to any given situation. It wasn't just the predator I had to study; it was also the people around him, because this predator was known to all of my family. I had to learn how others lived with him so I could navigate them too. I had to watch what they were willing to minimize, what they were willing to deny, and what they were willing to shut down in themselves in order to deny what was happening to me. I know what the justification of horrific behavior looks and feels like. I know it when I see it because I feel it everywhere. My unconscious mind is aware of the details and nuances that reveal the nature of a predatory man. I knew how dangerous Donald Trump was before I read about Ivana's original divorce complaint, complete with a rape allegation, before Trump silenced her with the obscuring influence of money. I knew it before I read the civil complaint against Mr. Trump for raping a thirteen-year-old girl. I knew it before I listened to the numerous recordings of the president describe women in demeaning, archaic, and overtly sexualized ways. I knew it before I watched Trump in interviews, sexually admiring his eldest daughter and then groping her onstage at the Republican National Convention. I knew it before he talked about grabbing women by the pussy. And I knew it before women backed up the story of his self-proclaimed sexual assaults. He wasn't trying to impress Billy Bush; he was telling Billy Bush exactly who was in charge. He was marking his territory. So much so, that Trump bragged about what he considers the ultimate show of power, grabbing a person's most private parts without consent. That, my friends, is a predator.

My roller coaster of emotions after the election continued as I read story after story from women and men who felt devastated and couldn't interpret why or defend their continued feelings of pain. I read in amazement as people I knew started to come out from the dark and defend the then president-elect. The shift came when someone I know well and trusted deeply, mocked Clinton supporters for feeling "triggered." That was as much as I could tolerate before I decided that Trump's presidency would not be my shame to bear. A bright white-hot anger coursed through me as I understood how much damage minimization could cause another person. It was the kind of anger I used to reserve for myself. But this time, it wasn't directed at me. It was directed at every person who voted for Trump—especially those I love, those who know the truth about my past and still voted for Trump. That betrayal is one my body will never forget. They are no longer a safe place for me as they cannot recognize a predator when they see one. I love them and I want them in my life—safely. Awareness is key for me as I have plans.

This anger is here to stay and I have embraced it. I've trained my whole life to release it in this steady, controlled, effective manner. And now that I have made the connections between the predator I faced and the predator America elected, I have a new purpose. To resist through truth and action. 2016 was not just the year we elected a predator: it is also the year I attended my first political rally, volunteered for a campaign, met Chelsea Clinton, attended my first local town hall meeting, made dozens of political calls to my representatives, wrote letters, marched in a protest, engaged in the grassroots effort to get precinct level recounts in Pennsylvania, and was labeled an *activist* in an article in *The New York Times*.

I am just getting started.

Stacy Robison, age 37
Software education and documentation specialist
Colchester, Vermont

I Almost Bled to Death

I WAS TWENTY WHEN I first knew with complete certainty that I was going to die and that my death was coming fast.

I had started my period, which is a pretty routine event for most women. For me, it wasn't as routine—I'd been getting my period roughly twice a year since puberty. I knew the pattern wasn't normal, but I had thought the problem wasn't something that needed medical attention. This time, however, I didn't stop bleeding. Not after seven days. Not after a month. Not after three months.

A friend told me about her mother who, after experiencing unusual hemorrhaging, was later diagnosed with endometrial cancer. My favorite aunt was diagnosed with uterine cancer when she was a young mother. She fought it and spent many years in remission, but decades later, it returned to steal her life. I was still suffering from losing her when the bleeding started. The ever present anxiety in the pit of my stomach whispered to me that I too was marching inevitably to the same fate.

I had no health insurance. As a college student, paying for

insurance was financially out of my reach, and having grown up in a house where we never had enough money, the fear of astronomical medical debt paralyzed me.

For seven months, I existed in a state of constant panic. My skin, already pale, grew sallower every week. My gums and nail beds turned white. I felt weighed down by crushing exhaustion in a way I had never experienced. The slightest activity winded me, and keeping up with my school work drained what little energy I had. The bleeding was copious enough that every day I had to be extremely careful not to destroy another set of clothes. Tears came easily, and fear gnawed on me, becoming my constant companion.

My friends were worried and convinced me to schedule an appointment with one of the on-campus doctors. After I told her what was happening, she admitted she didn't know what was wrong. She said oral contraceptives would stop the bleeding but wouldn't prescribe them without doing a pelvic exam, which she couldn't do while I was still bleeding. My only alternative was an ultrasound, at a cost of over a thousand dollars. There was no way I could afford to pay that kind of money. I left that appointment more convinced than ever I was going to die. I sank deeper into despair.

Months later when I was home for a break, I broke down and told my mother what was happening. She got me an appointment with a nurse practitioner whom she'd seen in the past, a woman who had worked serving women at Planned Parenthood for years before moving to a private practice. The walk into that office felt like an ascension to the gallows. The conviction that I was dying, which I had carried for so long, would be nothing to the grief I expected to drown in once my fears were confirmed. But the moment I told the doctor my symptoms, she said she thought she knew what was wrong with me: polycystic ovarian syndrome (PCOS).

PCOS affects an estimated ten percent of the female population. While I would still need a pelvic exam to rule out a more serious health problem, she reassured me that the diagnosis was the most likely explanation given my symptoms. Instead of leaving with the doom I had been anticipating for so long, I left the appointment with a prescription for birth control pills.

I also found out I was dangerously anemic, enough to be at risk of organ failure. The nurse practitioner wanted to admit me to the hospital for a blood transfusion, but since I had no insurance, she instead told me to take an iron supplement (double the usual dose) with vitamin C, to make sure I absorbed as much as possible. She made me promise to come back in a week to have my hemoglobin levels checked again. She referred me to Planned Parenthood to continue receiving care.

Because I had so little income, the counselors at Planned Parenthood helped me sign up for California's Health Access Planning program, which enabled me to get medical care at Planned Parenthood and my birth control prescription for free. I was also able to get the pelvic exam I needed to confirm the PCOS diagnosis; finally, I could really let go of the terror I had been dragging around for so long.

For a full decade of my life, I received nearly all of my medical care from Planned Parenthood. Years before I ever became sexually active, Planned Parenthood kept me healthy, and I never paid a cent for any of it until much later, after I obtained insurance. So I take it very, very personally when politicians and antichoice groups attack Planned Parenthood, and women's health in general.

Despite the assertions of "pro-life" groups, very little of what Planned Parenthood does involves abortion. In fact, according to their annual report for 2014–2015, only three percent of the services provided were abortion services, compared with seven percent for cancer screenings and prevention and thirty-one percent for contraception services. And when it comes to abortion, none of those groups seem to have any idea of how complex the need for abortion care is to the women whom they so callously disregard.

Donald Trump has shown complete disregard for the integrity of women's bodies, and he thinks that sexual assault is his sovereign right as a rich white man. His campaign felt like a personal assault—he has threatened my right to decide what happens to my body and threatened to take away my medical care. Election night was one of the worst nights I've ever experienced, as I watched in horror as our country legitimized everything that disgusting man represents.

The one thing we have in our favor: Women have more power now than we have had at any other point in history. We have greater personal and professional freedom, greater access to financial autonomy, greater access to education, and greater access to physical training. We won't be as easy to oppress as we were in the past. To me, it's clearer than ever that all of us must commit to tirelessly fighting this antiwoman agenda.

This election has taught me that the moral arc of the universe may indeed bend toward justice, but it doesn't bend of its own accord. It bends only by the conscious will and dedicated actions of people who believe in justice—not *just* for themselves or women's rights, but for *all* who suffer from inequality.

Southeast

"The truth does not change according to our ability to stomach it."[5]

—Flannery O'Connor

---

5 Letter from Flannery O'Connor. September 6, 1955.

KM Huber, age 65
Retired administrator
Tallahassee, Florida

Confessions of
a Closet Activist

I. No Solace in Open Spaces

IT IS OCTOBER in Wyoming, 1998. A cloudless sky sinks into an aspen-gold landscape.

Days like this are why I live in Casper, I tell myself—a disabled 46-year-old lesbian, partnered, with two children (hers, not ours—ever).

On this same day, Matthew Shepard is found hanging on a rail fence—alive—more scarecrow than human.

Hate comes to Wyoming is what the statewide newspaper headline reads, as if hate were new to us. We are the land of Gretel Ehrlich's "solace of open spaces."[6] Room for everyone.

Matthew Shepard is murdered and tortured by people who live in Wyoming, have always lived in Wyoming.

---

6   Gretel Ehrlich, The Solace of Open Spaces (New York: Viking Press, 1985).

Solace for some but not space for all.

The hate that arrives is the congregation of the Westboro Baptist Church. It is their life's work to protest any "fag" event.

The brutality of Matthew Shepard's death draws worldwide media attention. The Westboro Church finds the recognition it has been seeking.

On the day of Matthew's funeral, the blue skies go dark with winter: first gray rain and then white flakes, thick, as if being dumped from a truck bed. White on Wyoming white.

Signs of *Matt in hell* and *God hates fags* sway in their sturdy righteousness. They take all the space they need, these true believers.

With others, I stand on "our" side of a drooping police tape. We hold our umbrellas high, trying to block out a hate that is bigger than all of us.

We are so naïve in our whiteness. Soon umbrellas sag under the weight of snowflakes.

There is no privacy for the family and friends of Matthew Shepard who wish only to mourn and to remember.

In frustration, we scream at the Westboro Church members, whose First Amendment rights loom larger than ours. They know our fear; it makes them smile.

We don't have words or signs. In the stillness of snowflakes, our umbrellas completely collapse.

The sound of silence.

I look into the eyes of the bearded youth holding the *Matt in hell* sign. He looks straight through me—my rage unseen, my fear ignored. I do not matter.

Pure hate, one-on-one, white-on-white.

II. Implosion: The Vote in Florida

Eighteen years later, the glass ceiling still holds.

On November 8, 2016, I am old, a sexagenarian—the only

label that anyone notices. I live alone, and no one asks whether I am a lesbian or a feminist or Zen Buddhist.

I am wrinkled beyond my years; time and illness blur my sexuality. All I did never slowed either.

I am ten days out from the first of two hip replacement surgeries. Being old is being invisible, and what was once disability off and on for nearly forty years, is now the frailty of chronic illness.

I now live in the blue county of Leon, Tallahassee. It has voted Democrat since 2000, the other election in which the majority vote took a backseat to the electoral college. And just as in 2000, Florida goes the way of its governor.

All around me the trappings of my privilege unravel. It was never enough to always recycle, to be almost vegan or mostly Zen Buddhist, or to be selective in my support of causes, including which Member of Congress to write.

All necessary but never enough.

A hard, hard rain falls as hate reveals us. My own white privilege blinded me to the white women of my own generation who vote against reason and for . . . chaos. What could they possibly fear in a multicultural nation led by a woman?

On November 8, 2016, the eyes of the young man from Westboro look through me once again.

White-on-white, one-on-one, winning.

The win is uncertain, split between the popular vote—the people—and those who elect the president, the electors. The uncertainty is palpable, on either side of the chasm.

I frame my life one day at a time because yesterday is gone and tomorrow is a maybe. There is today. That's my sliver of light.

I trust in impermanence—no thing or no one ever lasts—the law of life. Chronic illness taught me the moment is all I have, and it is enough. Even when a sliver of light is the only offer on the table. I aim for even, stay open to the experience.

Before Zen, chronic illness was like being between a rock and a hard spot, a constant bumping back and forth between two knowns. Zen is a game changer. No rock, no hard spot, no buffers. There is only the experience of the election of 2016.

Ever there is an array of life lenses. I look through Zen.

III. The Safety of a Crazy Woman Hoodie

By mid-November, I can drive, my hip joint replacement recovery on track, praiseworthy even. Autoimmune illness—Sjogren's syndrome—flares, averse to even the mention of recovery.

Online, I send letters, call Members of Congress, make small donations, join groups—all from the comfort of my adjustable bed.

November 18 has a bit of spark; it dawns differently. I take my first trip outside my apartment since the election.

Rarely is it cold enough in Tallahassee to wear a hoodie, much less one from Wyoming, but neuropathy and spinal cord disease mean I am always cold. I pull on my *Crazy Woman* hoodie, warmth my only reasoning.

Being old is my greatest advantage. My three-wheeled walker has handlebars like a motorcycle's and wheels thick enough for freewheeling on beaches or down sandy roads.

On this day, the hoodie and dark glasses complete my look.

In the parking lot of the grocery store, people keep their heads down and look away when they see my smile. It's insistence all around, and I don't force a hello from anyone. I don't even think about my hoodie.

What has really brought me out is my craving for comfort food. I am drawn to the aisle of gluten-free, preservative-riddled cookies. I read the packaging promises. Knowing better, I put two boxes in my cart.

"I was wondering if I should just stay out of your way." It is a male voice coming from the other side of the aisle. The tone is sincere, maybe even with a smile in it.

"I thought it only fair to give everyone notice," I say.

He and I talk, staying on separate sides of the aisle. I hear his entire being open up as he talks about the "Big Sky Country" of Montana.

I respond in kind, telling him about Crazy Woman Creek in the Bighorn Mountains of central Wyoming.

The sky knows no boundaries.

Aisle after aisle, one person after another stops to acknowledge the hoodie and me, sometimes at the same time. Crazy Woman Creek is not a stream too wide.

No one looks through anyone.

White-on-white but a sliver of light where I least expect it.

IV. The Context of Curiosity

I have *namaste* printed on my message chalkboard next to the lock on my apartment door. A locked door and gesture of goodwill—mixed signals. I work with the reality I have.

Only an upstairs neighbor asks me about *namaste*. She is not a frequent visitor and never comes inside my apartment. We stand with my doorway between us. She is at least fifteen years my senior but comes to "check on me." She has heard about my Buddhism, but the word *Zen* is foreign to her.

"I don't want to deal with any foreigners," she tells me, looking me straight in the eye. She mouths the word *Black* in a whisper.

Soon there will be new neighbors in the apartment down the hall. "*Hispanics*, perhaps," she mouth-whispers. Her eyes return to the word *namaste*.

I do not give her the popular translation "I bow to the divine in you." I am no longer that kind of fool. Instead, I use words like *compassion, goodwill, peace.* She nods, not satisfied, but I know our moment is over.

In a few days, I will visit her on her turf. I have a stylus that may help her text with her smartphone.

It is slow this white-on-white, one-on-one. Often it feels futile. It's grunt work. Whether calling Congressional offices or visiting my neighbor, it's connection.

Mostly, it doesn't feel like enough, but I work with the reality I have.

The cracked ceiling holds—a prism. Slivers of light stream through.

Alyson Ritter, age 35
Independent contractor
Raleigh, North Carolina

The Making of a Warrior

I WAS ELEVEN YEARS old the first time I was assaulted. In the lunchroom one day, a teacher asked me to go to the principal's office with her. As an A student and a classic Goody Two-shoes, I had never set foot in the principal's office before. The office was bright, but also cold and gray. I immediately felt like an outsider, a bad guy.

I was brought into a room with a big round table. The principal, a guidance counselor, and two teachers were in the room. As serious as this meeting seemed, my parents weren't invited. After we all sat down, the principal told me that someone had witnessed my math teacher molesting me. He wanted me to talk about what happened and put it in writing. When I refused to say or write anything—because nothing had happened and I'm not a liar—I was told I could trust them and the school would protect me. Again, I told them nothing happened.

I had no idea where any of this was coming from. I was in sixth grade and knew what to do if someone was hurting me or making me feel uncomfortable. But I didn't know what to do in a situation where nothing was happening to me and no one believed me. I kept telling them the truth, but they wouldn't believe me.

I don't know the details of what the school administrators did from there, but they definitely didn't protect me. The math teacher in question had a daughter in seventh grade at the same school. The next day, I was welcomed into school by a bunch of older kids bullying me. I couldn't walk down a hall without someone calling me a name or pushing me around.

When I went back to the principal's office, I was told they had to use my name to get to the bottom of what was going on. I cried. I told them it was a rumor. They still didn't believe me, and the bullying continued.

One day during class, I left to use the bathroom. The halls were empty until I turned a corner and saw a student walking my way. He pushed me against the lockers with his hand on my neck. He told me he would make me do everything to him that I said the math teacher did to me.

I wanted to scream and cry, but I didn't because my dad had taught me exactly what I needed to do: I kneed him in the crotch and punched him in the face as he doubled over. I walked to the principal's office, told them exactly what I just did, and demanded they put an end to the witch hunt. I remember feeling so strong and so powerful that I even scared myself a little. That was my last visit to *that* principal's office, but not my last visit to any principal's office.

*   *   *

My dad taught me to fight when I was seven years old because as father to three daughters, he knew we would have to be able to protect ourselves.

The day was one of those unseasonably warm early spring days. My family had just gotten home from grocery shopping, and I was finally free to be as loud as I wanted, which was fairly loud. I did a lot of cartwheels. I ran the perimeter of our yard and made up silly dance routines. But I was still bored.

Then my dad came out the front door and told me to follow him to the backyard. He was the smartest person I knew, one of the two people whom I could count on for anything. I would have followed him anywhere.

When we were in the backyard, behind the garage, my dad held up his hands, palms facing me. "Punch my hands," he said. I was confused. Although my sisters and I fought on a semi-regular basis and often hit one another, hitting was not allowed in my house.

He repeated, "Punch my hands." So I did. I balled up my tiny seven-year-old fists and punched the palms of his hands as hard as I could. He didn't flinch. I kept punching. I wore myself out.

"Take a break," he said. "Watch me make a fist. See how I keep my thumb tucked in tight? That will protect you from hurting yourself. When you start punching me again, this time hit my palm with your knuckles, not your fingers. Use your whole body and move into the punch. Are you ready to try again?" I nodded. I used my whole body and punched.

My dad kept critiquing and giving me pointers. The lesson could have been five hours or five minutes, but as we were walking back to the house, he told me that whenever someone made me feel unsafe or uncomfortable, I should use what he just taught me . . . and no, I was still not allowed to hit my sisters.

I didn't really understand what he did for me until that day in the school hallway when that bully had his hand on my neck, pushing me up against the lockers. My dad didn't teach me how to punch to help me exhaust my energy—he taught me how to punch to protect myself. He taught me to be a warrior. He taught my sisters to be warriors too.

My older sister fights for social justice, is empathetic, and cares for everyone. She is not a physical fighter, but she doesn't let anyone push her around. She sticks up for herself with a grace I wish I had. My younger sister is a warrior of knowledge and dexterity with words. She remembers everything and always has a comeback. She is a force. She won't back down and can stump anyone with her wit. I like to think the three of us form our own little army.

*   *   *

The second time I was assaulted, I was sixteen and a cheerleader in high school. I had worn my uniform to school for game day. As I walked up a flight of stairs, someone grabbed my ass and said, "I'd like a piece of this." I turned around swinging and knocked him backwards down the stairs. Instead of going to class, I took myself to the dean's office and told him exactly what happened. The dean gave me a high five.

Sadly, but not surprisingly, this assault would not be the last one of my life. Assaults kept coming. I was a pretty blonde with unusually large breasts. Men wouldn't keep their hands to themselves or their mouths closed. As I got older, I put on weight but was still a pretty blonde with tits and ass to spare. It's as if men see my body as an invitation for them to act how they want.

When a leaked audio recording revealed that Trump said he could grab a woman by her pussy, I was horrified but not surprised. I have dealt with men like him all of my life. I knew deep down that he would never be our president and that Hillary would help change things for women. Hillary is a fighter. She would have my back. I told myself I had to deal with Trump only for a few more weeks until he lost the election in the most embarrassing way possible.

I watched the debates with disgust, a bag of chocolate, and

a bottle of wine. The knot in the pit of my stomach wouldn't stop growing. I wanted to be so sure Hillary would win, but I was terrified. I knew a Trump presidency would mean that men would think they had a right to my body more than ever.

And I wasn't wrong. One week after the election, I was baking and needed an ingredient. It was cold outside, but since I was in a hurry, I left the house wearing shorts, a tank top, and flip-flops. As I walked into the store, a man who was in front of me turned around to look at me.

"Aren't you cold?" he asked. He stopped walking.

"Nope," I said. I stopped walking too.

"Oh, I was waiting to let you pass so I can see how you look from behind," he said.

I kept my feet planted to the ground. "You'll want to keep walking, because if I catch up to you, you will be so sorry you messed with me. But if you don't believe me, stay right there, and I'll be happy to show you," I said.

"Wow, you're a bitch," he said, and walked away.

A week after that incident, another man decided he could say whatever he wanted to me. "Hey, baby. Wanna wrestle? I'd like that ass in my face," he said. When I told him he shouldn't talk to women that way, he said, "Trump is president now; I can say whatever I want."

With the glimmer of hope Hillary provided, I thought that maybe I wouldn't have to fight hard to stay safe, that rape culture would come to an end. I hoped that crimes against women would be seen as actual crimes and not just tall tales women were telling. That hope was shattered on November 8.

Now I have to fight more. I need to be stronger and fearless. It has been a long time since I punched someone, and I worry I'm out of shape for the next time I need to protect myself. I know there will be a next time. It's not enough to be able to protect just myself; I need to be able to protect all women.

The Trump patriarchy will do what it can to hold us back, push us down, and make us feel unworthy. So I'll be a warrior like my dad taught me. I will fight with my army of women. And I will never let the Trump presidency make me feel like less than what I am.

Andrea Nourse, age 35
Director of marketing
Nashville, Tennessee

For My Son

IT WAS THREE in the morning, November 8, 2014. I lay awake in bed contemplating relieving my bladder. My husband lay beside me, deep in slumber, oblivious to the world around him. I've learned this is a luxury of being born with a penis.

My brain began to wander to something other than my full bladder. I was now three days late, and the test I'd taken two days earlier had been negative. When you're over thirty and trying desperately to conceive, those missing blue lines are little assholes. You dread them. You yell and cry when they refuse to appear. Was I mentally ready for another negative? The aching breasts, late period, and cold symptoms were all good signs, but the negative test from two mornings ago nagged at me.

Fuck it. I threw the covers off and made my way into the bathroom. I fiddled with the wrapper, hopping around the bathroom with my legs crossed as I struggled to tear open the package. *Easy tear, my ass.* I whispered words of encouragement to my pee and to the stick, and let my bladder go. The feeling was pure bliss. Finished, I slid the test back in the wrapper, convinced if I watched it, I would jinx the result. Much like my bowling technique—throw the ball and walk away, don't look, and hope for the best.

I sat on the toilet and waited as the minutes ticked by on my phone. I reassured myself that if the lines didn't appear, it would not be the end of the world. *There is always next month,* I whispered. *There is always next month.*

I'd wanted to be a mom for as long as I could remember, but I denied that truth to anyone who asked. I am a driven, focused, independent modern woman. "Maternal desires are an archaic idea meant to hold women back"—that's what I'd say when asked about getting married and having kids. Inside, however, I longed to feel the stirring of a growing life. I craved a baby who would cuddle against my chest. I dreamed of the man who would hold my hand through it all. My outer feminist often shushed those fantasies. It took turning thirty, alone and childless, to understand I could be all of these things—a mother, a wife, and a career woman.

Our four months of trying to conceive really wasn't that long. I'd come off the pill in June, just prior to our Vegas wedding. I'd been tracking my cycle for months, and my mom assured me that we came from a long line of fertile women. We bought countless ovulation test kits; we should have bought stock in e.p.t.˙. For my husband, our inability to conceive was not much of a concern. He was the king of "we'll try again next month." But I didn't want to try again next month. I wanted *this* month to be the perfect union of egg and sperm.

Eight minutes. *Eight minutes was long enough,* I decided. Slowly, I slid the test back out of the wrapper and closed my eyes one last time. I reassured myself that a negative wasn't permanent, nor was it a reflection of my ability to be a mother. I opened my eyes. *Pregnant.*

Taking after his mother, our son decided to make a dramatic

entrance into the world on June 2, 2015. He arrived four weeks before our July 21 due date, one week after Donald J. Trump announced his candidacy. We'd always said we wanted two children. However, over the course of my son's first year of life, I often told my husband that if Trump wins the presidency, our son would, in fact, be an only child. What started as a joke became more and more serious as we approached the Republican National Convention.

*   *   *

Something about the 2016 race felt different from other elections. The racism that had been simmering in the people outraged that we had a black president, was boiling over. People on both sides were angry. Many felt disenfranchised and unrepresented. As a white college-educated, white-collar professional, I couldn't relate. Sure, I was outraged at what I was seeing in cities around the country, but it didn't affect me; I had the luxury of living in a bubble. But I felt the tension and the unrest. They made me uncomfortable and fearful of the future being shaped for my child.

I've always felt great empathy and compassion for those whose voices are silenced. I get enraged when people use their religion or fear of differences to violate the rights of others. But I'd never spoken up or tried to make a difference. Now, as a mother, I find myself wondering how I will teach my own son to embrace all humans and our differences.

Perhaps this is why the 2016 election felt different to me—I was seeing it through the eyes of someone who is responsible for another life. My fear of the future was no longer limited to that of my lifetime but included the future my son and future generations would see. What kind of world had I brought him into? This America wasn't the America I once believed in— these politics weren't the politics that had fascinated me as a child. This was different. This world was fueled by hate for others, masked in a false sense of patriotism. The true face of the movement Donald Trump represents is one of anger and hatred. Trump's Americans are so fearful of those who don't look, act, and think like themselves that they will willingly trade their own rights and future in order to diminish the rights and future of others. Did I really bring an innocent child into this world? Did I really want to bring another child into this world?

As I sat down to write this story, I initially thought and wrote about how I felt about the candidates, the primaries, and the general election. I mechanically went through the process of how I chose whom to support and why. But as I reread my words, I realized that none of it mattered. Bernie lost the primary. Hillary lost the election. The Electoral College is a bigger asshole than those missing blue lines that taunted me for months. None of this intense over-analysis is productive. Instead, I started focusing on where we are as a nation and where we are as a human race. How did we become a nation united in hate and divided in love? How do we bridge the gaps before they become impassable canyons?

As cliché as it sounds, in the month following the election, I did more and more soul searching. I wanted to do something more than blogging and venting on social media. I've always had a passion for politics and human rights, but I've always been incredibly one-sided. More than once I've joked I am more liberal than California. But for all my interest in politics, I never once tried to understand what the other side thought. I never felt I needed to.

My boss has a favorite saying—*Seek to understand before seeking to be understood*—which infuriates me. Now I understand the importance of that phrase. With the real possibility of a Republican-controlled government for the next four or eight years, that saying is more true than ever. While it is important and crucial for us to fight for our rights and for the rights of those who have been marginalized, I've come to realize that, in doing so, we've somehow created a culture in which nothing or no one else seems to matter.

How do we move forward? My idealism and optimism tell me we move forward with love. My pessimism and realism tell me to fight back and demand justice. The mother in me wants to flee with my child in order to shield him from the evil I see all around. The balance lies somewhere in the middle, and reaching that balance starts with action. Action is how lives change.

This election has inspired me to take real action so that I can help to shape the world my son will grow up in. I've resolved to get involved with local politics, both with the donation of my time and money. I live in a blue bubble in the middle of a deep red state; it's not the time to be idle. More important than getting involved in politics, will be how I engage with my community. As our son grows older, my husband and I will introduce him to volunteerism. In the meantime, I give my time back through mentoring and have a long-term goal of starting a nonprofit.

When I woke up the morning after the election, my eyes bloodshot from the bottle of wine I unintentionally chugged as the results came in, I walked into my seventeen-month-old son's nursery. He was just starting to stir and was doing his morning mumbling. I watched him for a moment and then leaned over the railing of the crib. I laid my hand on his back and simply felt him breathing. My eyes filled with tears.

"I am so sorry," I whispered into the darkness. "Mama is so sorry. We let you down."

My son, a white male from a middle-class family, has every advantage in the world. He will never know the struggle firsthand. But my hope as a mother is to teach him love, compassion, and acceptance. I want him to know and understand that tolerance is not enough. Tolerance is how we got where we are. He will grow up to know no boundaries or walls based on race, nationality, religion, or any other divisive label assigned to drum up hate.

I dream of a world where mothers don't have to apologize to their children for the wrongs of their fellow humans. I dream of a world where my son and his peers don't know the pain of hunger or the struggle of poverty. I dream of a world where mothers, fathers, sons, and daughters can walk freely and live without fear. I will fight for these dreams until my dying breath, and I will no longer apologize for believing that we, as human beings, are better than this.

Bobbi Adams, age 26
Speech-Language pathologist and poet
Charleston, South Carolina

I Can Still Hear Their Silence

"*I*'VE GOTTA ASK . . . *are you gay?"*
The comment appeared below an entry in my online journal.

The journal was stuffed with the usual naïve thoughts of a thirteen-year-old, but it also contained dreams about my friend Sarah. She was different from my other friends. She *got* me. That's why I talked about her all the time . . . wasn't it?

The longer I thought about it, the more I wondered if the commenter was onto something. Maybe I did like girls. It would explain a lot—like my daydreams of raising kids with my best friends and my need to frequently reassure myself: *I can think she's pretty and not be gay.*

And just like that—it clicked. I *was* gay.

* * *

I came out to everyone over time. My parents took it well. My mom worried my life would be more difficult. My dad said, "As long as no guy's *thing* gets near your *place*, I'm fine." The rest of my family followed suit, extending tolerance but withholding support. I suppose that's the Southern way when you're anything to the left of normal.

I had managed to garner a reputation in my comfortable suburban South Carolina bubble for being out and proud. Other LGBTQ teens began seeking my advice. I remember when a friend, following in my footsteps, came out to her parents. Her mother threatened to commit suicide if my friend didn't go back to being straight—as if that were even possible.

As a gay teen living in the South, you rolled the dice each time you came out to someone, knowing you could either be hugged or killed. I've met other members of the LGBTQ community who were disowned or who suffered beatings. I've met parents who had to bury their children. The kindness and compassion of Elke Kennedy still resonates. Her son, Sean Kennedy, was followed home after leaving a Greenville bar one night. His attacker punched him with such force that his face shattered and his brain separated from its stem. Elke had to bury her son, but she refused to bury his memory. She gave out sunflower seeds at Pride marches in hopes new life would bloom from the life of her child taken too soon.

The gay men and women of the South—I carry their words with me. These stories, these violent acts by strangers or family, taught me to be scared. I woke up every morning in the Bible Belt never knowing which redneck or frat boy or angry kid would decide it was my day to die. But due to a combination of luck and constant vigilance, nothing has ever happened to me. Listening to that inner voice may be the only reason I've survived.

My fear manifested itself in many ways throughout my life. There had been periods when it had been both legal and even *encouraged* to discriminate against me. Sex was illegal when I was fourteen—not because I was fourteen but because I was gay. Being gay was against the morality clause I had to follow as a teacher. Gay panic was a legal defense for killing someone who was presumed LGBTQ; killing a gay person wasn't a hate crime at the time.

Discrimination in my life hasn't been just fearing people on the street; I saw it in professors, coworkers, and supervisors. In college, I joined the Gay-Straight Alliance and the Future Teachers Association and was successful in remaining active in both, while keeping the latter from knowing my relationship with the former. It terrified me to think of trying to find a job after college as an openly gay woman. It was—and still is— legal to fire someone for being gay in South Carolina. I started to wear pearls and sundresses, longing to go unnoticed and thereby avoid scrutiny.

I attended graduate school in a small South Carolina town. In my multicultural studies class, the dean of my program asked, "In your family, were you allowed to wear your church clothes after you got home?" It was a very long and serious discussion. I don't remember what answer I gave; some lies are a coin toss. But that discussion did make me think back to my freshman year of high school, when my church refused to baptize me. Drug abuse and premarital sex were easily forgiven, but as an unapologetic gay woman, I could not be "saved."

I was still in graduate school when the ban on same-sex marriage was overturned. Not long after, I, along with other professionals in our school district, scheduled a meeting with a student's same-sex parents. When the parents failed to attend, the educators spent the allocated hour discussing whether or not the kid had seen his two moms having sex, eventually concluding his home life may be where his "deviance" was manifesting.

Even while I lived in fear, I found ways to make friends: Teachers would sit at a lunch table across from me; someone would offer to share my office; a stranger would welcome me to their church. Even when I lied about my girlfriend being a boyfriend and avoided pronouns at all costs, people tried to get to know me—and because I was lonely, I let them. I accepted the chicken casserole they offered. I was touched when they asked about my mom or how my presentation went. I began to trust them. I considered them to be the family I had chosen for myself, because it felt as if they had chosen me too.

In the end, however, I had to live my truth—even if it meant leaving my friends and family behind. After graduate school, I moved to California and met my fiancée. The West Coast changed everything for me. For the first time since coming out, I could exhale.

* * *

When the 2016 presidential election rolled around, I should have said, *If you care about me, you won't vote for Donald Trump,* to all the people I left behind in South Carolina. But I didn't. I was too scared. Once again I silenced myself and, in doing so, became complicit in the deprivation of my own rights. It didn't take long to find out that my own silence did nothing to help me.

Over the years, the stories I'd heard from the LGBTQ community—stories that have become a part of my story— had gone untold to the people who knew and loved me. After the election, when I voiced my concerns, they tried to reassure me: "What are you worried about? Trump's not gonna do anything to the gays." "Gays are a nonissue. Nobody cares anymore!"

I tried to tell them: "Don't tell me everything's going to be okay. Promise me that you will do everything you can to protect my life and my rights."

They never did make that promise.

Around Christmas, I went on social media and posted my fears of bringing my fiancée home with me for the holidays. Mere acquaintances commented with offers to escort us. My blood family, however, expressed zero concern. The family I chose for myself, the friends who chose me, were silent.

*   *   *

As I am writing this, a confirmation hearing for Donald Trump's candidate for the secretary of the Department of Health and Human Services, Tom Price, is underway. The congressman from Georgia is among the most conservative members of the House, calling Obama-era protections for transgendered individuals "absurd" and "a clear invasion of privacy." He has been openly critical of the Supreme Court's ruling that allowed same-sex couples the right to wed, and he has voted repeatedly against hate crimes legislation, nondiscrimination bills, and the repeal of "Don't Ask, Don't Tell."

But why should I care? No one cares about the "gay issue" anymore.

I have moved away from the South, and I am living my truth. But those changes don't take away the pain of being cast aside by the people I love most. I have struggled to reconcile the love I had for the friends and family who took care of me when I was at my lowest, and my bitterness when they carelessly chose to risk my life and my rights. I feel my emotions—anger, disappointment, anger, disappointment—spin like a coin in the air. This sense of betrayal motivates me to speak louder and more often. I will not let my story go untold; I wish those who said they supported me let their actions speak just as loudly.

I will never know who considered me when they submitted their ballot, but I can still hear their silence.

"In the end, we will remember not the words of our enemies, but the silence of our friends."
—*Dr. Martin Luther King, Jr.*[7]

---

7 Dr. Martin Luther King Jr., "The Trumpet of Conscience, Steeler Lecture," (speech, November 1967). Fellowship of USA Reconciliation Archives: http://archives.forusa.org.

Dolores M. Fernandez (aka, "Lola"), age 52
Interior designer
Miami, Florida

Our American Tyrant

THE BACKYARD OF my parents' house in Puerto Rico smelled like guavas. Tart, sweet, and pungent, they permeated my world. Lush and green, that yard was a child's paradise. There were several guava trees; banana, coconut, and lychee trees; a royal poinciana; and a chicken coop. I would climb those trees, play with the chicks, and scrape my knees. As idyllic as that world was, it had a particular drawback: I was not allowed to eat the guavas.

My grandmother had many elaborate reasons for this: If they were green, they'd certainly cause constipation. Or they might have worms, which she'd say would make their way to your brain and kill you. Guavas were the forbidden fruit.

My parents, busy with raising three children, running a business, and organizing the Cuban anti-revolutionary movement, counted on their parents to bring up the rear and take care of the house and children. No guavas allowed.

The house was a mid-century, modern split-level with a front porch, terrazzo floors, four bedrooms, two bathrooms, a kitchen, dining and living rooms, and a room for meetings to organize the counterrevolution against Castro. What I remember most about this house was the number of people coming and going at all times. It wasn't odd to zigzag around mattresses and cots in the mornings when we left for school. The bedrooms were inhabited by family members: My grandmother, aunt, sister, me, and my grandma's parrot were in the first bedroom. My parents slept in a smaller room across the hallway. My paternal grandparents were in the smallest room, and my uncle, cousins, and brother, in the largest bedroom, at the end of the hallway.

The people who stayed on the mattresses and cots, the ones who came and went, mostly were political prisoners. They had spoken up against a tyrant and paid for it with years of torture. They were tried in military tribunals made up of illiterate rebel "judges," no jury, no defense. They were broken and sent to jails filled with human excrement.

My mom would cook a pasta feast every Sunday. I have vivid recollections of one guest, a man whose fingers had been cut off by his captors, who told me he couldn't eat pasta because it reminded him of the worms in the food they were served.

There were many like him. Blinded, maimed, a man whose tongue had been cut off, yet he spoke through his poetry. The women—yes, there were women—who had been raped and mutilated, who went in as young girls and came out old ladies only a few years later. That was our life in "The Guava House," a refuge for the survivors of tyranny.

* * *

My family had been living in Puerto Rico on and off for ten years after the Cuban Revolution. We'd also lived in Miami, New York, the Dominican Republic, Louisiana, and then back to Puerto Rico again, many times over. That island had welcomed us with open arms, no questions asked. And it was in that house, a block away from the ocean, under the guava trees, where the seeds of dissent were planted in my soul as I watched my parents and those they knew fight against an authoritarian regime.

* * *

Both my parents were in their forties when I was born. I was the youngest child in our family. By the time I was born, they had been living in exile for eight years. My dad would read me books and write me poems. He would point to the letters, and I would say them out loud. He would couple them together and have me make the sounds of their conjunctions: "A- P- . . . app," "B- A- . . . bah," "M- A- . . . mah," "M- E- . . . me." At five, I could read the newspaper.

My father was, undoubtedly, a figure of authority who never lost his inner child. We would play games. I would be a doctor or judge, an architect or a cowboy, all of whom he named *Jerry* to his *Tom*. He never stuck to traditional gender roles. And to him, women were the perfect creatures, and fathers of daughters were more sexually potent than fathers of sons. His belief was that a woman could be what she wished, have children, and wear heels while she changed the oil in the car, as my mom often did. And she called the game, my mother. No *grab her by the pussy*; more like *pussy grabs back*. What she did mattered none if she did it well and felt fulfilled. I think that's what he wanted for his daughters: to do what they loved.

Several times during the day, my dad and I would sneak out to the backyard, and he'd pluck guavas from the trees. Hiding from his mother and my mother and everyone else, we'd sit on the ground and eat them. No constipation, no worms exploding my brain, just the tart, sweet, pungent taste and conversations with my father that started as soon as I could speak and go on in my head to this day.

He taught me how to catch. As I got a little older, he taught me how to pitch: a slider, a curveball, a fastball, and more. He'd say, "Keep your changeup grip ready at all times; use the fastball grip; add the extra finger. . . . You have to be ready to change at all times. Don't let them see what you're holding."

My mother would come out, screaming, "She's a girl! Not a boy!" She'd do this every time we were out there. He'd shrug his shoulders. I kept pitching. To counterbalance, she signed me up for ballet class. I could pitch in pliés. One day, we were out in the yard playing ball when she came out, screaming, "She's a girl! Not a boy!" Father looked at me, shrugged his shoulders, and said, "Oh, please, when she's grown up, women will be pitching in the majors or be president of the United States!"

Indeed, the day had arrived. I stood in line for early voting during the 2016 United States presidential election for two hours and forty-five minutes. I had never voted early before in all my life. But I had been waiting to cast *this* vote for a lifetime; why wait any longer than I had to? Trump supporters were behind me in that line. One young man kept saying he was voting Trump because "they weren't going to take his guns away!"

I tried my best to remain peaceful and quiet, enjoying a moment I had been waiting more than forty years for. As the man behind me kept talking, he mentioned he was on disability. I turned around and said, "Bite your nose; spite your face."

He got angry, yelling, "Shut up, old hag!" Insults flew out of him like bats out of hell.

Then everyone else around us stood up to him. The family in front of us was made up of all women; the grandmother called him "uncivilized and boorish," while the others told him no one wanted his guns and to pipe down. At that moment, I knew: we were in this together.

* * *

Over time in the United States, my father became, like most exiles escaping an extremist system, the opposite of what he'd previously stood for in his home country: a Republican. He had slowly veered toward the center right. When Fidel Castro started to gain prominence, with the hope for a free and democratic Cuba, the country followed like sheep to the slaughter. My father never liked him. Castro was an egomaniac who spoke for hours and said nothing; a vengeful man who rid himself of not only his enemies but also his allies if they in any way overshadowed him, as did Camilo Cienfuegos and Che Guevara. In my dad's view, the only thing that mattered to Castro was Castro.

*   *   *

Shortly after the revolution, my father, who was then president of the Cuban equivalent to America's Screen Actor's Guild, stood up and denounced Castro as a communist at a union meeting. After which, a tank showed up in front of our house. My father had to flee, or they would take him to the shooting wall at Castro's request. My mother, an American, called the United States embassy, and he was able to seek refuge and be safely escorted onto a plane by the American ambassador. The next day, Castro gave an angry speech, much like Trump's speeches before the election. Castro said that all dissidents should leave now or risk arrest, forfeiture of property and goods, and death as well. With every threat against counterrevolutionaries, the crowd erupted into enthusiastic applause and ovation.

*   *   *

My own political enthusiasm took me in a different direction. I registered to vote at seventeen, although I would not get a chance to vote in a general election until I was twenty-one.

A political junkie by nature and nurture, rejecting everything that my father now stood for, I registered as a Democrat. The Democrats had saved this country from the Great Depression; led it through two world wars; and gave us multiple Kennedys, FDR, Johnson, and, what hits me on a more personal level, the Cuban Enactment Act. That's right: The Democrats gave my ethnic group entitlement. Cubans were able to seek political asylum without having to go through the red tape to gain a path to citizenship. It prequalified Cuban refugees, even those living on the island under the regime, to immigrate. As long as they reached American soil, they could stay. The Republicans, on the other hand, only came by every four years, pandered to "Viva Cuba Libre," and left. They never helped my people and still don't.

* * *

For a year leading up to the election I had been knocking on doors, phonebanking, working the voter hotline, driving voters to their early polling places, and contributing whatever money I could afford. I was fully vested in my support for Hillary Clinton and had been since 2008. Maybe even since 1972, when my siblings and I followed our parents to the States.

On the day I went to vote early, I felt my father there with me. I wondered what my father would think of Trump. Trump, after all, has the same characteristics as Castro, Hitler, and Mussolini. Tyrants share the same mold; Left or Right is irrelevant. Trump is *our* tyrant who talks a lot and says nothing. I can't imagine my father's condoning a man who has such a divisive and hateful demeanor.

My hands started to shake when I was given my voting ballot. As I stepped inside the voting booth, I reached into my purse, pulled out a baseball, and sat it on the edge of the table.

The ballot for my county was seven pages long. The first item was the vote for president of the United States. Too nervous to look, I bypassed it and then went through all the other votes. I voted down-ballot Democrat, for the first time in my life, all while teary-eyed and shaky. When I finished voting for all the other positions and measures, I took a deep breath and looked down at that first page. There she was: *Hillary Clinton*, number eleven. Eleven is my lucky number. I was now sobbing, tears streaming down my face and landing on the ballot. I grabbed the baseball, gripped the changeup, and cast my vote. I voted for women's rights, for children, for clean air, for education; most importantly, I voted for that little girl and the father who taught her to pitch.

*   *   *

This country once held promise, freedom, and opportunity for men like my father. Not anymore. Incompetence has won. Lying has won. Hate won. And we all lost.

I had taken the day after the election off, assuming I'd be celebrating. Instead, I spent the day drinking, whining, and wallowing, bitter at everyone I knew who voted for him. *I don't need those people. I don't need anyone who stands with hate.*

But enough is enough. Although I will not move past this anytime soon (maybe never), wallowing is not going to change anything. So I'm fighting back. I walked into my local Democratic Congressional Campaign Committee office and volunteered. I volunteered for the cause of democracy, like I did for Hillary Clinton, all in and ready. For now, I am fighting in the trenches and hope for better outcomes in 2018, 2020, 2024, and beyond.

*   *   *

Several days ago, I received an email from the Clinton campaign with a letter written by Hillary. She wrote, *I believe it is our responsibility to keep doing our part to build a better, stronger, and fairer future for our country and the world.* Her words gave me the hope and resolve to fight however I can. And at this moment?

There're three men on, two men out, and my changeup grip is ready.

Marian Weber, age 42
Nurse
Lafayette, Louisiana

Woman Hating

I'M THAT FRIEND or family member in your life who has done almost everything and has done it all well. Served my country? You bet. Saved lives as a medic? Yeah, I saved a few. Succeeded in the male-dominated commercial diving industry? Yep. Finished nursing school? I did that too, and am still working towards my masters. I've worked for a top talent agency in Los Angeles, and one time bluffed my way into a temp job at NASA's Marshall Space Flight Center.

I also worked as a hostess in the red light district of Kinshicho Tokyo Prefecture, Japan. In the mid-nineties a boyfriend dumped me, and for a short time it broke my heart. I decided Los Angeles was too small a place for the both of us to live, and decided to leave the country. Without a job or a place to stay, I bought a one-way ticket to Japan.

I had never been to Japan, I didn't know anyone there, and I did not speak Japanese. To brush up on Japanese history, I bought a copy of *Shogun* to read on the plane. That was a big mistake—lots of samurai killing samurai and committing seppuku. By the time the plane landed at Narita airport, I was a sobbing mess. There was another American woman on the plane who took pity on me. She and her husband let me crash on the tatami mat floor of their tiny apartment for two weeks while I looked for a job.

Eventually I found a job as a hostess at a swanky, dimly-lit lounge in Tokyo called the President's International Men's Club. The acrid scent of cigar and cigarette smoke filled the club's quarters. In the center of the shadowy corners was a karaoke stage, and at the entrance was a waiting area decorated with stained velvet sofas where hostesses could lounge around and look gorgeous. We would strike our best pose to lure a paying customer into choosing one—or several of us—to be his hostess for the night.

My job was to nod, smile, pour drinks, and sing karaoke. The rules were simple: Be beautiful. Be flirtatious. Be submissive. Wear dresses or skirts only. Wear heels. Only cross your ankles, never your legs, and always have a beautiful handkerchief in your lap.

I was the only American, and with my sunbleached California-blonde hair, I did not have to work hard to earn tips. I'd pour a drink for a customer, pour myself two, and sing whatever was requested. (I must have sung "Hotel California" every single damn night.)

The men were respectful and often quiet. A few became good friends. When a customer began behaving rudely, the women generally teamed up and shut down the altercation before it had a chance to start. Sometimes we would encounter stalkers, men who would wait around after the club closed and try to walk us home; those occurrences were usually short-lived. Most of the men were simply looking for a beautiful, fun distraction from their dreary jobs and boring lives.

It was a sweet gig: Easy work, good pay, a fairly safe

environment, and most importantly—voluntary. No one was forcing me. I could have left at any time and returned home safely to my family back in the United States. I was having a good time and making enough money to travel the world.

While working in the red light district, I met women from all over the world—Filipinas, Colombians, Israelis, and women from Eastern Bloc countries who weren't all there by choice. Some were victims of a dishonest manager who had forced them into prostitution while holding their visas hostage. Others were choosing the lesser of two evil paths. I remember meeting a young Columbian girl named Isabella, who worked as a street prostitute. My fellow Men's Club hostesses and I were horrified at the thought of someone so young working the street scene, but she informed us that no matter how bad her situation appeared to us in Japan, life was still better there on the streets of Tokyo than back home. Over time, I met more girls like Isabella, girls who were doing whatever they could to be on the path to eventual financial independence.

*　*　*

After the abysmal presidential election results, I began to see a troubling trend—the so-called "slut shaming" of Trump's wife, Melania. I know people were angry and looking for anything Trump-related they could stick their claws into, and Melania's modeling photos made for easy prey. I get it—but I don't agree with it. Maybe we should start by calling this heinous verbal assault what it truly is: *woman-hating*.

Now, I'm a feminist in the sense that I passionately believe in *Her mind, her body, her choice*. I don't know Melania's entire history. It appears that she lived comfortably with her family in Slovenia, and that many of her decisions were made when she was a young woman trying to get ahead in her chosen profession. Her nude photos were taken when she was a model.

Her job was to look smokin' hot and sell products. It was her choice to pursue this career path. When I hear people *woman-hating* Melania for her choices, I reflect on my own decisions, which I've filed as the good, the bad, the ugly—and the stupid. But I've also worked hard and made many contributions to my community, none of which are diminished by *my* choice to party for pay in a foreign country at the age of twenty-two.

However, I can't help but think of women like Isabella and the other women I met with troubled histories, from areas rife with human trafficking and political strife. By participating in the *woman-hating* of Melania—and women like me who have voluntarily used our physical attributes for financial gain—we are also shaming women like Isabella, who saw no other way out of a bleak and destitute future. Our tendency to *woman-hate* sends a dangerous and irresponsible message to women like Isabella; a message of derision and shame, further marginalizing them—and potentially compromising their safety.

Annette D., age 46
Risk consultant
Charlotte, North Carolina

Election 2016

BIG DECISIONS, PRIMARIES, campaigns, canvassing for my party, making phone calls, attending rallies for Her.

Explaining to my girls what this could mean. But not to worry! We will prevail.

Primary won; feeling hopeful; I am with Her.

Debates, wondering if this is really a joke, horrible words, locker-room talks, hate and fear.

Urging others to vote early, holding candid conversations regarding promises being made.

Election Day approaches: anxiety, stress, worry.

My daughter accompanies me to the polling precinct; casting my vote, feeling secure.

Waiting, watching, hoping, doing the math, praying for swing states, nervous.

Polls still reporting, going to sleep with hope and a dream.

Waking up, *the news must be wrong*, sitting in disbelief, crushed.

In a fog, glued to the news, waiting for this to be a prank.

Fear sets in; then sparks of hope, recounts, popular votes, Electoral College.

Gathering new friends, identifying old friends who didn't stand with me.

Building a future with my kids—loving, caring, being kind.

Becoming more active in my community to make a difference, give hope, give love.

Marching for Love, showing my kids how to give back, praying for their safety.

Others say, "Wait and see"; I can't sit and watch it go to hell.

Pray for peace; be active—

Love trumps hate.

Corey Williams, age 40
Photographer
North Carolina

Four Days

April 9, 2011

THE WIND BLEW the rain sideways into the tent. We were wet and cold. The guests had gone, and those still in the mood for revelry had moved on to a local bar. But as the event committee, we scrambled around in our heels and gowns, rounding up unclaimed artwork.

I let myself have one of those lingering moments when I want to remember a visual catalogue of the night: Ana, racing about with her damp fir and green satin dress; the DJ, pulling speakers into the center of the soaking tent; tables with toy-themed centerpieces and Little-Golden-Books'-themed programs; and pallet-wood-lined walls hung with beautiful local artwork. We had worked so hard. Then the rain came. Had we a clear night . . . how long would people have stayed? I followed the revelers into the adjacent bar and settled into conversation with the committee, donors, and friends.

"Come sit down with me. I want to get to know you," said a man's voice.

His name was Ryan Cross; he and his wife had won my auction item. As a photographer, I'd offered up a year of photography services. He'd paid thousands for it. I was grateful, *so grateful*, when I saw a number go up for my item. Nothing is more humiliating than having your personal auction item sit out there without bids.

I didn't know him well. But his children were enrolled at the same private school my children attended, and we shared many mutual friends. Our conversation was easy, filled with laughter. He was flirty, but in that way that's societally acceptable when your wife is nearby and she slaps you on the wrist for your comments. Everyone laughed.

I looked around to realize there were few people left. My husband had gone home, and the folks that remained were mostly committee members.

"Hey," Ryan said, with a wide smile, "let's grab one more drink down the street. I know the owners at The Tavern, and we can have one more there before we call it a night."

I hugged girlfriends goodbye and ran, laughing to the Tavern. When we opened the door, the bartender gave a chuckle. We looked like wet rats. Ryan in his tuxedo and me in an evening gown, drenched by the rain.

The bartender handed me a vodka tonic, handed one to Ryan, and made one for himself. We continued to talk, but the conversation had taken a turn that was making me uncomfortable. Ryan could tell. He asked about my relationship, which was, I'll admit, rocky. Something about the way he asked felt off. He told me about his wife—whom everyone liked and whom I had hoped to get to know better. Ryan told me he wasn't attracted to her anymore.

"I'm attracted to you," Ryan said. His face twitched into an unreadable expression. Not lust or desire—but more sinister, craven. Suddenly, the room melted around me. Information began to swirl. The door was locked, but there was another man, the bartender. I was not alone. Ryan began to take off his pants. Startled, I looked over my shoulder at the bartender. His eyes stared back, dead empty, and he began moving toward us to assist in my rape.

October 7, 2016

My legs were falling asleep. I shifted on my boyfriend's sofa and resettled my computer on my lap. It was the height of my busiest season, and I was culling through the week's family photo shoots. The room grew dark, and my monitor glowed along with the television, tuned to one news channel or another.

It was election season—and a strange one at that—and I'd been following along with the rest of the country. I couldn't believe that Donald Trump had become the Republican Party's nominee, but at least it made for good political theater. The news had never been so interesting.

I got up to get a diet soda, thought about how I should really give up soda, and walked to the kitchen. The glass was cold in my hand as I walked back to the living room, and I stopped and picked up the remote. There was breaking news.

The channel was broadcasting audio of Donald Trump and some host, still in the bus, awaiting the start of a news magazine: "I don't even wait. And when you're a star, they let you do it, you can do anything . . . grab them by the pussy."

I realized I was sitting about the time that I realized that my lips were numb. A hot pressure burned in my chest, a sensation that brought with it a familiar panic. *When you're a star, when you're rich, when you're a white man . . . I don't wait . . . grab them by the pussy . . . I'm attracted to you. . . .*

I was not back there. I was not locked in that bar. I was not in the hospital, where they dyed my vagina blue and looked for tears. I was not having fifty pubic hairs ripped from my body.

I was not in a police station having my bruises photographed. I was not surrounded by the committee friends, showing them handprints on my body while they shook their heads in disbelief.

I was here, on the sofa I loved because it was marshmallow cozy. In my boyfriend's house, waiting for him to return from the restaurant. I was strong. I had already fought this battle. I'd made it through the tumultuous pain of the end of my marriage. I'd pulled myself together when my friends apologetically abandoned me because of the "drama." I'd sat with attorneys; I'd gone to counseling. I had made it through the other side.

The burning in my chest was back. And the numbness in my lips. They sat on my body like a weight. And crushed me. I felt the room grow long, and I curled into a ball on the sofa. I wanted to be as small as I could be. I cried into an exhausted sleep.

November 8, 2016

I was tired and cold when I finally made it to my best friend's warm house. I had been out all day with my college roommate, Adam. We had wandered the Raleigh city park adjacent to the bus station, wearing signs offering rides to the polls.

The plight of one young pregnant woman, Samantha, who was waiting for a bus, tugged at my heart. She was living in a homeless shelter after losing her job. But she wanted to vote. We had found her precinct, drove her there, talked about candidates and her beliefs, and dropped her off at her bus station. But not before exchanging numbers. I was resolved to help her.

My best friend and I settled in to watch the election results. We poured wine as we waited. I told her about Samantha, and we began a debate about personal responsibility, social services, and the working poor. But our attention turned sharply when we heard Wolf Blitzer's voice calling Florida.

My mouth hung open. Donald Trump had a path to the

presidency. The weeks of believing that Hillary's win was a forgone conclusion, shattered like glass in front of me. There was still hope: Wisconsin, Michigan, Pennsylvania, even Arizona hung in the balance. Slowly, those states were called for Donald Trump. There was no more conversation.

I went home and heaved myself into bed. Donald Trump was winning. The tears came fast and hard. I lay in the dark, trying to tease apart why I was so upset. The answer hit me like a fast hard wind that knocks the breath out of you.

America didn't care. America didn't care that Donald Trump said that he didn't wait, that he can do whatever he wants and get away with it. America didn't care that sixteen women came forward with sexual assault charges against him knowing that the media and public would crucify them. America didn't care about their assaults, nor mine either.

The burning was back. I swallowed back a huge scream. Ryan had never been charged; he'd hired detectives to shake friends up. The district attorney told me there would be no charges. Ryan was still walking around town, where I would see him. Nothing had changed for him. He had gotten away with it. No one cared.

My rapist and men like Trump were white, powerful, and wealthy. They could get away with it. No one cared about women like me. Not only could they go on with their lives like nothing happened but also America would still elect a perpetrator as president. America didn't care.

December 13, 2016

I kissed my three children goodbye and headed home. Client orders weighed on me. I took the stairs to my bedroom. My friend Mary's social media status lit up my phone. She was on her way to the North Carolina General Assembly building to protest. Our legislature was attempting to curtail the powers of our newly elected governor and to pack our state's supreme court.

Damnit. I had talked about Judge Mike Morgan to so many people I knew. On the day I drove people to the polls, I'd suggested him to voters. He'd *won*. The balance of the court was changing because that's what we, the people, wanted, and now the legislators in NC were changing the rules. I don't let my seven-year-old change the rules after the game starts, and I wasn't going to let these guys either.

As I reached for my keys, my chest was burning again. But I wasn't afraid. I was angry. Really, really angry. And I was going to use that anger.

I packed my camera, my laptop, and jumped in my car. I laughed. Turned up the radio and buckled my seat belt. I was ready. Ready for a long fight.

Katherine Dupont Phillips, age 71
Retired teacher
Raymond, Mississippi

For the Sake of History,
I Must

I HAVE BECOME A crazy person since the election on November 8, 2016, another day that "will live in infamy."

Not many of us Americans remember much of anything, it seems, from history. Why? Did the Trump supporters sit in the back of the room and nap with dribble cascading down their overprivileged flesh? Cause trouble so that conscientious pupils had to strain to hear? Daydream of owning empires? Lose all sense of a moral compass? I hope to God it wasn't my former students who did this to us.

I first realized I was descending into madness when I looked around the other day and saw flags flying at half-staff. *Oh*, I nodded knowingly. And then I realized it was Pearl Harbor Day.

We know the number of people who died on December 7, 1941; we know how that day affected people. We still don't know the body count on this latest thing, the presidential election. And half of America don't even know it is a *thing*. One of my beloved ones is a veteran, and he doesn't know. He called to check on me yesterday. He's not one to talk much on the phone, but maybe he suspected my pending descent into madness.

"What are you doing?" he asked.

"I'm decorating the Christmas tree and listening to Christmas music," I responded.

"Good. . . . Good," he said.

Toward the end of the conversation I broached the subject of this "new thing." I could almost hear him sigh. He responded with his standard answer of remaining neutral politically.

"You don't understand. I'm seventy years old. I've never seen anything like this in my life." I think I must have sounded like I was drowning. He himself was winded; he was rushing back to his office in DC so that he wouldn't go past his allotted lunch break. He's an Eagle Scout, you see. He has a family to feed. And I love him beyond measure.

He started into his "gotta go" part of the conversation.

"Wait, wait!" I said. "Would you pick me up a few things? An Obama mug? Something with his name . . . his picture on it . . . before they are all gone?"

"Sure, sure. Love you." And then he was gone. He was a top student and member of the academic competition team in high school. He should know better.

* * *

Oh, I was having a pity party yesterday. Somehow I had managed to latch onto some soul-gripping Christmas music channel on my smartphone while searching for "O Come, O Come, Emmanuel." It followed with "Mary, Did You Know?" and "Have Yourself a Merry Little Christmas," which is a tear-jerker for me. In 1964, it played as part of the score of a movie in which executions during World War II were being shown. The high school friend who sat in front of us in the theater died that weekend from a drowning accident. Later, we would all think that at least he didn't die in Vietnam.

Sounds terrible, doesn't it? It's how most of my generation thought back then.

At our fiftieth high school reunion a few years back, some of my former classmates and I talked about what happened on November 22, 1963, the day President John F. Kennedy was assassinated. This was before integration in the Deep South, so I was a senior at an all-white high school. When the president's death was announced over the intercom, the vast majority of the students stood up and cheered. It was a big, two-storied brick building, and you could hear the resounding whoops of glee coming from all directions.

I checked out of school as soon as it was announced that we could. I also checked out of a lot of friendships that day. Only a handful of us were devastated, and we soon became a small band of brothers. I had loved JFK since the ninth grade when, for a school assignment, I had taken notes during those famous debates between him and Nixon. I was attending a small Catholic high school in Louisiana then, and our civics teacher inspired us to pay attention to politics. Now *those* were debates.

* * *

I sure as hell do not want to talk about the night of November 8, 2016. For the sake of history, I must.

My husband and I live in our ubiquitous ranch-style home in Raymond, Mississippi, where a Civil War battle took place during the Vicksburg campaign. My husband is a subject of the Queen of England and cannot vote. I was watching CNN. My husband, the documented "alien," had gone to bed because he leaves for work each weekday morning at 4:45 a.m. (I'm retired, and he has me and the cats to feed. But I do have my state retirement and social security to supplement our income—at least for now.)

My daughter, whom our Republican cousin/governor has called "Hillary" since she was twelve years old, was texting with me. My retired schoolteacher cousin from the Mississippi coast, who disdains cell phones, was emailing back and forth with me. By 10:00 p.m., there was no doubt the impossible had happened. My alien husband, after waking to "pop loo," stumbled through the living room on his way to the screen porch for a "fag" (cigarette). He instinctively knew something was amiss and plopped down on the sofa beside me. We hadn't been this dumbfounded since 9/11 or since Hurricane Katrina tore off part of our roof. I think we finally headed down the hall about 2:00 a.m. My daughter and cousin were as incredulous as we were. Pantsuit Nation, other groups, we were all just stunned. How had this vile, unprepared individual won the election?

The days following have seemed to all run together. Almost immediately, there was talk of a "Million Woman March" in Washington to protest Trump's win. I got my plane ticket to DC before the prices went too high. The Women's March on Washington? Hell, yes! My daughter and I were going and taking her twelve-year-old daughter, my wide-eyed wonderful granddaughter whose other grandparents happen to be Muslims from Turkey. "We'll be part of history," this little beloved said to me when I drove to Texas to visit for the last two weeks of November. It was good therapy to care for my four Austin grandchildren, but now it all seems a blur.

I was in Texas because daughter "Hillary" and her boyfriend had gone to India to a wedding. On the way, they had a layover in Zurich, and Hillary texted me picture of the front page of a newspaper bearing the president-elect's picture and which proclaimed *Ende der Welt*—"End of the World"—and I whispered, "As we know it." But none of *us* felt fine.

*   *   *

Thanksgiving Day: My older daughter, Aunt JenJen, had voted for the "Emperor with No Clothes." I love her dearly, and she had been through a dreadful week, having been made redundant due to a corporate takeover. We were trying to cheer each other up. As we were taking the turkey from the oven, Jen said, "AHA! I'm taking a picture and putting it on Hillary's Facebook' page." (Family inside joke. Hillary is a vegetarian. Cousin/governor used to threaten to send her deer sausage made from deer that he had actually killed.)

Then it happened.

"Wait!" said Jen. "Has Hillary unfriended me on Facebook?"

"Uhhhh . . . well, I hate that you had to find out on Thanksgiving."

"That heifer!" exclaimed Jen.

I just stood by sheepishly.

"Is it because I voted for . . . ?"

"Yes," I admitted.

We ate our nice dinner, and I volunteered to take all four children to the nearby park while Dak Prescott continued to work his Dallas Cowboys magic. Jen and I love football, but I wanted to give her some peace and quiet.

The park was lovely, and I had many happy thoughts as I sat there while the children played. Austin is a cool city, and every demographic was represented on the playground that day. *Can't we all get along? YES, WE CAN. There's No Hate in My State*, I thought. But there *is* hate. And it is deep-seated. And it has been dormant since November 22, 1963, or thereabouts. I just didn't know it. And knowing it hurts like hell.

We were the last ones to leave the park. The full moon and the posh lanterns led our way back to the apartment building. The four grandchildren, despite their age differences, were skipping along and laughing together. Then from a balcony in the apartments across the way, we heard a young male voice, probably a University of Texas student who had elected to stay home for the holiday. He did what my husband would call a proper "Tarzan yell." The oldest granddaughter answered him with her preadolescent call. He answered in kind. We were all laughing so hard. A middle-aged couple walking their dog joined in the merriment. It felt a little bit like the French Quarter in New Orleans, The City that Care Forgot. For a moment, we were lost in the world, and that was just fine by us.

Later, after everyone had either left or gone to sleep, I began to reflect on other times in my life when I had felt alienated from my own country. "Is this America?" Mississippian Fannie Lou Hamer asked at the Democratic National Convention in Atlantic City, New Jersey, in 1964. There was no Trump Casino back in those days. "I question America. Is this America, the land of the free and the home of the brave, where we have to sleep with our telephones off the hooks because our lives be threatened daily, because we want to live as decent human beings, in America?"[8]

* * *

Where am I five weeks into this nightmare? I am asking the same question Fannie Lou Hamer asked all those years ago. Now with new allegations of Russians' tampering with our election.

---

8 "Fannie Lou Hamer's Testimony," YouTube video, 7:24, from a speech delivered at the Democratic National Convention on August 22, 1964, posted by "Pamela Cook," June 10, 2010, https://www.youtube.com/watch?v=ML3WaEsCB98, quoted in Peter Dreier, "'I Question America'—Remembering Fannie Lou Hamer's Famous Speech 50 Years Ago," *The Huffington Post* (August 2014): http://www.huffingtonpost.com.

The Russians were the bogeymen of my nightmares when I was my oldest granddaughter's age. Now they are back.

But you know what? None of us everyday people, whether Americans or Russians, are even on this chess board. None of us. And that is why this whole "mess" seems off and *is* different from anything in our history. I have never been much on conspiracy theories, although my hero JFK was embroiled in some major goings-on that we may never know about, including Norma Jean. But something is rotten in Denmark. I know it in every fiber of my being, and not just because I have a master's degree in history from a prestigious little college. The hairs on the back of my neck are standing up from the wariness that has served us humans well since we stood upright.

Above all, I am a teacher, and others like me will lead the charge. Let it be observed that people like Donald J. Trump— who didn't apply themselves in school, who cheated their way through life, who recklessly destroyed thousands of lives for financial gain, who lied to get their way, who couldn't be bothered to take their daily duties seriously, and who showed no sense of responsibly or remorse—will never again be allowed to gain this type of power in the United States of America.

Robin Rosenberg Spence, age 62
Retired
Lewisburg, West Virginia

Everything They Vote For

MY DAUGHTER AND I were in a long line at our local grocery store. My daughter started flipping through a magazine, reading the latest escapades of Tom Cruise, and commenting on the absurdity of Scientology.

When we got up to the register, the cashier leaned over and said, "Do you know what the real problem is?" When we didn't answer, the cashier continued, "The real problem is, Hollywood is filled with rich Democrats. Rich Democrats and homosexuals who believe everything they hear!"

My daughter and I exchanged a bemused glance. I leaned over the register and quietly replied, "There are Democrats and homosexuals right here in this town, and I really don't think they are the problem." (I didn't defend the rich. Sorry.)

As we were walking out of Kroger, I turned to my daughter and said, "This country deserves everyone they vote for."

Kristen Chapman Gibbons, age 46
Storyteller
Nashville, TN

Whiteout

There are ways
to survive
a winter you weren't prepared for

a storm even the most beloved prognosticators misread
there are instructions to heed
when you are trapped in blizzard conditions
and
horizons disappear

you tell yourself
the day started with defiant, bare arms
and then
like a fickle Tennessee afternoon,

the clouds signaled
a temperature drop
and it did,
even as the electoral map grew bloody,
it began to snow.

Wet, white, and unceasing.
Suddenly, the familiar markers are
blurred and indistinguishable,
voices
like bells
get muffled
when covered.

And you waste time immobile—
wondering why no one thought
this whiteness wouldn't blind us.

Why have so many lost the ability to
see the villain?
Who walked right into
the spotlight,
announcing his sorry intentions
on an Access Hollywood bus.
How could they not see?

We believed each new horror

would be enough.

Our privilege sustains this delusion still . . .

even as we are forever falling apart.

I wanted so badly

to be believed this time.

I needed for everyone to

recognize The Bad Guy.

And they didn't.

Or they did, and they didn't care.

And the snow keeps coming.

It doesn't care what it smothers.

The How-To is as follows:

Focus on what is in front of you.

Conserve resources.

Protect skin and eyes—vulnerable areas require extra protection

Build shelter—snow can be sculpted, hollowed out and burrowed into—but you must insure ventilation.

Follow footsteps if there are any.

Avoid panic.

Focus your mind.

Aim for slow, steady breath.

In times of additional snowfall, anticipate avalanches.

Stay hydrated, dry, and warm.

Keep moving, lethargy will lull you to fatal stillness.

Know that each step forward keeps your blood flowing.

Stay alive as long as you can.

Laura McDaniel, age 28
Recruiter
Birmingham, Alabama

My Impolite Life

W HEN I WAS six, my absolute favorite movie was *FernGully: The Last Rainforest.* This became a problem when I eventually realized that my father owned a logging company. I lived with the enemy. I spent months begging him to stop cutting down innocent trees and erasing entire populations of fairies and fruit bats, but to no avail.

After weeks of debate with my poor father, I had an idea. I woke up early one morning and walked through the sparse woods between our home and the family business. I arrived just in time to body-block the last employee from leaving the lot and heading into the forest. It was my father's oldest employee, a semiretired grandfather, currently wearing a worried scowl. I calmly explained to him that if he wanted to steamroll a population of fairies and fruit bats, he would have to steamroll me first. After a few minutes of arguing with a six-year-old, he left me alone to step inside the shop and call my father at home.

In his absence, I unsuccessfully attempted to attach myself

to his vehicle with a large rope I'd found behind the shop. By the time my father arrived to assess the situation, I was tangled, rope-burned, and frustrated, but I hadn't lost my resolve. My father wasn't as much surprised as he was impressed. He laughed as he put me kicking and screaming into the front seat of his fire-engine-red work truck—I don't think he stopped once in the quarter-mile drive back home. After he filled my mother in on my tree-hugging antics, my father sat me down for a discussion. He explained that he was a hardworking small business owner who wasn't killing the rainforest, delightful fairies, or well-meaning fruit bats. After my eventful morning, I was tired and eager to see my father once again as the hero he'd always been, so I forgave him. I had one condition: he would keep an eye out for any creatures—magical or otherwise— lurking in his jobsites and would do his best to keep them safe. My good-natured father agreed, and our relationship returned to what it had been before my self-discovery.

If my parents didn't realize when I was six that I was a bit more progressive than my peers, they definitely got the picture a few years later. When I was twelve, I came home from school sobbing. I had been attacked at recess for announcing that if I could have voted, I would have voted for Al Gore. I don't know what hurt more: receiving the right hook of a fellow seventh grader or realizing that at twelve years old, I wasn't like everyone else. I desperately wanted to be average. My mother attempted to teach me two things that day: that being "average" wasn't necessarily something I should strive for and that discussing politics wasn't polite. Sixteen years later, I still haven't learned the latter.

Fall 2006, during my freshman year of college at the University of Alabama, I was asked to write a piece on an up-and-coming figure in American politics for my Introduction to American Government class. I chose Barack Obama, who was, at the time, a little-known senator from Illinois, and that was it—my descent into the United States Democratic party was complete. At eighteen, I was a Southern sorority girl with a secret too big to be hidden in my voluminous hair. I realized I didn't belong; for the first time in my life, I liked it that way.

Fast-forward to a chilly February morning in 2016. I huddled in a gym in South Birmingham with a few hundred other men and women, awaiting the main event. I didn't realize how excited I was until a petite woman clad in pearls and a slate-blue woolen pantsuit walked to center stage; gave a broad smile; and proclaimed, "Good morning, Birmingham!" Those simple words made my eyes tear up. I cheered until the crowd calmed, and then I listened to Secretary Hillary Clinton tell a gymnasium full of progressive Southerners everything we yearned to hear. Right there, in that brightly lit college gym, I knew I had found my candidate. I knew the woman standing on stage would fight for me, and at that moment, I realized I would fight for her too.

I spent the next months telling anyone who would listen about the great things Hillary Clinton was going to do for America. I spoke of how she would fight to end discrimination and poverty and work to reform our educational system. I provided candidate breakdowns to all my friends who were undecided voters. I watched the polls roll in, all of them indicating the same thing: Hillary Clinton would be the next president of the United States. November 8, 2016, came, and I proudly voted. That night, I snuggled up with my dogs, turned on CNN, and eagerly awaited the announcement of our first woman president.

It's been months now, and I still feel like I'm waiting for that announcement. I struggle to come to terms that the world I knew in the months leading up to November 8, no longer exists.

In the wake of that awful day, however, a funny thing

happened: I found hope. The men and women who had cheered with me before the election weren't fading away now that it was over; they were standing up for themselves and one another, shouting to be heard over injustice and prejudice, smiling in the face of adversity. *We're here for you, a big wave of blue in our very red state. Bring us your struggles; we will make them our own.*

The election is over, but our vision for America isn't. We remain a proud and tireless group of warriors united by a common goal, a mutual enemy, and a tireless blonde in pearls and a pantsuit.

Monisha, age 19
College student
Tampa, Florida

Stronger than Hate

I LIVE IN FLORIDA, one of the most important swing states in the country. Born in Indiana to Bangladeshi-born immigrants-turned-American-citizens, I am a Hoosier through and through. I grew up in Indiana, and moved to Florida when I was nine. We lived in particularly red areas in both states. I grew up with my parents' telling me to hide who I was and the beliefs I held, fearing harassment and bullying. I was lucky I had a loving group of friends who supported me and shared similar views. However, there were moments in my life when I did face retribution for my opinions. One of these moments happened in my tenth-grade American Government class.

The assignment was to debate a controversial topic, and we were to argue abortion. I chose the pro-choice side to defend. I decided to start with my parents. I asked them to share their thoughts about abortion and listened as they explained feminism and the right for a woman to decide what to do with her body. Afterwards, I felt I understood and agreed with their points. I did my own research and created my argument and questions for the pro-life side.

The day of the debate, I was harassed by my classmates because of our differing views on this issue. They didn't respectfully disagree with me as one should in a debate; instead, they berated me and treated me like an enemy, not an opponent. It was my first brush with those who had a political view different from mine. This moment should have made me start speaking out more, to be unafraid to speak my mind. Instead, it urged me to stay quiet and hide my views, out of fear of being different.

* * *

I've called myself a Muslim, but I am not a typical Muslim. Both of my parents are from Bangladesh. My mother is Muslim, but my father is a former-Muslim-turned-atheist. So I grew up with two very different views. I strive to remain neutral while still religiously respectful. I'm still unsure of where I stand on religion, except that people should be allowed to practice without fear whatever they choose. I mention this because at some point I generally tell new people I meet that I come from a Muslim family; lately, I've learned to be cautious about disclosing this fact. I've seen so-called friends become uncomfortable when I talk about my Muslim heritage. I hope that when I tell them about the problems I've encountered with Islamophobia and xenophobic bigots, they feel as uncomfortable as they've made me feel.

I faced an even greater challenge in 2016. I'm a college student, and I live in a dorm room with friends who voted for Trump. They are all Republicans and voted for him for "their own reasons." I remained quiet and friendly. The week following the election, I left the building and stayed with family and friends, because I would not let my roommates see me in my distraught state. They lost the right to see me at my lowest point when they decided that Donald Trump's actions—including making disparaging remarks throughout his campaign about immigrants, Muslims, and Mexicans—weren't deal breakers for them. They lost the right to say they care about all people, after I'd spent two years listening to them support Trump, who has stated to his followers that Muslims are terrorists, that Islam is a violent religion, and that he is considering the possibility of an internment camp. Did they not understand such a policy would result in the locking up of my own friends and family?

When I went back to school in the new year, I continued to be polite to these people, but I've realized even in friendship, I can't look past certain things. I will not be a token person-of-color friend, whose inclusion in their life is meant to ease their consciences. I will not be a friend to those who decide that xenophobia, Islamophobia, and a lack of human decency are minor, easily ignored character flaws. I realize I may end up burning bridges along the way. But I'm personally affected by almost every policy Trump plans on diminishing or replacing, while others have privilege keeping them safe, whether it be white privilege, white woman privilege, or class privilege. A president is supposed to act for and represent us with our best interests at heart. But Donald Trump does not have my best interest at heart, nor does he speak for me. Until he shows me respect, he does not have mine.

*   *   *

As I write this, President Trump has signed legislation banning Muslims from entering the United States, including refugees. While I was shocked that such a thing could even be legal, I was not surprised at the selectivity of the ban. While not directly affected by this executive action, I have never felt more pain than I did that day. I lost track of the times I cried as I read online articles and posts on Twitter. But later that day, my desolation once again turned to hope and love, sparked by the courageous men and women who stood in airports, telling those affected by the ban that they are welcome, that they are loved, and that this hateful action does not represent the views of the entire country. Because of these protests, and the lawyers who showed up in force to start putting together legal representation for detainees, the ban has been temporarily lifted.

Two days after the ban, my university held a rapid-response protest against the Muslim ban. I stood in solidarity with those directly affected by the ban and with those like me who were there to lend support. Muslims and Muslim Americans spoke of their stories, of their backgrounds, and of how lucky they are to have the opportunities they have been afforded. Together we chanted, "No Ban. No Wall. You come for us, you take us all!"; we made our support heard and felt. Afterwards, we marched around campus to the main building where the president of the university resides, and protested outside. While a majority of the protesters were there for the Muslim community, other groups suffering from civil injustices were present. There were speeches about immigration reform, about supporting the undocumented, and about Black Lives Matters, all stressing how we must stand together. People from all walks of life were supporting one another, vowing to stand together, all of us knowing our fight has just begun.

I am a girl who loves my family, who is loyal to my friends. I go to school. I read books. I watch the news. I am no different just because I learned about God as Allah. I wake up every day knowing there are hundreds of people who hate me just because of my religious affiliation, but I still get up out of bed. I am stronger than the hate that surrounds me, and together, we are that much stronger. We will all survive this.

Noelle Buttry, age 47
Photographer
Little Rock, Arkansas

The Compassionate Path

I GREW UP IN the 1970s and 1980s in the small, rural community of Bernie in Southern Missouri. The economy was dependent on the farmers who worked the surrounding land, the blue-collar factory workers who toiled daily in the shoe factory, and the employees of the locally owned mill that made ax handles. My dad, Norm, was a professional portrait photographer, well-known in the area for weddings and family portraits, which placed us in the upper class of this tiny enclave of eighteen hundred people. He was also the municipal judge in the town, which added to his image of success and wealth. I remember children referring to me as "rich," and it often angered me, because even at a young age, I knew my social and financial status was primarily one of perception and not reality. I had a good life and I was loved abundantly. But we did not have a large home, a fat bank account, or brand-new cars. My mother and father had split in an ugly, contentious divorce the year before I began kindergarten. My dad and I lived in a small bungalow with my grandmother Dorothy, a nurse at the town physician's office, and my great-grandmother Lottie, a homemaker. Our home lacked central heat and air, which didn't seem like something a rich kid would have to endure, so I was truly mystified by the label my friends stuck me with.

During elementary school, I became keenly aware that, although not I was not wealthy, I was fortunate to have more food, clothing, and toys than many of my fellow classmates whose parents were unskilled, uneducated, and caught in unending cycles of poverty and alcoholism. My dad and grandmother spent much of their time quietly offering assistance to members of our community who struggled to find food or warm coats.

One of my favorite memories of my father is from an especially cold winter, just a few days before Christmas. He called the owner of the local department store and asked him to open it one evening because I had come home from school and mentioned that a classmate of mine had no winter coat. Dad bought coats for the whole family, parents included, and we left the coats on their front porch under the cover of darkness. It was incredible experiencing the warm rush of compassion and kindness that floods your heart when helping someone in need.

Grandma Dorothy was a yellow dog Democrat who regularly sang the praises of FDR and JFK. She was also a passionate supporter of Jimmy Carter and Walter Mondale. We kept our thermostat set on sixty-eight because "Jimmy Carter wants us to, honey," and I was the only child at school who sported a pair of blue jeans she had embroidered with the names of the Democratic candidates running for office that year, including Carter and Mondale. I looked forward to election day and the three-block drive down to the local fire station with Dorothy, where I would be allowed to accompany her into the curtained tent to mark her straight-ticket ballot for all the candidates I had unwittingly endorsed with my embroidered attire.

As I neared age ten, I noticed that my dad's political views were somewhat different from those of my grandma and that he held Ronald Reagan in high regard. His business had suffered terribly after his divorce, and he credited Reagan economic policies with helping save it from ruin. I began to feel torn politically as I neared my teenage years. Being a Democrat felt like the more compassionate path to follow, but it seemed everyone around me except my grandma leaned Republican. This was the Bible Belt. The majority of people who lived in and around Bernie were white, Christian, and still living in close proximity to the towns where they were born. We had one Jewish family in town, but people avoided discussing their religious affiliation as if it were a skeleton in their closet. Not one person I grew up with was openly gay, though there were whispers about some. My hometown churches were fundamentalist in their teachings and often used God to justify excluding people who didn't fit their idea of the "perfect Christian."

My family differed somewhat in this respect but were not entirely accepting of others. My grandma and dad helped people local to our area, no matter their circumstances, skin color, or religious affiliation, yet they were still reluctant to accept outsiders—people my family had never actually met and who were markedly different in beliefs, traditions, or values. On summer vacations we would bypass motels with dark-skinned desk clerks in search of places that were "American owned." Even today, if my dad gets a customer service representative who speaks broken English, he is immediately out of his comfort zone, and he grows angry.

I chose to attend a large state university upon graduation from high school because I believed there was more to experience in life and so much more to learn, not only about others but also about myself. Throwing caution and security to the wind and heading off to a much larger city remains one of the best decisions I have ever made. Though the university was still in the Bible Belt and in a rather homogenous area of the Midwest, I met fellow students from other countries and professors of many different faiths, including my first atheist. I lived in a town with a large Vietnamese population and an abundance of Chinese and Mexican restaurants. It wasn't until college that I ate my first (and definitely not my last) taco. I tried Chinese food, cooked by actual Chinese people, something I could never have experienced in my hometown at that time. I lived in the dorm with a practicing Buddhist. I had friends who were gay. I knew good people who had abortions. I would love to say that by the time I graduated I was an all-loving, compassionate, accepting woman who didn't rush to judgment of others and who opened her heart to all, but I was still incredibly far from being that woman.

I eventually married a hometown boy who was raised two blocks from me in Bernie. Our family backgrounds were similar, and he was a staunch conservative, having been brought up attending a Southern Baptist church. He listened to Rush Limbaugh, and I gave being a conservative Republican my best shot. I agreed with some of the more idealistic ideas of the Republican party, but as I grew older and became a mother, I started to feel strongly that life didn't usually present itself in situations that were conducive to these idealistic concepts. Yes, we should all be drug-free, self-reliant, hard-working people who uphold high standards of personal responsibility one hundred percent of the time, but that isn't reality. Sometimes people need help, and as my children grew older, I was motivated to provide some of that help in an effort to be a good example to them. I found myself envisioning a world where everyone wanted to help those who had less and found themselves in unfortunate circumstances. I wanted to be an example of unconditional acceptance of others for my children to see. While I was busy envisioning myself on this journey, I witnessed the Far Right descend into a state of panic rooted in the feeling they were losing control. Rather than admit that some of their ideas and principles might be harsh and unaccepting, the Right seemed to respond to the Left by spouting conspiracy theories, spewing hate and vitriol, and invoking God as a fear tactic to scare people into supporting their platforms. The Republican Party was no longer the party it once was, and I no longer wanted to be associated with it.

The presidential election of 2016 was a remarkable turning point for me in my journey to be a better human being. Nothing I had supported politically in the past made any sense to me. Sometimes the hatred and meanness I saw on television and in my own daily life with my friends and family became almost too much to bear. I had been a Republican in theory, but my heart was never in it. The realization that prejudice and isolationism still prevailed in Bernie struck me hard as I attempted to interact with some of my friends on social media. Facebook became a stressful place to hang out with fake news and uneducated statements being shared faster than you could read them, often by childhood friends.

The town of Bernie has changed tremendously since I left. The shoe factory closed, leaving much of the town jobless. The ax handle factory was sold, and they closed the local mill. The downtown I grew up in became a shell of its former self, with stores closing at a rapid pace. Poverty and drug use are evident as one passes through the once flourishing community, with homes and buildings falling into ruin. The little home I grew up in was sold and turned into a rental; it fell into such a state of disrepair that I could no longer drive by it. The population has changed a bit, with Latino people moving into the area, usually to work at the chicken processing plants. You can now get a taco four miles from where I grew up and travel a few more miles to dine at an Asian buffet. To this day, however, the town's demographic remains largely white and overwhelmingly fundamentalist Christian. A neighboring town still has a reputation as being "unwelcoming to Black families."

My interactions with friends on social media have shown me that the residents still fear those unlike them and are unwilling to educate themselves about other religions, races, and issues facing the country. In my Republican days, I criticized Barack Obama for claiming Midwesterners clung to their guns and religion, but that characterization is astonishingly accurate. One of the hardest things for me to accept during all of the mudslinging and propaganda the election produced was the fact that all that stood between most people and change was a simple admission they might be wrong. All it takes for change to happen is for someone to hold out their hand to a person in pain and say, "Let me try to see how it feels from your perspective." This is not happening as it should.

The compassion I have developed for immigrants who come to our country to contribute and try to make better lives for themselves and their families was inevitable. I grew so weary of my own acquaintances' making blanket statements about people they knew little or nothing about. Then, after the election, the widespread stories of discrimination and hate began to surface. With each story of a hijab being ripped off or an immigrant being refused service, the anger in me grew. I was inspired to find a way to tell the stories of people who have become marginalized in this country that is supposed to be a melting pot and the "land of opportunity." I began to notice people around me who were not originally from the United

States but in a leap of faith had moved here and were making a life for themselves and their families. I realized they were enriching *my* life too.

I cherish the relationship that has formed between my children and the Eastern Indian owners of our neighborhood convenience store. The owners have watched my children grow up and compliment them when we are there to buy soft drinks, chips, and candy. We shared in their joy last year when they brought another beautiful baby into the world. When I attended the funeral of a murdered boy the same age as my daughter, I looked over my shoulder to see the owner of the convenience store, dressed in a suit, head hung in sadness, paying his respects to the kid who frequented his store over the years. These are the people I want in my country. These are people I want to know better in order to facilitate change and to help others understand that not everyone who comes to the United States is here to do harm. The vast majority of immigrants want to raise their children in a safe nation, free of suicide bombers and war. They want to contribute to our economy, celebrate our successes, and feel that this is their home. I want to create an avenue to broadcast their stories of hope and survival.

No one has ever inspired me to do more to help others than Hillary Clinton and the "nasty women" of the United States. I feel more empowered as a woman and am sporting a level of confidence that was barely present before. My fellow Hillary supporters have lifted me up like no other. It's my hope that in 2017, I will seek out immigrants and photograph them in their everyday surroundings, doing what they do on a daily basis to make the United States their nation too. I want to interview them and tell their stories using blogging as my outlet.

My children worked hard to help get Hillary elected and

were heartbroken on November 8, 2016, when the results rolled in. I want to show them that the work must not stop and we can each do a small part to continue to pursue the hopes and dreams we had that evening in November. We can't stop being stronger together just because the electoral vote didn't go our way. I like to think that somewhere, in a pair of embroidered pants, my grandma is looking down at my children and me, beaming proudly.

Maranda Joiner, age 35
Poet
Jackson, Mississippi

America "the great"...

July 13, 2013.

The world zoomed in on me as I sat rooted in my grandmother's floral-printed couch.

Strange Fruit on the TV caused me to have anxiety.

A flat-screen color TV was broadcasting to the world that my colored life don't matter.

Not guilty was the murderer who cried wolf.

But anyone with eyes and a moral compass could see that he was.

I guess the jury's justification was that you should never bring Skittles and Tea to a gunfight.

In shock, I turned the TV off along with my hope in humanity.

They will never let me forget that I'm black.

America "the great"...

1963.

Police used dogs and hoses on protestors.

America chose sympathy as their way to cope as these images hit their black-and-white TVs.

Civil Rights Movement was not the end of inequality, just a transition to a more systematic form of racism.

Possibly causing more damage to us than it did to my ancestors who had to wake up to their morning Joe dangling like dead leaves from trees.

Strange Fruit, they called them.

America "the great" . . .

And now . . .

Nothing worse than living in Mississippi in 2017, but it feels like the Mississippi of 1963.

The year my mother was born.

The year Dr. King Jr. had a dream.

Now a dream turned nightmare.

Living in skin that can range from the color of dead leaves in the fall to sweet caramel candy at the top of spring.

Beautiful yet every day is a fight for self-love in a world committed to reminding me how much my black ass don't matter,

Not worth the dead leaves under white-privileged shoes or the penny candy my mama chewed growing up in the projects.

No matter the shade or hue, my melanin is always just enough to keep me behind the curve.

They say time heal all wounds.

But there hasn't been a time when my skin or my gender weren't abused or misused.

Blinded by my anger towards the anger lunged at me, I lash out as I hear echoes of "get over it already. "

But how can I when every channel between FOX and CNN exploits my skin.

Again . . .

America "the great" . . .

Police have traded hoses for guns and dogs for cameras.

Seeing eyes caught on tape.

Catching death in the air like the violent Chicago winds.

Our black lives still don't matter.

Black president pushing hope.

They tear it down.

More gunshots.

You hear the sounds.

Then . . .

Just when I thought that they couldn't hate us any more . . .

they gift us Trump.

Obama, booked back to back, and then they pull a Trump?

Guaranteed joker.

Hide your wives 'cause he's bound to poke her.

This is our America,

land of the free.

They want me to stand to pledge allegiance knowing that line was never written for me.

I placed my right hand over my heart and my left hand to God as the results rolled in on election night like a plow truck spreading white snow *back* over black streets,

taking us back to that cold numb place of seeing dead black bodies on TV.

A whiteout Trumps everything.

Now my gender is up to bat like grabbing pussies at an animal shelter.

Take the lead and pick your cat.

Avoid the black ones: they scratch.

The orange ones will need a wall, you know.

Damn.

Here we go.

November 9, 2016.

America was made "great again"?

It was reminded, again, that I was "*The* African American."

Of 1963 . . .

Susan E. Stutz, age 48
Litigation paralegal and part-time student in women/
gender studies with emphasis on race
Port Saint Lucie, Florida

The World Went Red

NOVEMBER 2015. IN a bid to be hired for the highest office in the land and one of the most influential posts in the global community, presidential candidate Donald Trump mocked a disabled reporter for *The New York Times*, and Trump's supporters went wild with adulation. Blood rushed my brain and the world went red.

In that moment, for the very first time, the election hit home. No more was the victim of ridicule out there in an indeterminate *somewhere*; the victim was seated on the couch across from me. He was my son, Patrick. I was beyond crazy with anger.

July 29, 1993. One of the most path-altering days of my life. The colors, smells, and emotions of that day are as vivid to me now as they were then. Heavily pregnant with my second child, I sat in the lounge of the birthing center, patiently waiting my turn for my weekly exam. I can see the gloss of the magazine pages between my fingers as I read about how to be the perfect mother. I can feel the cushions on my back as I sat on the couch. I can feel the warmth of my daughter's body sitting next to me.

The birthing center resembled a home more than a doctor's office. The antiseptics of a hospital room or traditional doctor's office were nowhere to be found. Live plants hung from the ceiling and sat on shelves. Expectant mothers gave birth in real beds, with pillows in shams, in bedrooms you could actually envision living in. A dining room offered tables and chairs made of real wood. I wore one of my favorite pregnancy outfits—a red-floral-printed Laura Ashley˚ jumper, a white T-shirt with a Battenburg lace collar, lace socks, and white leather Keds˚. My hair, which hung to my waist, was braided down my back. My husband, Dan, was there, as well as our daughter, Jessica, who was four years old at the time. My pregnancy was a family affair, and everyone participated where and when possible. I was young and healthy, and I had no high-risk factors. My pregnancy had been routine. I anticipated giving birth to a healthy baby within the next week or so.

The birthing center was running behind that morning because many of their mothers-to-be had delivered their precious cargo the night before, and virtually all of the birthing staff had been called in to assist. As a result, we waited almost three hours for our turn. Finally, they called my name, and off we went to an exam room. I assumed the position, my tummy was appropriately gelled, and we waited while the midwife located the heartbeat. It was there, then it wasn't, then it was again—but it was really slow. The wand circled my rounded stomach, first in one direction and then back in the other. I knew we were in trouble even before I saw the look in the midwife's eyes. The heartbeat was gone.

My birthing center was in partnership with an OB-GYN practice located right behind the building. After several harrowing minutes, the door of the exam room opened, and in walked a doctor I had never seen before. He was so young, but his eyes were filled with compassion. He continued the wand-work of trying to find the heartbeat and, being unsuccessful, decided I needed to be transported to the hospital across the street. Doc—who has been my physician since that day, some twenty-three years ago—told me afterwards that he had wanted to pick me up and carry me to the hospital but that we had had to wait for the ambulance. I was not at all prepared for this. I had had no complications during the entire pregnancy, nor had I experienced any difficulty when I was pregnant with my daughter. There had been no sign of trouble, no forewarning. I was completely adrift, not able to process what was happening.

Once we reached the emergency room, I was immediately wheeled into a surgical suite, and my dress was flung up over my stomach and chest. The anesthesiologist leaned in and said, "Time to go nighty-night," and the world went black. I awoke to find my dress in the same place it had been in when I closed my eyes. I still had my shoes and socks on. Dan was sitting next to me crying. I had never seen him cry. In fact, that day was one of only two times I have witnessed him cry in more than two decades. The tears running down his face scared me like nothing else could. Dan realized I was awake and looked up at me. I asked him about our baby, and he told me that we had a son and that he was in serious trouble. The world went black again.

The next time I woke up, I found myself in a private room. My clothes had been changed, and I no longer wore my shoes and socks or my favorite red jumper. I cannot say what happened to them, but I never saw those belongings again. I spent the next three days in the hospital, but our Patrick was transported to the neonatal unit of a hospital forty-five minutes away. I saw nothing more than the heel of his foot before he left. I didn't know what he looked like, whether he had any hair, or how much he weighed. The painkillers had made me almost incoherent; however, I knew I must be lucid if I was to be released from the hospital and to see my son. My identical twin sister, Paula, did my hair, applied war paint to my face, and propped me up in a chair with every pillow she could find. Doc came in, and I was momentarily brilliant. Paroled, first time up. Now let me see my son!

Dan and I made daily trips to the neonatal unit over the next two weeks, viewing Patrick through a plastic tent; reaching in and around wires, tubes, and lines to hold his hands in the enclosed crib; feeding him; singing and reading to him, all while trying to digest the knowledge that he might not survive. When Dan and I left the hospital each day, Paula would arrive. I could not be there with Patrick twenty-four hours a day, but she wanted Patrick to see his mother's face—my face—whenever he was awake, so while Dan and I took the day shift, Paula took the nights.

For reasons that remain unknown to this day, Patrick had gotten into serious trouble in the womb. My C-section was performed in record time, but when Patrick was delivered, he was essentially stillborn—no heartbeat, no respiration, Apgar scores at zero and zero. I learned much later that, at that time, the protocol for CPR on a newborn delivered in Patrick's condition, was no more than six minutes. Doc brought Patrick back at five minutes and twenty-three seconds. Thirty-seven seconds became the difference between life and death. It was only with hindsight I recognized that had my appointment taken place at the scheduled time or had I decided not to wait, my son would likely not be here today.

I do not recall how we got on their radar; however, almost immediately upon his release from the neonatal unit, the then Department of Health and Rehabilitative Services began monitoring Patrick. They offered us testing to determine the extent of Patrick's abilities and thus his challenges. This allowed our family the possibility to get in front of whatever he was sure to face. We knew from the onset it was going to be an uphill battle, but we now had the resources to begin conquering the obstacles.

Patrick was almost immediately diagnosed with microcephaly, which means that his head is smaller than it should be. In turn, his brain is not as developed as it should be, either. He began life with a deficiency of gray matter, which not only develops in utero but also continues to grow with you following birth. As a result of that deficiency, together with the prolonged lack of oxygen, Patrick is both developmentally delayed and intellectually disabled. The various milestones of childhood came late to him. Holding up his own head, rolling over, and crawling seemed to take forever. Walking didn't come until he was well past a year old. Tasks such as toilet training took more than a year to accomplish, as opposed to a few months.

Patrick has had the benefit of occupational and physical therapy to deal with the incredibly high tone he has in his muscles. He has also had speech therapy to overcome the adverse effects of a submucous cleft palate, which was repaired when he was about one but has still adversely affected his speech patterns and ability to communicate properly. He was diagnosed with ADHD at the age of three and began taking medication for it at that time. As a young child, he experienced separation anxiety to the extent that he had to be within sight of me at all times except for when he was in school.

As Patrick has grown older, his difficulties have become more pronounced. He does not read or write well, and his comprehension levels are very low. This means that everyday concepts you and I find minimally challenging, such as putting a puzzle together or playing a board game, can be especially difficult for him to grasp. Socially, he is very awkward and has a difficult time with common social behaviors around those individuals with whom he is not very familiar. He suffers from chemical depression, and at age twenty-three, he has the mental acuity of a very young teenager. Patrick does not, and may never, have a job or live independently. Additionally, although not formally tested, he exhibits signs of being on the autism spectrum. Although he cannot remember how to spell simple words like the days of the week, he has an almost encyclopedic memory when it comes to sports, both professional and collegiate. He can give you the rundown on virtually any athlete's college or professional career. Given the right athlete, he can even tell you about where they went to high school. He spends his days and nights glued to ESPN and SEC Network, and I happily pay a king's ransom for cable and internet so that he never misses a play.

Over the course of Patrick's life, I was a permanent face at every preschool program, day care, before- and after-care program, and school that Patrick attended. I volunteered in classrooms, some of which were Patrick's and some of which were not. I knew by heart every educator's name and the rules of engagement for students with disabilities. I became friends with the exceptional student education (ESE) professionals who were largely responsible for Patrick's day-to-day education. I became his most ardent supporter and his most visible and vocal advocate. I shouted the loudest in support of him. I attended every single meeting or function at both children's schools, regardless of the perceived importance. I signed off on every academic change or update to Patrick's education. I made sure that Patrick received each and every benefit that could be reaped from our public education system. My husband and I also did the work of parenting at home, making sure he always got his work done and in on time and shaping and molding him to grow and become a valuable member of society.

Being the parent of person with intellectual disabilities has been one of the most rewarding experiences of my life. While Patrick grew from infancy to young adulthood, I became a better and stronger person, more than I would have had I not been so fortunate to have him as my son. I learned to fight for him and for our family because of the lessons I learned being his mother. I learned to have greater compassion for those who do not have the same abilities as mine and to appreciate some of the smaller things in life.

The year 2016. The 2016 election was the first that Patrick participated in. It thrilled me that his first political experience happened at the same time we had our first female presidential candidate to be nominated by a major political party. Over the course of the election, Patrick and I talked a lot about the things Trump said about people with disabilities, immigrants, and women. We spoke often about how the world is filled with people of differing abilities, backgrounds, races, ethnicities, and sexual orientations and how different does not equal wrong. We also talked about what we, as humans, have in common. We all love, laugh, face adversity, and have the capacity to grow and be quality individuals.

Often, these conversations were somewhat one-sided, as Patrick has difficulty articulating his thoughts. But on this occasion, he listened. I know he did. When it came time to cast his vote, he supported the candidate who held his interests close at heart.

So my question is this: if my intellectually challenged son can recognize the inherent problems of a diatribe that ridicules differences and the people who applaud it, who then deserves to be the butt of a joke?

My son is precious, unique, funny, humbling, and amazing. He will be no one's punchline.

Robin Elise Weiss, age 45
Mother, doula, and author
Kentucky

Mother Material

"*M*OM, ARE WE *red or are we blue?*"
I remember asking this when I was in elementary school, during the 1980 Carter-vs.-Reagan election. We were living in my grandparents' basement, my mother having left my father the year before.

"We are red! Republican red," my grandfather said, with a growl that was not unaffectionate. "We're not raising any of those liberal-ass feminists in this house!" I'd never heard the word *feminists* before, but I knew by the way his lips curled and the spittle gathered that the word must be powerful and frightening. We weren't feminists. We were red. Republican red.

* * *

"*You're not mother material.*"
Said to me from an early age, my family's opinion wasn't intended to be cruel, but it was said often and stated as fact. "You should probably learn to type," they'd say, as if my only two

options in life were a station wagon full of screaming children or an IBM˙ Selectric typewriter.

Why was I not mother material? Wasn't mother material simply someone who had a kid? What kind of person did it take to be a mother? Everyone had a mother. Not everyone had a father, as far as I knew.

I learned to type, as instructed.

*   *   *

"Those are her ass-kicking boots."

Being seventeen, female, and a military police officer was an interesting combination. The fact that I was *female*—not a *woman* or *girl*, as defined by the military—was my first clue I wasn't in Kansas anymore. The guys didn't respect me in training. The army didn't want me to train with a .45-caliber pistol because, you know, I had a vagina. Too bad for them: my next unit didn't have women, so it didn't have the army's preferred .38s for me to carry. They had to train me with the .45-caliber. I outshot every one of them.

When I enlisted, I asked to be sent as far away from Louisville, Kentucky, as possible. I was assigned to Fort Campbell, Kentucky. At first I didn't get any respect there, either. But eventually my hand-to-hand combat skills and a pair of boots—known as my ass-kicking boots—got their attention.

*   *   *

"You're going to grow up to hate me."

That was my response when the nurse handed me my first child—a girl.

During my pregnancy, people would ask, "Are you having a girl or a boy?" I would smile and say that we didn't know. Surely you have a clue, the stranger would press, because didn't all mothers instinctively know? What I'd admit to few but felt in my heart was that I was carrying a baby girl—because I so desperately wanted a boy, and I never got what I wanted.

I was right.

* * *

What's a political moderate doing married to the red likes of me?

With these snapshots of my life, you might wonder what my story is doing in a book of Nasty Women, liberals, and feminists. The truth is that if you had asked me that question even ten years ago, I would not have had an answer. The change happened slowly.

The decision to have kids didn't come lightly. It was a mistake. A birth control failure, to be exact. My husband and I felt we were grown-ups, and an accidental pregnancy was the risk we took in being sexually active. We were young and didn't really know exactly how pregnancy worked. A few weeks and many tears later, our pregnancy ended in miscarriage. We'd grown to like the idea of being parents, and now we had lost our baby.

This point is where my earth shook. Immersing myself in pregnancy and birth was my defense. Even though I was an active military police officer, I started offering help to other women when they gave birth, and my career as a doula was born. It would be several years before I realized what I'd actually birthed, but in hindsight it's so clear.

My husband was the first person I knew to say out loud that he was a feminist. I rolled my eyes. How stupid. Women were equal to men. Who needs feminism? Not me. We were a case of opposites' attracting. He was the blue to my red, the feminist to my ignorance. We tolerated each other politically.

Raising a family, going to graduate school, and working all at the same time was hard was the true grit of how I made my life fulfilling. My votes became bluer. My words became more centered. Then one day I heard myself explaining to my grandmother that while I would never have an abortion, I felt it wasn't my place to tell other people what to do with their bodies.

I'm not sure when it happened, but I started claiming I was a feminist too. In Kentucky, you'd probably get a better reception as a Communist than a feminist.

* * *

"He's so . . . ugh!"

Donald Trump came to town for a rally. On a whim, I decided to take my almost-sixteen-year-old daughter to see him. At the last minute, she begged to use the second ticket to invite a friend.

The bubbly girls whom I dropped off were not the girls I picked up. They were angry and astounded. "Mom, he's so . . . ugh!" Her friend added, "And the people . . . ugh!" This was the first rally where violence had broken out.

* * *

"That cat is better than half the candidates."

Many of my older kids are politically active. My son ran a cat for president, as a way to get the Federal Election Commission (FEC) to change the rules on how people register to run for Office. It worked. He and his sister managed the cat's campaign and had more social media followers than Martin O'Malley. Their presidential pet debate wound up on the *TODAY* show.

"He's so mean." My eleven-year-old didn't understand. My husband and I told her that mean kids don't win, that good triumphs evil. "Why did Republicans pick him to run against Hillary?" she asked.

I tried to make excuses for my fellow humans, but I was baffled. I muttered some crazy ideas that I'd read on the Internet, as if they were truths.

* * *

"Do people hate her just because she's a woman?"

My eight-year-old daughter cut right to the chase. She saw right through me as I tried to tell her that being a woman, that simply having a vagina, was not a reason to be hated.

"That's not what they say at school. They say women can't be president."

Oh, yeah? We'd show them.

* * *

"Don't forget to get out and vote tomorrow!"

My oldest daughter was going through a rough time in her life, but at the campaign headquarters, working on the Clinton campaign, she was bright and alert.

The day before the election, with six girls in tow, we went to make calls for Hillary. The force in that room was palpable. It was so crowded that we worked in a back stairwell. The older girls went to work right away, but I had to help my eight- and eleven-year-olds as they started making calls from a script. I knew my son was making similar calls in a different red state while at college. I was so proud.

We canvassed and left *Get Out the Vote* materials. The kids met some neat characters that day—some positive, and some not so positive. It began to get cold, and the rain started to fall. The little ones were the first to complete their tasks. Soon only my 25-year-old daughter and I were finishing the job. The campaign had said we could skip it, but she felt it was important. Having watched her battle depression, I loved seeing the life back in her body and the spirit in her eyes. She was on a mission to elect the first woman president.

* * *

"Hillary's wall in Florida isn't holding."

On election night, we turned to the televisions and waited for the returns. In a matter of minutes, I felt panic. Florida was not the anticipated wall of protection. I started looking around, and no one was jovial; everyone was staring intently at a screen. The tiny seed of panic was quickly growing, and I knew I had to get my girls out of there, to shield them from the horror to come. Home and to bed!

That worked for only the younger ones. My oldest stayed up, watching and asking questions. I tried to hide. *I'll take a bath and all will be right—Wisconsin will save us.* Nope.

In the wee hours of the morning, I was left holding a puddle of tears that was my eldest. She was shattered. She felt as though she somehow personally failed the campaign, that Hillary's loss was a reflection of her worth. The despair in her reflected my own feelings.

* * *

What is a feminist mother?

To me, being a feminist mother means to allow my kids the options and space to be who they are, to the best of my abilities. To acknowledge that I am flawed: as a mother, as a person, as a woman, and as a human being. They are too.

I reflect back on the oft-told advice that I should avoid motherhood, that I was "not mother material." I don't know what that means now, even though I knew exactly what that message meant when I was growing up.

Was the matriarchy holding me back or propelling me forward? My belief depends on which day you ask me. I like to believe they saw something in me that said I would do great things. Though if I believe that, then I have to believe they thought motherhood would bring me down. But I say motherhood made me the strong feminist that I am today.

*   *   *

What would you tell your sixteen-year-old daughter?

"I bought us bus tickets so that we get to walk in the Women's March on Washington together."

Her eyes sparkled, and she ran off to tell her friend—the one who also had gone to the Trump rally—that she gets to go to the real march. Turns out I am mother material after all.

Rosemary Forrest, age 65
Retired Journalist
Augusta, Georgia

Looking Back and Ahead

M Y IMMIGRANT GRANDFATHER, who entered this country without knowing the date of his birth, took the Fourth of July as his birthday to show his high regard for his new home. My father served during World War II, and my brothers served during the Korean and Vietnam conflicts. My mother and her sisters were true Rosie Riveters, working in the factories to support the war effort until the men returned. They would strike the famous pose showing me their muscles. Patriotism and strength were fed to me with mother's milk.

In high school, I petitioned for the right to take a boy's class in printing. After much debate and many denials, the school allowed me to audit the course, but I was told a girl could not receive credit for a boy's course. That taught me much more than the California job box.

As the war in Vietnam consumed my male friends, spitting them out dead or damaged, I stuck out my thumb on the New Jersey Turnpike and rode into Washington, D.C. in a

Volkswagen Bus so full I sat on the stick shift the whole drive. It was my first march, but not my last.

While working as a reporter at a major newspaper's community bureau, I was told by my editor that women should not be reporters and that therefore his bureau had no restroom for women.

When I married, I kept my maiden name until a banker told me my husband and I would not receive a loan for a car, or a house, or even a credit card unless I changed my name to my husband's.

When I became pregnant and miscarried, I was fired from my job because my pregnancy indicated I wanted children and my employers did not want such inconvenience.

I eventually gave birth to two daughters and raised them alone to be independent women. In my divorce, I got nothing but my name back and considered it a win. One daughter is both a mother and an engineer working on the HiRISE Mars project. The other has a master's degree in counseling but stays at home with her three children. Their children are the reason I am willing to again pick up a protest sign and fight to preserve the rights for which I fought in my youth.

All during the campaign, my ten-year-old granddaughter would ask me, "How's Hillary doing?" She kept track of her wins in the primary and as we drove around town, she would excitedly point out Hillary signs when she found one. When it began to look like Hillary would win, I made plans for election night. My granddaughter and I would watch together as the first woman in history won the presidency. At least that was the plan.

I took my granddaughter to the polls with me. She had questions so I had her ask the poll manager, who explained the voting process. When we went out for lunch, her excitement was evident. I bought special treats and later that night we sat together as the results rolled in. I had promised her mom she would be in bed by ten p.m. because I expected a win before that time. As the states began reporting, I sent her to bed and stayed up until the bitter end. In the morning, she crawled into bed with me and asked who won. I stroked her curly brown hair, as I tried to explain what happened. We had studied the electoral college together ahead of time, but words failed me. She said, "People are stupid." I nodded.

Since then I have watched in dismay as Trump has appointed disastrous cabinet members. I have been appalled at his refusal to take daily briefings. His business and his refusal to release his taxes present the country with unprecedented conflicts of interest. His massive, yet fragile, ego is a danger and his foreign policy by tweet is more than disturbing.

I watch as a Republican Congress dismantles the healthcare upon which so many Americans depend. I listen as these same men make plans to turn the clock back to the 1950s when abortion was illegal and women without means died from dangerous procedures while the wealthy simply went abroad for little vacations. I listen to the threats against Planned Parenthood.

I fear for my granddaughter. I fear she will grow up in a country where her reproductive rights are denied, where her middle-class family is burdened with taxes, where sexism, racism, and nationalism taint everything. I fear for her brother, who has a rare genetic disorder. Will his life be less valuable in this brave new world? Will he be able to afford the care he will need for his entire life? And I fear for myself. Will my Social Security and Medicare be reduced? If so, how will I live?

I am embarrassed for my country. We have kept an archaic election process to our own detriment. We have elevated wealth over freedom. We are blind to the white privilege we have created and continue to deny. We have gerrymandered ourselves into an administration we may not survive. We have ignored our own

Constitution and are drifting toward fascism and a dictatorship. It is some comfort that Hillary won a massive popular vote, but it is damning that so many supported someone so unfit, so despicable, so wrong for our country.

I am sixty-five and have seen many election results I have not liked. But nothing like this. I weep for my country and for my grandchildren's futures.

Midwest

*"We are each other's harvest; we are each other's business;
we are each other's magnitude and bond."*[9]

—Gwendolyn Brooks

9 Brooks, Gwendolyn. Family pictures. Detroit (Mich.): Broadside Pr.,
1973.

Kirsty Sayer, age 40
Blogger, personal trainer, and mother
Bowling Green, Ohio

Snow Globe

I STARTLED AWAKE, LYING rigid, staring wild-eyed at my bedroom curtains, trying to regain a sense of security in the waking realm. The soothing familiar patterns were gone; in their place, the leering face of a mocking gargoyle stared back at me. I refused to blink. I would stare the creature down. I wouldn't look away until I had beaten the image with the knowledge that it wasn't real. Still, my heart pounded furiously; cold sweat trickled down my spine to the small of my back.

*   *   *

Later that day, my therapist explained that this phenomenon can happen after you wake up from a traumatic flashback nightmare; inanimate objects can appear to be alive and threatening. It is common in PTSD sufferers. The previous summer, I had been diagnosed with Complex Post Traumatic Stress Disorder, a condition I had been unknowingly suffering from for about thirty years. It was the result of having been sexually abused from around the time I was ten until I turned eighteen and moved away from my home to attend college on the other side of the world.

I remember everything about the abuse—nuances of faces, strained voices, footsteps, the sound of the door creaking open, calculations of how long I would be alone with him, heartbeat racing as I heard him approaching. Closing my eyes, I can recall the numbness that I'd will to overcome me. I would tell myself I couldn't feel it. *It didn't matter. It was okay. It was okay. It didn't happen. Nobody would know. I could keep this secret, and everyone would be okay.*

At age thirty-nine, I finally told my family about what I had experienced. I braced for the worst. Not being believed. Being rejected. I was wrong. They were shocked, outraged, deeply sympathetic to me, and overwhelmingly supportive—absolutely brokenhearted by the secret I had kept with my childish hope of protecting them, of protecting everyone.

I reveled in the relief while it lasted. It was predictably short. My abuser started backpedaling. Most of my family members started interacting with him again, with strained civility at first, but outwardly, to the observer who knew nothing of my revelations, nothing was different.

Alone and removed from them on the opposite side of the world, I was left to process my PTSD in a whole new dimension. What had been buried was now in stark relief. The deep and dulling pain was coming to a head.

The rest of the year was a blur—confusion, suicidal ideation, flashbacks; going in and out of periods of my life with my damaged psyche. Nightmares. Every single night. All night long. Exhaustion. A sense of low-grade panic at all times.

I distanced myself from my husband. Our once happy, easy marriage was now something completely different in my eyes. The sweet innocent narrative of how we had come together in the most unlikely of ways suddenly felt sinister, instead of "meant to be" I started to imagine it having been engineered in part by a powerful patriarchy. I started to mentally chronicle all I had lost, the person I was supposed to be versus the person I had been manipulated to be.

While I was locked into processing the trauma of my childhood, I was stripped of my identity as a mother. My relationship with my children up until that point had been loving and easy. My affection flowed toward them as naturally as the daily tide. My eyes lit up when I saw them; my arms automatically reached for them. Now they were just faces. I loved them, I worried about them, but they existed on another plane. I couldn't access my maternal instincts; it was too overstimulating to interact with anyone on a consistent basis. I knew I was losing time I could never get back. I felt trapped on the outside of a snow globe. But I could only hold my life in my hand and watch numbly as the seasons went by and the people I loved lived without me. I felt the acute regret of the things I had missed before I even missed them. I was a ghost.

Publicly I tried to put on a face of happy, healthy competence, but at work, I would slip away, hunched in a fetal position, feeling guilty and threatened for no discernible reason. One day, I confessed to a friend that I had written a suicide note to my children. I was out of options. It was clear to everyone that I needed intensive therapy.

I saw my local therapist three, sometimes four or even five, times a week. I took a medication to take the edge off my anxiety. My psychiatrist also suggested yoga twice a day to rewire my brain responses to adrenaline. I made other changes too: I quit my job, focused on eating for optimal nourishment, and went running in the woods each morning. My body grew leaner and stronger, an external reflection of the state of my mind. I started looking familiar to myself again; the good days came more frequently than the bad. I sought out social interactions. I allowed my husband back into our room at night. My mothering instinct slid back into place; I basked in the company of my children again.

* * *

Because I was so totally immersed in the work of healing, I had paid very little attention to politics that year. Then reports of Donald Trump's sexual assaults began making headlines, and everything changed. My therapist, who had graduated me to "maintenance" visits, started seeing a lot more of me. Tension, hypervigilance, the desire to isolate became a familiar urge again. The nightmares slithered back.

* * *

As the election grew closer though, there was hope for resolution. I counted down the days, picturing myself holding, white-knuckled to my progress until such a time where this awful man wouldn't be blaring from every news-source, triggering my darkest demons. With steely optimism, my friends and I planned a "Nasty Women" party for the night of the election. On the drive over, I was on the phone with a friend of mine who had accurately called the way Obama's second election night went down. He seemed to think Hillary was a forgone conclusion.

But around eight in the evening, he texted me: *We need to talk about the strong possibility of President Trump.*

What the hell? Don't mess with me like this. It isn't funny, I replied.

I'm sorry was his response.

The election results unfolded just as he said they would. State by state. The ashen faces and brittle commentary of the news anchors on PBS echoed my bewilderment. My friend sat beside me on the couch, tapping on her laptop keyboard, crunching the numbers as I drew my knees closer and closer toward my body. "We can still win, we can still win . . . ," she repeated. "I want to wrap everyone in a blanket; I want everyone to be safe in my living room," I heard my voice saying over again, to nobody.

On the way home that night, I thought about the first question I had been asked when with excruciating pain, I told my most trusted adult confidante the barest details of the abuse almost twenty years ago: "Did you seduce him?"

That question. It had sucked the air out of my twenty-year-old world, and I would never be the same from that moment on.

Did you seduce him?

What? How? Oh my God. Why would you ask that? I was a child! A victim.

I'm sorry. But this is very serious. I had to ask.

She had to ask.

Message received. He did a bad thing, sure. But what did *you* do? You must have deserved it. From then on, I would default to blaming myself for anything bad that happened. That terrible prolonged miscarriage when I was twenty, sexual harassment more times than I can remember. Somehow, I had brought it upon myself.

Nothing happened to my abuser. Life as he has always known it, goes on. No consequences. Bad Men Win. They always win.

*   *   *

I surprised myself with the force of my angry tears. I was in the bath; it was the day after the election. A wave of furious realization washed over me: My two years of hard-won progress, my triumph in escaping the thirty years of pain and denial prior to it—all of that had been wiped out with the shocking election results. President Trump. His win felt so incredibly personal. America was laughing at me. At women like me. Women like me don't triumph. Bad men win. They aren't accountable. They take what they want. They do what they like, they destroy lives. And they still win. The darkness gathered around me, I could feel its curling tendrils, preparing to begin its grim work of clouding, of strangling, of burying me again.

I resisted.

I picked up a shampoo bottle; in slow motion, I saw myself throw it, watched it bounce off the sea green wall. It crashed onto the floor at the same moment as the white-hot resolve bubbled and rose up from deep in my consciousness washing over me, pushing back and eviscerating the black fog. *NO*. No. *I* would write this story. *I* would decide the outcome of this fight. Thirty years of my life had been sacrificed to a man like Trump; I wasn't about to be a victim all over again. I wouldn't retreat back into the catatonic grave of PTSD. I would keep fighting. I would be angry. I would live out loud. I wouldn't give a *damn* about the people who said I was too emotional or I was unhinged over this—

This. This travesty of decency. This abuse of power. This blatant reward for evil behavior.

This man may be president, but he will *not* send me back to my bedroom with the gargoyle curtains. Those curtains were *paisley*, goddammit. No man would ever bury me again.

To the cynics out there, know this: Women like me? We are not delicate flowers. And hell *yes*, we are special snowflakes. Emphasis on the *special*. We have overcome more than people can ever imagine. For women like me, staying alive is a heroic act in and of itself, and we have done so much more than breathe in and out. We have raised good children. We have built communities; we have supported other people in pain. We should never, ever be underestimated. We are fierce, and we are more awake than ever. Bad men are now on notice. And they will not win.

Kenyona "Sunny" Matthews, age 35
Bailiff, and cofounder of Dimensions of isms, a diversity
consulting firm
Akron, Ohio

Answering Trump's Call

In the 21st century . . .

We chose a president who believes my child is less than because she is black.

We chose a president who believes my child is less than because she is a girl.

We chose a president who believes my child is less than because she is not wealthy.

In the 21st century, there is no justification for our choice.

COLORED. NEGRO. AFRICAN American. Black. The "race" section of the birth certificates dating back to my grandmother's time changed with each generation. The power of these words and how they defined my people amazes me. While race relations did not improve dramatically from generation to generation, the terms used to describe us improved slightly over time.

As an African American woman, I thought I was luckier than my ancestors. I thought that America had, for the most part, become a progressive and culturally sensitive society and that the majority of Americans would not blatantly speak or act upon hate. I knew systemic and institutional racism affected us still, but I thought political correctness limited the impact of direct personal racism.

On November 9, 2016, I learned I was wrong.

* * *

I was not completely naïve; I knew that we didn't live in a utopia and that racism was still very raw and real.

During my second year of law school, a few students were dismissed from school for low academic performance. The loss of some of my African American classmates was all the more visible because there were so few of us to begin with. Once, while rounding a corner, I overheard some white students talking about my former classmates. I stopped and heard them call us all "affirmative action babies" who could not handle the work and should not be in law school. I took a deep breath, held my head high, and walked around the corner. The conversation stopped, but I heard them snickering under their breath.

I didn't stop to speak or educate them. I buried my hurt, knowing that expressing it would only justify the *angry black woman* stereotype. It wasn't the first time and would not be the last time I would bury those feelings.

These moments are common for me—moments when people question my intellect and my place in the room, moments when people write me off as a politically correct answer to equal opportunity. They see only an African American woman when I enter the room. Well, I am an African American woman, and am proud to be, but I am not at all lesser because of it. At what point will society start to see the humanity in people of color? When will we break free of this history? When will our differences stop dividing and conquering us?

Not in Trump's America. Trump did not invent racism, but he purposefully exploited it, playing to the fears and hate so present in Middle America. Conservatives in Middle America want the status quo to continue, ensuring privilege and opportunity for themselves, even if it is denied to others. I didn't realize how many white Americans felt betrayed by the cultural shift toward an inclusive society. Their feelings of betrayal became evident as Trump gained momentum.

I came to terms with the reality of just how divided we were when I heard Trump's slogan, "Make America Great Again." I thought, *Wait a minute, when* was *America great for people who look like me? How far back are we trying to go: Jim Crow or slavery?*

African Americans are strong people. We are survivors. But we lack the unity of our ancestors, and as a whole, we are more combative, angrier, and more divided than ever now.

An Underground Railroad simulation illustrated this to me years ago. I played the role of a slave leading high schoolers through the woods toward freedom. They were laughing and joking until the slave catchers shouted in our direction. The students responded by hurling violent threats.

I stopped and whispered, still in character: "They will kill you and no one will care! Run for your life!"

The kids laughed, not grasping the fear and desperation of the moment.

The African American community cannot live in an America reminiscent of yesteryear. We won't survive a throwback to Jim Crow. We are barely surviving the current age.

* * *

I work in the criminal justice field and am a firsthand witness to one facet of this new adaptation. The American justice system tries to impersonate a restorative justice system but is, at heart, all about punishment. Most cases are drug offenses or crimes committed to support someone's drug habit. In the 1980s, when crack cocaine was destroying the African American community, the solution was to lock them up. This policy devastated communities by affecting unity, family structure, and economic stability. Drug users, sellers, and their families faced harsh sentencing, a lack of rehabilitation options, and the stigma associated with crime.

The population affected by drugs is now shifting from brown bodies to white souls, and it is no coincidence that the judicial system is now shifting to a more balanced view. We are considering drug use a public health issue and criminal epidemic. The only difference between now and then is the drastic increase in the number of whites using drugs. Courts are beginning to help defendants through recovery programs instead of jail time. When crack was merely a problem "in the hood," it was not an important issue to address.

Racism is prevalent in all of our political and social systems. It affects everything from our justice system to our political system. It helped a man who had no government experience become president of the United States. Our divided country elected an openly racist and sexist president. I am still in shock.

* * *

The days after the election were a blur for me. At work, Trump supporters high-fived each other, grinning from ear to ear and congratulating one another on "taking back" their country. I heard one man say, "Now Trump can fix everything Obama messed up!"

I came home that evening and hugged my daughter. She

is biracial, and some of her father's family voted for Trump. I haven't spoken to them about the election. I don't know if I ever will speak about race relations or politics with them again.

* * *

This dark chapter in America's history has a silver lining because we are forming coalitions of powerful people. Hope lies in these coalitions. In today's society, I am able to stand up for what I believe in: equality and a society working for us all regardless of race, class, or gender.

As we enter a Trump presidency, I will remain a proud liberal. For the next four years, I will live in fear as a person of color, as a woman, and as a middle-class citizen, because his platform is aimed at minimizing me. I will not remain quiet so that you who voted for him can remain comfortable with your choice. You chose a man who hates. You need to deal with that, just as I must now deal with my fears. My daughter's future depends on it.

I will find the strength of the Negroes before me and fight vehemently for our rights. I accept the challenge and vow to fight as Trump's racist and sexist administration tries to strip us of our rights. In the African American community, we believe in call and response. Trump's call: "Make America great again." My response? "Make America great, for the first time, for all of us."

Anonymous, age 50
Retired chief of security,
Oklahoma Department of Corrections
Muskogee, Oklahoma

Here I Am

PRIOR TO NOVEMBER 8, 2016, I had been skipping along happily in my pro-Hillary fog. I thought Donald Trump was not a viable candidate and, at most, would provide us with a few laughs while he fulfilled his need to get the attention he so obviously craved.

My fog evaporated two weeks before the election. My sister and I were waiting for my brother-in-law in the parking lot of the hardware store where he worked. After he approached the vehicle, just to be nice, I commented on how professional he looked. He thanked me, then looked at my sister, pointed at a lawn mower, and told her he wanted to save up to buy one. Then, in a loud tone, he said, "Forget it; what am I thinking? I need to save up to buy guns; because if that bitch Hillary or that old fucker Bernie gets elected, those fucking liberals are going to take all our guns." His sneered, spitting out the words as if he had tasted something disgusting.

I was in shock. He knew I was a Democrat. We have had a long-standing truce that, in order to keep the peace, we would not discuss politics. He broke the truce that day, along with our relationship and, later, my relationship with my sister.

After that incident, I started looking around and listening to people around me. Living in Oklahoma, I knew guns would play a big part in this election, and in some areas, race would as well. But I believed (wrongly, as it turned out) that common sense would prevail and that Trump and his cronies wouldn't be allowed anywhere near the White House.

On the day of the election, my eleven-year-old daughter stopped me as I was getting into my car to go vote. "Here, Mom," she said, and handed me my MP4 player with earphones. "You might need them. Because more than likely, people would be talking about things you don't agree with, and I don't want you to get angry." The wisdom of children!

Thanks to my daughter, I spent my time at the polling place listening to fun eighties songs like "Walk like an Egyptian," instead of the antiliberal chatter going on around me. When it was my turn to receive my ballot, I handed my voter ID to a smiling older lady waiting behind the table. She looked down at my card. When she looked back up, her smile had faded. "You have to wait," she said in a stern tone. "Those people are ahead of you." She pointed at a group of people who had been in line behind me.

"I was in line ahead of them," I explained.

The lady shook her head and called a couple of the people in line by their first names. She motioned with a wave, letting them walk through without writing down their information.

After waiting thirty additional minutes, I was finally allowed to vote. I am not sure if the people behind me were voting more than once or if the woman was trying to silence my voice by making me wait longer. Maybe she was hoping I would get frustrated and leave. I don't know, but I was determined to cast my ballot.

Still, the whole experience left me with a sinking feeling.

*   *   *

My sinking feeling grew stronger throughout the day. I tried to tell myself to stop worrying: there was no way Trump would get elected. The radicals were louder, but sanity would prevail. For reassurance, I reached out to some of my friends who lived in more progressive states—but as it turned out, they were worried too.

I went to bed early that night, unable to bear watching Hillary Clinton concede to that monster.

*   *   *

After a couple of days of trying to get over the fact that I now viewed most of the American population as morons, I took a closer look at the people closest to me. One sister voted for Trump, one sister didn't care to vote at all, and my mother voted for Hillary. All aunts, uncles, and cousins on my mother's side voted for Trump.

I had almost as much disdain for those who didn't vote at all as I did for those who voted for Trump. So when it came time for Thanksgiving, I knew I could not sit with a group of people who went to church on Sundays; bent down on their knees to pray every night; read the Bible every morning; asked for "unspoken prayer requests" on social media; and yet, somehow, didn't care enough to vote against everything Trump stands for.

My nonvoting sister was not happy with my decision

not to partake in the Thanksgiving festivities. She informed me that I needed to get over myself pretty quickly—that I could not avoid my Trump-loving family members forever and that something might happen where I would have to be around them. I told her that, in my heart, I could not accept anyone in my life who had voted for what Trump stood for.

My sister, the Trump supporter, has a biracial niece and nephew. Her niece and nephew's father is an illegal immigrant. She has a gay sister (me) and marks *Hispanic* on employment applications, just as the rest of my family does. She owns a home day care business, and every one of her clients is on state assistance. (Every last one!) The last time a Republican was president, her husband couldn't find a job. For three years, he was unemployed. She spent a majority of that time on social media sites, asking churches for money just to pay her bills. Her vote was almost totally influenced by her husband and the NRA. She voted against her own interests and the interests of her family. I couldn't comprehend it.

I recently had a conversation with my mother. "I cannot be close to people who believe I shouldn't be able to marry the person that I love," I said. "I cannot be close to someone who thinks if my child is raped, she must carry that baby to term. I cannot be close to someone who thinks grabbing someone by the pussy is acceptable presidential behavior."

My mom then told me that it was their right to their own beliefs under the First Amendment. I told her I agreed with her, but why wasn't I being given the same courtesy when I said I didn't want to be around the family members who are Trump followers? Why was I being labeled narrow-minded and selfish?

Her response? "Because she is your sister and you love her."

But here is the frightening part—I don't love her. I don't hate her either. I feel nothing towards her—nothing . . . like I have hit a wall. And that worries me most of all.[10]

* * *

So here I am—in a state where every county went red. (Every. Single. County.)

Here I am, in a state where the governor recently issued a proclamation of "National Day of Prayer"[11]—not for people who are poor or homeless, not for any human beings, but for oil fields. *Oil fields.*

Here I am, in a state so bankrupt by poor management that we were forced to buy new license plates because we needed more revenue.[12]

Here I am, in a state that did not update its state identification cards as ordered by the federal government, because state officials thought it would be harder for terrorists to duplicate our cards if we kept the old ones. (Soon we will have to use our passports at airports or to enter federal buildings, because our state identification will be worthless.)[13]

---

10 "Oklahoma Results," *The New York Times* (January 4, 2017): http://www.nytimes.com/elections/results/oklahoma.

11 Claire Lampen, "The governor of Oklahoma created 'Oilfield Prayer Day' in hopes of saving the state's oil and gas industry," *Business Insider* (October 13, 2016): http://www.businessinsider.com/oklahoma-oilfield-prayer-day-governor-mary-fallin-2016-10.

12 Bill Schammert, "OK Budget: Senate approves new license plates to generate $12.7 million," Fox 25 (website) (March 24, 2016): http://okcfox.com/news/local/ok-budget-senate-approves-new-license-plates-to-generate-127-million.

13 K. Querry, "Denied: Oklahoma's request for Real ID Act extension denied," KFOR (website), (October 11, 2016): http://kfor.com/2016/10/11/denied-oklahomas-request-for-real-id-act-extension-denied/.

Here I am, in a state with a governor so inept that she was appointed to Trump's transition team.[14] That same governor had her daughter move her trailer house onto the grounds of the governor's mansion. And who footed the bill for her water and electricity? You guessed it. Taxpayers.[15]

Here I am, in a state being rocked by earthquakes because of our governor's love affair with big oil companies and their fracking.[16]

Here I am, in a state that uses state taxpayer monies to settle sexual harassment cases, such as the one involving Representative Dan Kirby, at the price tag of $44,000.[17]

Here I am, a little speck of blue in a red volcano.

But here I am, and here is where I will stay.

---

14 Rick Green and Chris Casteel, "Oklahoma Gov. Fallin named to Trump transition team," *The Oklahoman*, NewsOK (website) (November 29, 2016): http://newsok.com/article/5528996.

15 Abby Phillip, "Millennial daughter has parked her trailer at the Okla. governor's mansion for months," *The Washington Post* (July 29, 2015): https://www.washingtonpost.com/news/morning-mix/wp/2015/07/29/millennial-daughter-has-parked-her-trailer-at-the-okla-governors-mansion-for-months/?utm_term=.bc50860f5e4f.

16 Jackie Wattles and Matt Egan, "Oklahoma orders shutdown of 37 wells after earthquake," CNN Money (September 4, 2016): http://money.cnn.com/2016/09/03/news/economy/oklahoma-earthquake-fracking-oil/.

17 Barbara Hoberock, "Rep. Dan Kirby rescinds resignation given after sexual harassment allegations," *The Oklahoman*, NewsOK (website) (December 28, 2016): http://newsok.com/article/5532463.

Anne DeTraglia, age 47
Internal audit director for United Airlines
Geneva, Illinois

It Happened

Before It Happened

I was befuddled.
Mostly amused.

Staring at the Republicans.
The clown car.
So worrisome.
This is the menu?

Staring at the Democrats.
The virtuous.
So annoying.
There is no free lunch.
That's not how it works.
And those Wall Street speeches?
Much ado about nothing.

So frustrating.
But she prevailed.

ROAR!

While It Happened

Rallies.
Press conferences.
No press conferences.

Email.
More email.
God, more email.

Racism.
Bigotry.
Pussy-grabbing.

The alt-right.
Twitter˙.
And the F. B. I.

And Putin?

ROAR!

Election Day

Optimism.
Verklempt.
A badge of honor—I voted.
Smiles for all people.

Oh, to be alive.

A woman will be President.
A woman.
A smart woman.
A capable woman.
And then . . .
Election returns.

"Don't worry. Those states always vote red."
"Oh, that's not good. She should've won that state."
"And that one too."

Shock and horror.
The unthinkable.
She didn't win.

ROAR!

After It Happened

Existential despair.
Anger.
At family.
And friends.
And colleagues.

How could they?

Strangers on the street—did *they* do this?

ROAR!

Today

ORD–DCA.
I will march.
With my daughter.

They held us down.
But we're getting up.
Like thunder, gonna shake the ground.

ROAR!

Erin Bentley Wyatt, age 37
Stay at home mom and registered nurse
Bloomington, Indiana

Without a Home

FOR THE FIRST fourteen years of my life, I lived in southeastern Michigan, until the factory where my dad had worked for years announced it would be closing. He was transferred to another one of the company's plants in Marion, Indiana. I'm thirty-seven years old now. I've lived in the Hoosier State for over half my life. Until November 8, 2016, when I traveled out of the midwest, I'd always told people: "I'm from Michigan," because it seemed so much more progressive. Now I am so pissed off at my beloved birthplace for what it helped do to the rest of the country that I feel like I'm without a home.

I should provide full disclosure: I was a Bernie Sanders supporter for the majority of the 2016 election season. However, after Bernie's defeat, I reluctantly began to support Hillary; by the time Donald Trump had been exposed as a pussy-grabbing kind of guy, I decided the whole "lesser of two evils idea" was bullshit and wholeheartedly embraced Hillary as my queen.

In 2008, I had taken my ten-month-old daughter, who is

now nine years old, to see Hillary when she came to my city to campaign. In regard to Hillary's more recent bid for the presidency, I thought, *How amazing would it be for my daughter to be alive when the first woman president was elected, and she had even been in the same room with her at one time!* Yet as I started contemplating Hillary's positions on issues, I realized that maybe she wasn't as far to the left as I would have liked. However, after living in one of the most conservative states for twenty-three years, I realized that she wouldn't win over a majority of voters by coming across as a radical. I remembered just how smart, fiery, compassionate, dedicated, and beautiful I had always found her to be—until I was seduced by that wild-eyed, wind-in-his-hair Bernie Sanders, who was always saying what I wanted to hear. But now Hillary needed my support, and I was excited to give it to her.

I found the presidential debates shocking, horrifying—and completely hilarious. I gasped as Trump displayed his complete lack of understanding of how the entire world works, but laughed as he sniffed and lurked around the stage. I thought there was no chance in hell a joke like Donald would ever be elected.

My kids, however, were scared out of their wits. My daughter would ask, "Mommy, what will happen if Donald Trump becomes president?" My six-year-old son would say, "He can't win! He's mean to ladies!" I reassured them that everything would be okay, because Hillary was ahead in the polls, and joked that if she lost, we would move to Canada.

I voted early, as soon as it was possible. I swore that I would cast my vote and not watch any more news coverage until Election Day. On Election Day, even though my ballot had been submitted, I put on slacks, a cardigan, a string of pearls, and my *Nurses for Hillary* pin. I began worrying that morning when I arrived to a scheduled doctor's appointment. My physician looked at my Hillary button and said, "You are only the second person I've seen in the office today who is for Hillary, and the other person is me." What? How can that be? I thought health-care workers surely vote Democrat. They're supposed to be caring!

My fears began to grow as my daughter and I filled in her Electoral College coloring page. The states I expected to win were too close to call, or, even worse, they had gone red. My kids went to bed a little worried, but I gave them hugs and tucked them in. As the hours went by, I became more and more disillusioned, angry, and scared shitless. When the news stations finally declared the winner, I went to my room, turned off the lights and bawled my eyes out.

The next morning, as I told my kids about election results, my daughter cried. My sons were too young to fully understand. For the next few days, I felt crushed. I couldn't accomplish a thing.

But a few weeks ago, I visited an event in my child's classroom. My kids' school has an enrollment that is about 30% international students. The students in the class were reading their writings to their classmates, and their teacher was working with another group at the time. One child had some sort of developmental disability, and another child spoke very little English. When I was a kid in the early '90s, my classmates would have probably made gestures similar to Trump's when he mocked Serge Kovaleski or whispered a few ethnic slurs when the teacher was not around. The children in this classroom quietly moved closer so that they could hear and understand these students better. They clapped when their classmates were finished. I left that morning feeling that while it might take a generation or two, things will be okay. If we continue to encourage and nurture the qualities of empathy and mutual respect in our children, we have a chance at peaceful world where women can have autonomy, people of color are no longer marginalized, our LGBTQ friends can openly love their partners without fear, and non-Christians will also be able to have true religious freedom. There is hope for the future.

Jane Lohman, age 60
Retired; small business owner
Liberty, Missouri

My Blue Heaven Is Red

I AM A WOMAN of a certain age. One of my first memories is peeking out over an armchair to watch my mother and her best friend apply rose-colored lipstick in front of the living room mirror. I was fascinated; the same woman who had punished me days earlier for drawing on my arms was now voluntarily spreading red paint over her mouth.

"Where did mom go?" I asked my father as he was tucking me in bed that night.

"To Crestwood Plaza," he said. "To see John F. Kennedy."

"Who is John eff Kenwady?"

"He's running for president of the United States, Janie," my father said with a laugh—as if I was supposed to know that. I was three. I could barely remember the names of my aunts and uncles, much less who was running for president.

Another early memory: Robert Kennedy's assassination. I woke up in the middle of the night to my father shaking me. "It doesn't look good," he said. Our family sat vigil in the living room for hours. I left for Girl Scout camp the next morning, not knowing if Kennedy would live or die. I returned days later to a house heavy with unspoken sadness.

*   *   *

In 1972, Missouri went red for the first time since Eisenhower's win in 1952. My die-hard Democrat parents were beside themselves. It was as if John and Robert Kennedy had been murdered all over again.

The day after the election, I accompanied my mother on a shopping trip to JCPenney˙. At the checkout counter, my mom and the clerk engaged in political small talk. It was quite friendly until the last second, when the clerk handed the bag to my mom and said, "I bet no one will admit they voted for that other guy today."

My mom's back stiffened. She opened her mouth and said very loudly, for everyone to hear, "I did, and I would vote for him again!"

*   *   *

My parents didn't live and die by politics. They had other interests too. They believed in traveling for education and fun. They would save all year so that when summer came around, they would pile my two sisters and me into the station wagon with a new raft and a sand bucket and drive down to Florida, making many detours on the way.

I had a ball splashing in the Gulf of Mexico, laying out on the beach to soak in the sun. On our way there and on our way back home, I did notice the white-only drinking fountains and the separate bathrooms for "colored" people, but as a child, it didn't dawn on me that anything was wrong with these limits.

Not that Missouri didn't have its own brand of discrimination, back then and today. The racial tensions have been well-documented, in fact, but some of those incidents don't make the headlines. For example, my 23-year-old nephew was in second grade before the first minority student joined his class. The day before the new student started, the school held a special meeting with the second graders to explain that a black student would be joining their class. A meeting like that had never been held before when other new students, who happened to be white, joined the class. I get it: the meeting was done with good intentions, but still—it just goes to show that for many Missourians, race mattered.

* * *

After high school, I didn't detour too far from home, choosing to enroll at the University of Missouri in St. Louis, instead of leaving for an out-of-state college like many of my liberal-minded friends. With my parents' encouragement (and influence), I chose political science as my major. Later I became a proud law school dropout. I also had a stint interning at the Missouri Equal Rights Coalition.

My career path eventually changed, and I ended up spending most of my life working logistics and data quality management at a large conservative privately held company. I stayed in corporate hell for over twenty years until I finally broke away and started my own company.

* * *

On November 8, 2016, I prayed St. Louis and Kansas City would carry the rest of the state for Hillary. It was a Hail Mary, because I knew deep down, her winning Missouri wasn't going to happen.

I knew because I had travelled outside my blue urban bubble to more rural areas in the state. I had seen firsthand the influx of white Missourians wearing Trump T-shirts and *Make America Great Again* red hats. I had watched them gather together in the town squares of small towns, fists raised and voices booming, "Build the wall, build the wall!"

I knew because I had travelled to several small-town festivals and observed the local county Republican Committee members walking around, out and about with the people, making idle chitchat, sharing cotton candy and posing for photos with their constituents, while their Democratic counterpart was nowhere to be seen.

I knew because I had travelled to the western part of the state, where I had met up with the local Democratic Committee members. "Where are your election pamphlets?" I asked when I saw their office was absent of any literature from the Hillary Clinton campaign.

"We don't feel she really represents us," one of the members had answered.

I know because I kept travelling: east, west, and east again. The voices grew louder. *Obamacare is no good. Obama is trying to take away our guns. Hillary is a liar. Hillary is a crook. We need to reduce government regulations. We need more jobs. We have been forgotten. We have been forgotten. We have been forgotten.*

* * *

I think one of the ugliest outcomes of the election has been the severance of so many relationships. I have been determined not to let that happen to me. My friends vary across the spectrum of different races, religions, and backgrounds. Our beliefs are huge to us, but so are our ears and our hearts. We love one another, so we listen to one another's concerns. We try to understand the *why* behind the beliefs that are opposed to our own.

Empathy works. I have yet to lose one friend or family member due to this god-awful election.

But the election has earned my dissidence in other ways.

Each night I go to bed with a partner named *fear*. Fear snores and disrupts my sleep with *worry*, and *worry* sounds different every night. Some nights it sounds like my sister's fussing over medical bills, wondering if she'll still have health insurance a year from now. Some nights it sounds like my daughter's Marine husband's marching off to a war sparked from one of Trump's ridiculous tweets. Some nights it sounds like my three granddaughters' yelling *no* and hearing a reply: "But the president says it's okay." Some nights it sounds like the whole state of Missouri collapsing into a sinkhole of its own making.

So what can a woman of a certain age do?

To be honest, I don't know. I'm still working that part out.

But here's what I do know: Every morning I wake up, and my sleep partner is gone and so is his snore. I look out my kitchen window, and I see a bright sun shining down from a midwestern sky clear blue like an ostrich egg, and the blue stretches out for miles and miles—blue to the east and blue to the west, as far as the eye can see. Sometimes the beauty is so overwhelming that all I can do is close my eyes; take a sip of coffee; and think about something William Faulkner once said: "They kilt us, but they ain't whupped us yit."[18]

---

18 William Faulkner, "Wash," *Harper's Magazine*, February 1934.

Leigh W. Stuart, age 41
Writer
Switzerland via Missouri

Reality Show

WHEN THE COUNTRY came together on Election Day, my husband reassured me that people would make the smart choice. "I have faith in Americans," he said. He is Swiss and doesn't know Americans quite as well as I do. I told myself to trust him, despite my apprehensions.

I did my part. We traveled from Switzerland to Missouri in October to visit family, and I cast my absentee ballot in person to make sure it was counted correctly. Back home by November 8, 2016, we were in bed long before the results started rolling in.

My husband woke up first and left to get breakfast on the table for our daughter, but returned only a few minutes later. "Trump is ahead, but there are still several key states that don't have results in yet."

He still had hope, but I knew. I grew up side by side with these people.

It sounds trite—I feel trite when I put the feeling into words—but my bubble was burst wide open that day. *Poor little white girl,* I can hear people say. It's true. I am a sheltered White woman.

I spent much of November thinking of our stay in Missouri, especially about my dad and stepmom in their comfy middle-class, predominantly White area in a lakeside community not far from Kansas City. It is a place where the division of sides is felt and seen, but the tensions are rarely explosive.

One of my dad's neighbors had peppered his lawn with Trump–Pence signs until it resembled a poppy field in the French countryside. Another neighbor had arranged her two stately Hillary–Kaine signs to glare at the mess across the no-man's-land of the street. Trenches were dug, but shots weren't fired. Not there, at least.

During our October visit, we went to my grandparents' house for coffee, and my grandmother looked both my husband and me in the eyes. "I just can't believe that man said. . . ." And she paused.

My ninety-year-old grandma, as sweet and mild-mannered as a tough midwestern girl raised on a farm during the Great Depression could possibly be, was about to repeat the grab-'em-by-the-pussy line. *Sweet angels above, preserve us.*

". . . that word."

That *word*? That whole disgusting recording! A crumb on the pie of everything else he said and did up to that point, but a perfect representation of his true self, in my humble opinion.

I was furious. Call me ridiculous, but it seemed that, at my grandma's age and after her having lived through deprivation, fear for her husband at war, and bouts of cancer, she should at least be spared having to listen to obscenities from the mouth of a man being lifted towards the highest office in the land. But I could no more shelter her than I could protect my adopted, eight-year-old daughter from being picked on at school for her brown skin and Thai features—in Switzerland.

Racism knows no boundaries. A gleeful ultra-right-wing party in France celebrated Trump's victory with predictions of their own; Swedish neo-Nazis marched in Stockholm, chanting about the world revolution; German officials tweeted about the world's crumbling—to give only a few examples. A new world order was on the way.

In Switzerland, a couple of my neighbors practically offered their condolences for my loss. "We heard. We're so sorry. Are you all right?" they asked.

"I'm much better off than a lot of people right now." At least in Switzerland, my daughter was picked on, not assaulted, and I wouldn't have to experience firsthand my insurance's being ripped to shreds.

Flash forward to Christmas. We were invited to spend the day with my in-laws and extended family on my husband's side. In the small group was a retired Swiss couple with plans to move to the States soon, and naturally, the conversation turned to politics later in the evening.

By then, I was used to being in the majority with my opinions. I could show contempt and outrage, and my Swiss interlocutors would cheer me on.

But suddenly, it was like getting up in the middle of the night for a drink of water and stepping in cat vomit. One second, you were fumbling in the dark, befuddled and slightly apprehensive, but it wasn't so bad because you thought you knew the territory. And the next, you were toe-deep in bilious slime.

My ensuing argument with the relative, the only pro-Trump one in the family, was carried out Swiss style—a polite mix of French, English, and a smattering of Schwizerdütsch over cups of coffee and slices of cake.

"We need to give him a chance," the woman said.

"He is appointing KKK supporters to his cabinet," I replied.

"He's a brilliant businessman."

"With how many bankruptcies?"

The grab-'em line was inevitably mentioned. "Oh, that was just something he said a long time ago."

"But my grandma had to listen to that crap! And one day, both my kids will hear it too!"

"We have to wait and see all the things he can accomplish."

"This is exactly what I, and millions of others, am afraid of." So, so afraid of.

"You know, Hillary has such a cold heart. I can't trust her to do what's right." Her voice was smug. *Brains in women must not count for much.*

She was in her trench, and nothing I could point out in the way of facts, examples, or historical parallels could make her want to see my side.

From now on, we will choose presidents based on the warm fuzzies they give us. Sounds about right.

* * *

Reality shows have never interested me. Give me fiction shows based loosely on real life, or pure fantasy for the escapism. But not reality shows; they are shams, full of pretenders and false gods. You take something real—real people's playing at being themselves—and then shake them up in a snow globe of entertainment, and *Voilà*! Wealthy girls on farms, normal people thrust in the limelight, and young people locked in lofts. Nonreality shakes to be gobbled by the masses.

Bear with me a just little longer. I'm something of a word-nerd, and I wanted to point this out. The Renaissance saw the arrival of thousands and thousands of words such as *dishearten, lackluster, unreal, emancipate, absurdity,* and *fact* (oh, and *chocolate,* thank goodness). Every age sees the birth and death of words, but for comparison's sake, consider that the Oxford Dictionaries Word of the Year in 2016 is *post-truth.* Despite the fact that the prefix *post-* means "after" and the root *truth* means "fact or in accord with reality," this trending word actually describes a fabricated event's becoming an accepted event in the minds of select people because of their emotional response or personal beliefs.

Unreal.

Hard on *post-truth*'s heels is *post-factual*, a word naming a similar phenomenon in which people who are faced with unassailable facts will continue to believe what they choose. And the most recent spin on truth, to date, is Alternative Facts for a different perspective on quantifiable data.

We've been emancipated from the truth. Not bad work for 2016. The country has been taken hostage by people who want the reality show—the reality of their choosing. A person unfit to lead has been placed in a position of power because of his peddling to populist opinions. He did not offer viable solutions, reasonable debates, or forward-thinking possibilities. He just promoted racism, bigotry, and misogyny—more often than not in random social media posts, #becauseNewWorldOrder.

If this election has a bright spot, for me it is that after my little bubble burst and the world seemed to crumble, I began to find amazing, kind-hearted people crawling out of the rubble. Some men, but many women who were ready to fight back. Women different from me, not just because of the color of their skin or sexual orientation but through their rich and varied lives.

They have stories to tell, stories that break my heart and stitch it together and make it bloom all at the same time. I grew up side by side with these people and never had a chance to truly know them until now. To borrow a quote often attributed to Eleanor Roosevelt, "a woman is like a tea bag—you can't tell how strong she is until you put her in hot water." We are going to see more and more strong women emerge in the future, and

I am honored to have some feisty new friends who are coming out swinging.

And as I stand with others who oppose hate-mongering policies, the vast majority of the world will stand with us. That solidarity might be shown quietly and politely or might be forced by the threat of war. But sooner or later we will burst the bubbles, end the show of counterfeit leadership, and put *post-truth* in the garbage where it belongs.

Anonymous, age 59
Pastor
Missouri

Elephants

I HAD A BIBLE study to facilitate on November 9, 2016, the evening after the election. As I drove the thirty miles to my church, I realized I was grieving. I was grieving not only my candidate's loss but also the loss of all she stood for.

I serve a church in a small town deep in the heart of a red state. Most of the people who attend our Bible study are privileged—white, middle-aged or older, retired from white-collar professions. Several of them do not worship with our congregation but are members of other churches. Therefore, I try to be politically neutral in both the pulpit and the Bible study.

As the session began, I carefully avoided the elephant in the room. Continuing this tack throughout the evening, I focused on the topic of this session—facilitating discussion around questions that bubbled up from the week's assigned Scripture. It was like any other Wednesday evening Bible study, until the time came for our closing prayer.

I said, "I need to say something. In yesterday's election,

about 80% of the people who voted in our county voted for Donald Trump. While I know the people in this room do not statistically represent the people in our county, I suspect there are many people here who are happy about the election results. I am not. I am like the 50% of the voters nationwide who did not vote for Donald Trump. While some people today are joyful, I am not. While some people today have been celebrating, I have not. It wasn't until I was driving here this afternoon that I recognized it, but I have been grieving today. I'm grieving still, and this surprises me. I never thought I would grieve an election—not that I thought my candidates would always win. They haven't. I mean, I never thought I would respond to the results of an election with bone-deep, soul-deep grief. Yet, here I am grieving. I ask those of you around this table who are celebrating the election results to be aware there are people, like me, who are grieving those same results. I ask you to pray for me and the others who are grieving. I ask you to show me in the days and weeks and months to come that I have no reason to grieve. Prove to me that my fears are unfounded." I continued by asking for others to share their joys and concerns for prayer. As always, I included these in my prayer as we held hands.

Exposing myself as different from others in the room, naming my feelings, and requesting prayer for myself were difficult things for me to do. Who wants to ask for help in a culture that celebrates independence? Who wants to be vulnerable in a culture that elevates power? Of the eighteen people around the table, I knew of only one who, like me, would be frightened by the election results—because she had confided those fears to me earlier in the fall. After the closing prayer, she came and hugged me.

Then I realized a woman was standing behind her, waiting to talk with me. She was new to our study. She hugged me and said, "Thank you. I'm so worried about our country now. I didn't know if there was anyone else here who might also be worried. Now I know I am not alone."

After she left, I turned around. The matriarch of our church stood in front of me, her arms wide open. "Thank you," she said. "I couldn't sleep last night. I was so afraid. I barely made it through this day. You named it for me: grief."

Another person walked up, hugged me, and said, "Thank you."

Another person said, "Thank you for sharing your fears. I don't understand, but I will pray for you."

A married couple stayed after everyone else left. The wife said, "Our adult children are devastated by this election. We've been talking with them all day."

*   *   *

When we pray at the end of the Bible study session, we stand in a circle, holding hands. Each person's left palm is up and right palm is down. Our prayer posture models that each of us is supporting someone else—holding them up while at the same time, each of us is being supported by another—we are being held up.

After our Bible study ended on November 9, I realized we have built the kind of community that can hear one another's fears and accept them, whether or not they are our own fears. Our community has made it safe to be vulnerable with one another.

Two weeks later, I received a *thinking of you* card in the mail from the woman who said she did not understand, but she would still pray for me. Inside, she wrote how she is praying for me, and I don't doubt her. You see, I have prayed for her in the past, when she was facing fears I don't share but were still very real to her. I keep the card near me when I work because it reminds me how we lift one another up and pray for one another—not because we all think the same way or support the same candidates and causes, but because we are connected together by threads of love—loosely in some places, tightly in others—woven into a community of grace.

Jessica Hair, age 39
Communications professional
Cleveland, Ohio

This Little Light of Mine

I STOOD AT THE door between my son's room and the living room. In one ear, the TV—loud, changing from one commentator to the next. In the other, the whirring, comforting sound of my son's ventilator as he breathed, deep in sleep, the steady beep of his heartbeat coming from the pulse oximeter (pulse ox) machine. I paced the floor back to the living room where the map of the United States was being overtaken by red; commentators were dumbfounded. I looked at my husband, Adam, who was sitting there utterly shocked. "I knew it. I knew this was going to happen," I said.

It was too much. I walked back to Declan's room and stood over his bed. He slept with a smile, his arms wrapped around a Curious George˙ doll, his little hand pressed against his *Kung Fu Panda* DVD case, which he studies and karate chops as he falls asleep.

My sweet boy. I was supposed to protect him. *We* were supposed to protect him—Adam, me, our friends and family—the people who supposedly love him.

What the hell did they do?

* * *

During the election cycle, I shouted from the rooftops: "My son may die if Trump is elected!"

And how did people respond? "You're being dramatic! Trump would never take away anything Declan needs!"

Every morning Declan and I walked the neighborhood—he in his wheelchair, with his vent—and every morning, a new Trump sign would appear in another neighbor's yard. I sped by the owners of those houses without taking part in the customary niceties. I was outside, but suffocating. Who were these people? What was it about that man and his antics that made them love him? Did they not believe making fun of a disabled person was wrong? Did they not believe that my son should have access to health care?

My neighborhood told me something the polls had not: we were screwed.

* * *

My son arrived a month early on Thursday, March 1, 2012, gray and unmoving. My obstetrician was speechless as he had Adam cut the cord. The Neonatal Intensive Care Unit (NICU) team rushed the newborn baby to the corner and brought him back minutes later in an isolette.

I touched his tiny hand before he was rolled away from me. Chaos turned to silence. My husband and I waited for the unknown.

A NICU doctor came in. He told us that they thought our son had had a stroke and that they needed to transport him to a different hospital. Adam rode in the ambulance with our son, while I stayed in the hospital room due to blood loss.

Adam sent me a picture a few hours later of Declan covered

in wires and tubes and a head full black hair. "He's doing a little better."

Doing a little better.

There began our life in the NICU. Like many other families, we went through a battery of tests trying to get a diagnosis (he had not had a stroke). We spent weeks watching Declan to see if he'd start to move, if he'd open his eyes, if he'd be able to breathe on his own. We had no idea what the future would bring, whether he would make it out of the cave-like NICU. There were books I refused to read him and songs I refused to sing; I couldn't sing "Twinkle, Twinkle Little Star" if he'd never see the night sky.

Doctors approached us about providing "comfort care" (a gentler name for end-of-life care), and we turned them away. They warned us what the future would bring if our son couldn't breathe or eat on his own—surgeries, illnesses, doctor visits, home nursing, 24-hour awake care, constant therapies. But we'd seen him slowly get stronger. Moving a finger. Opening his deep blue eyes. Making the tiniest of fists. We knew Declan was in there. We were rarely allowed to hold him, but when we could, we could feel his soul.

We eventually made the difficult but necessary decision for Declan to undergo a tracheostomy and the placement of a g-tube, procedures intended to provide him a more stable airway and a way to receive nutrition even if he couldn't swallow. We hadn't known the surgeries would bring more "life" to him, but with the extra support, we suddenly had a baby who was awake more often than not. He wanted to play and take in the world.

Sure, he had a few extra appendages, but we would grow used to them.

After 104 days in the NICU, in June of 2012, we were transferred to a rehab facility. A therapist told us to expect to be there for at least six months.

We were there for sixteen.

When we could, we slept in the hospital. When we couldn't, we came home late. If we weren't by Declan's side, we were calling to check in. We were watched, evaluated, and discussed during staff shift changes. Zero privacy; living in a bubble. We ate in random spurts (when we remembered to eat) and sometimes had to "gown up" to enter our son's room. We watched our baby grow into a toddler within the sterile confines of a white-walled facility.

Declan's ultimate diagnosis was handed down to us by a cold matter-of-fact neurologist. *XLMTM, an orphan genetic disease.* We searched the specialist's face for signs of hope, but . . . nothing. As Declan played on the exam table, the doctor told us to enjoy our time with our son, because he probably would not live to see his first birthday. He was already six months old.

My husband and I drove to a park and sobbed in each other's arms. I blamed myself. I was a monster. My genes had done this to our son. My husband scolded me: "We had no idea. This is from *us*. He got this from *us*." Even with the genetic confirmation, Adam refused to let me take the blame. We were in this together 50/50.

We made a promise that day: no matter what, we would not give up on our son.

* * *

The complexity of caring for a medically fragile child is nothing you could ever understand unless you're "in it." It's heartbreaking. It's joyous. It's often infuriating.

Because of the extraordinary costs of caring for the medically fragile, even those with private insurance can qualify for Medicaid for supplemental coverage. In cases that require home nursing, families can also qualify for a Medicaid waiver program, which waives income maximums and makes home care possible. Both college-educated professionals, Adam and I had no choice but to enter the proverbial "system." Declan's trach and ventilator support would require 24/7 "awake care," and he couldn't be released until we had care in place.

In September 2012, Declan was deemed medically ready to come home from the hospital. We applied for the Ohio Home Care Waiver program, and upon evaluation, a social worker declared Declan to be "too stable" to qualify. Too stable. Living on life support. So we were forced to celebrate Declan's first Thanksgiving, Christmas, New Year, and birthday in purgatory, stuck between the hospital and our future as a family.

On October 16, 2013, we finally brought our baby—who was no longer a baby—home from the hospital. Loaded down with supplies and nearly two years of gifts and cards, Declan did a little dance in his stroller as we made the long trek down the corridor to the exit. Our first car ride as a family—alone with our son—was when he was 19.5 months old.

When we got home from the hospital, we were greeted by boxes of equipment, visits from Help Me Grow, the county, Medicaid, social workers, therapists, and nurses. With weekly physical therapy, occupational therapy, speech-language therapy—PT, OT, and SLT—and specialist appointments, we learned to navigate our sea of new acronyms.

Out of the original nine nurses, today we are now down to two. We've had nurses fall asleep, cause him personal harm—knocking his two front teeth out, dropping a tablet on his head, or sitting on him and breaking his femur (all accidents; some we have on video)—forget certain meds, neglect to turn on his humidifier (causing a near miss for needing CPR, and an ambulance ride). We've had as many as twenty-one call-offs in one month. We've had no-call no-shows, mostly for night shift, which meant learning around midnight that we wouldn't be sleeping.

We can count on at least one hospital stay each year, both for routine procedures and emergencies, such as respiratory viruses, ear tubes, and emergency gallbladder removal. After his femur fracture, we discovered just how weak Declan's bones are and that one of his ankles had also been fractured. Every emerging health issue had to be reported to the state. After self-reporting Declan's ankle, Adam and I were investigated for physical abuse. We had to speak with the state, county, and Board of Developmental Disabilities before we were cleared.

Unbeknownst to us before having Declan, an entire world is dedicated to kids like ours. Amazing assistive and adaptive inventions: speaking devices to give him a voice, a power wheelchair to give him independence, specialized car seats and van adaptations so that he can explore the world. All such blessings, but they come either after a fight or with an incredibly steep cost.

We've been fortunate that a decent chunk of Declan's expenses have been covered by our private insurance. When they haven't been covered, we've had Medicaid or funds raised through an annual fundraiser our family holds. Without these supplements, giving our kid the chance to be his best self—or taking him anywhere—would be impossible.

We used to joke that it was good Declan was born to two people who have never really been "stable"—always moving, changing jobs, slightly more in flux than our peers. But the constant chaos of life in fight-or-flight mode is wearing. Medicaid waiver is an intricate system of regulations and fine print. We have had eleven case managers in three years, each with a different set of standards and a new method of evaluating our son's needs.

In June 2016, we were informed that Declan—again—was

too stable for the program. Being on life support was his "norm," so he no longer needed skilled care. We fought back and were awarded with a temporary stay—but the next evaluation is never too far off. We live on pins and needles every day, waiting for the state to kick us out of the system we despise, but so desperately need.

* * *

On March 1, 2017, Declan will celebrate his fifth birthday. Each day with him is a gift, but birthdays and his "home-iversary" are special milestones. Our little fighter has worked hard to get here. He went from zero movement and a one-year-to-live diagnosis—to being a wiggly dance machine. He is cognitively on par with his peers and is learning to communicate with both American Sign Language and a communications device. He loves animals, especially his dog, Penny. He loves looking at the night sky, signing "outside" and "stars" each time we get home after dark. He captures the heart of everyone he meets. I never imagined that I could love anyone as much as I love him or that anyone would ever love me as much as he does. He is my whole heart.

I take personal offense to those who chose to put my son's life at risk by voting for Trump. Trump wants to repeal the ACA and dismantle Medicaid. Trump's nominees like Jeff Sessions say that disabled kids are the downfall of public education.[19] Betsy DeVos sees no need for states to uphold the Individuals With Disabilities Education Act.[20] Donald Trump, the president of the

---

19 Laura Clawson, "Jeff Sessions: Protections for disabled kids are ruining America's schools," Daily Kos (website), (November 29, 2016): http://www.dailykos.com/story/2016/11/29/1605134/-Jeff-Sessions-Protections-for-disabled-kids-are-ruining-America-s-schools.

20 Valerie Strauss, "The telling letter Betsy DeVos wrote to clarify her

United States of America, mocked a reporter with a disability, and it was brushed off because the reporter "deserved" it.

When people with whom I am the closest—who know Declan's story and *every single fight* we've gone through—say that my son didn't factor into their vote, it fills me with rage. I'm told not to take it personally, there are other factors, like keeping the world safe from "terrorists." But my son is *my* world, so you bet your sweet ass I take it personally. I'm pissed; I'm afraid. When I think about what Adam and I have been through with Declan, and how we may have only touched the tip of the iceberg in our fight, I feel a tightening in my chest.

It literally takes my breath away.

position on U.S. disabilities law," *The Washington Post* (January 28, 2017): https://www.washingtonpost.com/news/answer-sheet/wp/2017/01/28/the-telling-letter-betsy-devos-wrote-to-clarify-her-position-on-u-s-disabilities-law/?utm_term=.9fcdcd4ac07a.

Linda W., age 58
Court reporter
Hardin, Illinois

Fault

I WAS RAPED WHEN I was fifteen. I had had too much to drink at a party, and a family friend offered me a ride home. Except he didn't take me home. He took me parking. When he reached for me, I said no. Over and over, I said no. It didn't stop him.

I have told my story only once before today. The first time was a week after the election of November 8, 2016, and I told my parents. To this day, and after forty years of marriage, my husband still does not know.

*   *   *

Prior to the election, I was excited and even proud that a woman would soon be our next president. Hillary Clinton embodied everything I stood for. Her opponent, Donald Trump, was a buffoon, a woman hater, and a complete and total moron. No one in their right mind could vote for him, right?

Wrong.

My parents were Trump supporters. We had so many fights prior to the election that we simply could not talk politics. Our first conversation after the election was via a telephone call from my mother.

My mom began, "Your dad and I would like to ask you to stop posting anti-Trump comments online. Our friends are calling and wanting to know what's wrong with Linda. What should we tell them?"

The astonishment of her and her friends astonished me. I had been voting Democrat ever since my first election in 1976, when I was an eighteen-year-old. The 2016 election would be my eleventh time to vote as a Democrat. Then my astonishment turned to anger.

"You can start off by telling them to go fuck themselves, and then start looking for new friends," I replied. "I'm your daughter. You should be supporting me. Who are these friends? Is it Judy?" Judy is the mother of my rapist.

My mom didn't answer. Instead, she handed the phone to my dad.

Dad's voice came on the phone. "Why do you hate Donald Trump so much?"

I took a deep breath. Time to break the news to them about their little girl. "Well, Dad, I was raped," I began and went on to narrate a story I had hoped would never become part of my life's narrative. When I was finished, I added, "So you can see why a man who boasts about *grabbing pussy* really brought back some raw memories for me."

I waited for my dad's response, but all I heard was silence. "Hello?" I asked.

Another moment passed; then I heard my dad say, "Why didn't you ever tell me?"

"What good would it have done? It would have just been my fault," I replied.

"Well, you were drinking," I heard him say. "You contributed to it."

My heart plummeted to my stomach. His reaction is why I never told anyone. Women are always made to believe it is their fault.

I have a few coworkers who feel the way I do. The rest of them crossed party lines to vote Republican. I don't understand why. To my dying day, I will never understand why. These people are not idiots. They're not Confederate-flag-waving rednecks. They are judges, attorneys, people who read and have college degrees.

A friend from high school added me to a secret women's group right before the election. The group has been my saving grace. I plan to march with them in Washington, DC, the day after the inauguration. I won't be marching to protest President Trump, although my husband served in Vietnam and certainly bought and paid for my ticket to protest.

I am marching in support of every ten-year-old who has been bullied. I am marching in support of every woman who has ever been groped, raped, or fat-shamed. I am marching in support of every ethnic group who no longer feels welcome in America because some fool wants to get rid of them to "Make America Great Again." I am marching in support of the LGBTQ+ community. I am marching against hate.

Lisa Talamantez, age 57
IT guru, metaphysician, and pastry chef
Chicago, Illinois

Abracadabra

SINCE THE ELECTION, I feel like my eyelids have been removed, and not in a tidy, surgical way. Bright lights suddenly blaring; layers of vermin are scrambling. Their waste products are hate, misogyny, xenophobia, ignorance, intolerance, and racism. I suppose I was somewhat sightless before the election, like so many liberals, believing Hillary was going to win in a landslide. *People couldn't ignore history and elect a madman to power.* Then it happened. The crawling mess is everywhere.

I knew trouble was brewing on election night when a series of old white male Republican heads kept popping up as winners on the results coverage. Red. More red. Too much red. Red everywhere! I stayed awake until the bitter end, and when Hillary conceded, I cried. I was and am still unashamed of my response to what I now call an act of domestic terrorism—the election of Donald Trump. Since then, my emotions have vacillated among sadness, anger, frustration, loss, grief, denial, panic.

*   *   *

The blurry holidays came into focus. Typically, I love the holidays, but this year? Merry? Happy? Barely. Cheerful holiday ads rang false. I could not pretend everything was okay. I skipped Thanksgiving. I pushed through Christmas for my niece and nephew.

I'm typically a wildly optimistic and happy person. I'm also a magician and a hereditary good witch, descended from a long line of magical folk. I believe in and practice magic. Not the top-hat-and-rabbit variety of performance magic, but rather using will to cause change magic. Think Patrick Swayze in the movie *Ghost*, in the scene where he is unable to push the bottle cap until the might of his emotion, his will, is behind his ghostly finger. Though my optimism and general joy have definitely taken a hit, I still believe deeply in the power of magic, despite the results of November 8. Without a doubt, magic is still working, rumbling underneath all of this funked-up weirdness.

Speaking of weird, I spend a great deal of time outside of my body, which has been a habit of mine since birth. My mother told me that, as an infant, I slept twenty hours a day and that she had to wake me up to feed me. I'm still quite an Olympic sleeper. These days I find myself having to make an effort to actually stay in my body when awake, and, frankly, I can't wait to go to sleep at night. Sleep is my safe place out of this upside-down world. Being a magician in a human disguise has been a lifelong challenge, though I've been far less confounded with living as I've aged. I'm thrilled with the popularity of the Harry Potter stories, at last giving a magic lesson to millions of humans. Not that mortals don't, but we wizard-types struggle mightily to cope with earthly phenomena like gravity; physical limits; stress; entropy; and the maddening human concepts of time, money, and death. Up until now, I've described my approach to living on Earth as sitting in the front car of a roller coaster, hands up, wind in my hair, trying to enjoy the crazy ride. By assuming a lofty perspective, I can also be staunchly neutral regarding even some of life's worst twists and turns. These days I'm wondering, as this ride appears to be heading directly into a pit of rotating knives, flaming vipers, and high-volume screams (Inauguration Day), if we will hit a sharp turn just before we collide, or not? This kind of nasty isn't supposed to happen! I mean, really, Universe? If there's a higher purpose in this massive, churning stew of events, it's eluding this metaphysician.

Back on Earth, I feel lucky to have landed on this blue planet into a blue-/pink-collar Mexican family in the city of Chicago. Our "blue" city carried this state for Hillary Clinton. Despite Trump's characterizations of Chicago as "hell," this big-shouldered town is an official sanctuary city and a true-blue refuge in the broader red Midwest landscape.

I'm writing this in the frosty final days of 2016, on the north side of Chicago, while house-/pet-sitting for my brother and his family. My brother, who has always voted Republican, has two small children and a lovely wife. For personal reasons, she chose not to vote in this election. My 87-year-old mother also likely voted for Trump: "His sexual assault has nothing to do with his politics!" I feel surrounded. Well, mostly. My eleven-year-old magician-in-training niece wore a safety pin on her jacket when I saw her post election. We had a talk about what wearing the pin meant and although she'd witnessed no bullying at her school, she claimed she was ready. She's one old soul!

We magicians often have animal companions, like Harry Potter's owl, called *familiars*. My niece raised a tiny tadpole into a fist-sized pet and named her Cookie. Cookie is an African clawed frog. This utterly prehistoric-looking species has clearly evolved just enough to survive, and not a bit more. Cookie is highly sensitive and aquatic and must live alone. She has no teeth, no tongue, and no eyelids. She has tiny T. rex front arms that do nothing but shovel prey into her gaping mouth. She will eat anything living or dead, including other African clawed frogs. Cookie ate her smaller sibling, and several apparently delicious guppies purchased to be aquarium friends. Despite these facts, my niece loves this pet deeply and tells her so quite often.

I feel like I'm channeling Cookie these days—feeling territorial, predatory, and without eyelids, in what feels like a space too small for my jostled psyche. Despite these facts, the universe loves me deeply, and yes, it tells me so quite often. Synergy's clues are everywhere always and are consistently added to our horizons, if we only have eyes clever enough to see. Being a magician helps, but in a pinch and with a little focused effort, everyone can harness the power and magic of synergy. For me, a small frog's lidless eyes laser-focused on her prey demonstrate utter present-moment awareness.

Cookie's lack of eyelids leaves her no choice but to see everything, all of the time. She lives her life as naturally as she can, given her limits. She lives without hate or anger and kills only to eat. She certainly lives without self-imposed limits, judgment, or discrimination. She lives completely without malice. Her example helped pull me back from practical narcolepsy to a state of eyes wide open. She reminded me to widen and prolong my gaze: to include ugly truths I had been ignoring, commit to live life genuinely and to be fully and fiercely myself in every moment.

We humans tend to see what we want to see, need to see, if we see anything at all. Sometimes we make it all up. We sift and sort through our underutilized brains a fraction of the available information generously placed before us. We spend more time gazing back at the horizon or forward to a nebulous future than at what is in front of us. We declare our species the most evolved on the planet. Nope. Not by a long shot.

I believe during this lifetime that I am back here on Earth to be as present as I can be. Not to do anything specific or through obligation—only to live as I am, wherever I am, contributing my unique energy to the mix. In these confusing times, I wonder if that's truly the case. What's going to happen in the next four years? Is "being" enough of a contribution? Without an obvious answer, my tendency is to fly right back out of my body.

Speaking of out-of-body experiences, I am a medium and have been since I was a child alone with a Ouija board. Believe it or not, I possess the gift of communicating with beings who are no longer in physical bodies—human, canine, feline, you name it. When I was nine, I sat eating a Dilly˙ Bar outside a Dairy Queen˙ restaurant. It was unusually warm, and I was watching dark clouds roll in on Good Friday. My family wasn't religious at all so I didn't know why I knew about the phenomenon of sudden, angry storms at 3:00 p.m. on Good Friday; I just did. I decided Jesus was cool for rising out of that tomb and proving there was no such thing as death. I started wearing a lot of black, much to my mother's chagrin. In any case, when I was a young teen, I had a distinct vision. I had learned how to play the guitar by then and decided that in the event of a nuclear holocaust, if my guitar and I survived, I'd try to comfort fellow survivors with humor and songs. I pray this vision never comes to be.

Regardless, I'll always do what I can in these times of confusing transformation, knowing the universe loves all of us deeply, even politicians who may thoughtlessly damage or destroy our precious planet. I now encourage all sensitive, intelligent, kind, caring souls to stroke the fire that's been ignited inside, and to do all they can to add to the layer of positive energy surrounding our planet. Certainly, no matter what, my eyes are now wide open, forever.

Do you believe in magic? Might be a very good time to start.

Sheila Reynolds, age 41
Corporate vice president
Mankato, Minnesota

I Won't Go Quietly

I N THE DAYS leading up to the 2016 presidential election, I was filled with the righteous indignation that can felt by only middle-class white people. I knew deep in every fiber of my being that we would wake up on November 9, 2016, victorious. I mean, surely common sense would prevail, and that orange moron couldn't possibly win.

I spent the entirety of November 7, reading post after post by my fellow liberals. With each successive post, my certainty grew. I barely knew anyone who was voting for Trump. All of my college-educated, middle-class friends were voting for Hillary. How could they not? We are all progressive and open-minded.

I have my very own gay son and a young lady I love like a daughter, who is Muslim. So obviously, I am the change the world needs. The world will be conquered by yoga-pants wearing midwesterners.

I walked into the voting place—a local Assembly of God church—with my head held high. Today I—I mean, the United

States of America—would be victorious. Our candidate would win. (Full disclosure: I was a Bernie girl, but hey, beggars can't be choosy, so "Go, Team Hillary.") I waited my two full minutes in line and marched to the voting booth to take my place in history.

I left the church so giddy that I stopped to treat my coworkers to donuts. I spent the rest of the day reading post after post on social media, tears of pride streaming down my face. Sure, I didn't help my 95-year-old grandmother vote in her first election. I didn't take the day off from work to drive senior citizens to the voting booth. I didn't knock on doors and rally for my candidate. But frankly, in my mind, I did my part. My vote counted. Minnesota always goes blue, so I did more than enough.

I went through my day proudly wearing my *Voted* sticker. I looked my fellow Americans in the eye everywhere I went. When I saw other women, I gave them that head-nod smile, assuming they too voted for my candidate.

As one of those progressive, cut-the-cable people, I don't have cable at home, so I spent my evening binging on streaming videos and periodically checking election result updates, and that's when the panic started to set in. *How in the world were we losing? How does that happen? Why the fuck did so many seemingly reasonable people vote for the "Mango Mussolini"?* I was flabbergasted. How does a man with zero political experience get to be elected leader of the United States of freaking America? I uttered the phrase *what the fuck* many, many times that night and in the weeks that followed.

I went to bed that night hoping for the best but expecting the worst. My husband woke me up and said, "You're just going to want to say, 'Screw it,' and stay in bed today." That's when I knew *he* had won. Donald Trump would be our next president.

For the first time in a very long time, I cried. I'm not one of those emotional people. In August, I left my only son at college twelve hours away, and I didn't shed a single tear. Yet on the morning on November 9, I cried.

The following days were spent in a fog. I listened to my coworkers tell me that "they let a 'nigger' be president for eight years, and there was no way in hell they would let a woman be president." Of course, none of my coworkers who were saying these things actually bothered to vote—but that didn't stop them from gloating and bragging about Trump's win.

I quietly unfriended a couple of people on social media. Not in a blaze of glory, as some people do; just the ones I knew would say hurtful things and brag about their candidate's winning. They were people who didn't really know me in real life anyway, so what did it matter if I unfriended them?

Then I came to realize that my single vote wasn't enough. I needed to be more active.

I've continued volunteering as a mentor for middle school girls. I've vowed to not be that quiet person in line who lets the racist woman in front bitch and moan about immigrants. I've come to the startling realization that America stopped being great on November 9, 2016. We have the potential to reclaim our greatness, but not under the current tyrant.

I won't go quietly. I'll be kicking and screaming the whole way. My single vote wasn't enough, and my single voice won't be enough either. But, God willing, the seventy-two million voters who voted "not Trump" have the potential to be more than enough.

A. Darabos Curry, age 42
Photographer and writer
Midland, Michigan

Tell

ABLINKING CURSOR ON an empty page stares back at me. I am repelled by anything that hints at telling me what to do. In this moment, the cursor is at the top of my shit list. Tell. Tell. Tell. The cursor and I are staring each other down in a pointless game of chicken. We both know I decided a few weeks ago exactly what the tapestry of my words was going to look like. It's a fabric I wouldn't have chosen, in a color that makes me feel uneasy and sad. Like the extra weight I carry, my plain appearance and the mole I hide, I'm ashamed of the embroidery of my life. Recently I've realized I'm at an impasse. I have only two choices going forward: (1) I can hoist this burden back up on my shoulders and continue to stumble through life loathing myself for being weak, or (2) I can decide right now to stretch that tapestry out on the floor, corner to corner, and expose its homely brocade for others to see.

I have chosen to lay my burden down.

*   *   *

My entire devoutly Catholic family identifies as Republican. I did too. In fact, I'd never voted for anyone other than a Republican until this past year. My mind didn't change because I especially liked Hillary Clinton and it didn't change because I hated Donald Trump. It changed because for years I had been struggling with accepting that I'm different from the people I came from.

I don't want to be different. My whole life, all I've ever wanted was to fit in and be accepted. I don't want to be unique. I want to be "them." Because if I'm them, then they have to love me. There would have to be a place for me no matter what. I'd belong.

As a teenager, I didn't belong anywhere. I had fewer friends than I could count on one hand and none whom I would confide in. Boys didn't like me and girls were afraid if they associated with me, boys wouldn't like them either. When I cruised the hall in the morning before school, a group of boys in my graduating class would bark at me. Loudly. I am forty-two and I can still hear it. I can still close my eyes and see their mouths snarled up, barking.

I voted the way my family did for years because I didn't want to be different. I wanted to believe that if I voted their way, it meant we shared the same ideals. I rationalized that I matched them and that someday they'd see me as one of their own. I resisted casting a vote opposite them because if I did, I'd be admitting I'm still a castoff.

The year my daughter turned twenty, I turned forty. I began to look at my voting record less as a concern for myself and more of a concern for her. She was now an adult, and the legislation that would pass from the officials I elected would affect her in new ways. I worried what would happen if she suddenly found herself with an unwanted or unsustainable pregnancy. It quickly became clear to me that my dogma from years of Catholicism, did not match my desires for my child. What I wanted for her was far more important than the desire to be accepted by my family.

I began to embrace a new set of ideals and set out to discover who I am, absent the fear of knowing. I discovered that I am pro-choice. I'm an opponent of the death penalty. I believe poor people should be fed and kept warm and given medical care if they cannot afford it. I believe giving compassion is always less of a risk than withholding it.

When my mom arrived at our viewing party on election night, I jokingly asked her if she had brought tissues for all of her tears. She was good-natured and said she'd brought plenty for mine. We laughed. I still believed Hillary Clinton was going to win. The night was early, and my faith in America was solid. America was not those boys in the hall. Even some of those boys aren't "those boys" anymore. We've grown up. We are the generation engrossed in preventing bullying. Stomping it out. Protecting our kids. There was no way a man who openly made fun of a person with disabilities was going to be rewarded with the presidency.

A month earlier, the *Access Hollywood* tape had been leaked. In it, Trump had bragged to Billy Bush that he'd sexually assaulted women multiple times and that he always gets away with it. I watched as, overnight, Trump's candidacy became personal for women everywhere. I had close friends who bravely revealed their own sexual assault stories. My heart tore for them as they each opened a vein and bled their truth. While they bared their souls, I retreated into a hole. I was equal parts angry and terrified. I desperately wanted to stand on the front line with them, but every time I thought about bleeding my truth, I couldn't put the razor to my arm.

So I watched as my friends showed me what bravery is, and I waited for the day I'd join them. When the polls started closing on election night and the news began painting the map red,

I felt a panic rising in me. As a family, we joked around and mildly debated policies while we waited for updates. But as the night wore on, my world was shrinking. I was speeding forward toward the head of the pin, feeling smaller by the minute. My skin was hot. My throat stayed dry no matter how much diet soda I poured down it. My head was beating like a drum, and when Florida's result came in, I felt nausea rise up. My eyes burned. I needed air. I was certain if I didn't run out the front door immediately and gulp some fresh night air, I'd vomit.

Today I can better identify the reason for my acute reaction. I was watching the world morph into a mutant version of itself, and I believe what I needed was to verify I was having a bad dream. I hoped that if I went outside and the sky looked the same as when I had come in, it meant the sky wasn't falling.

My parents' faces began to register concern. If I looked anything on the outside like I felt on the inside, that would explain their expressions. They were confused at a breakdown they thought was extreme and uncharacteristic. I was having a visceral reaction to being cut open. I was watching the blade inch towards my arm. My truth. My truth was building up, pressing from the inside out, pushing on my flesh. I felt enormous panic. My family couldn't have known why. The words were shoving against my lips, screaming to be let out for the very first time. *I was raped.*

I didn't say it that night. Instead, I wept and my voice cracked, explaining how heartbroken I was. I thought we were better than this. We grew up, didn't we? We raised our kids not to bully, didn't we? We raised our kids to be kind and to show compassion, didn't we? So why do I hear a dog bark every time another state turns red?

It wasn't because I was realizing the bully was going to win; it was because I was absorbing that he still existed. I said everything except my truth. Not out loud and not in print. Ever.

I came so close that night. The rage boiled inside me as I looked around the room with shifting eyes at a handful of people who had never been forced to have sex against their will. None of them had ever felt the weight of an attacker on top of them, shoving their legs apart while pinning their arms down. None of them had been ripped open, a victim of a deviant's sweaty, smelly thrusting. None of them had fought and screamed, "No!" over and over again until they just gave up and lay still, crying. They'd never been crawled off of and discarded like trash. They'd never worn the kind of filth that only germinates from shame. They'd never despised their own weakness and loathed the kind of humiliation I'd known.

I could have said it. But when confronted with the opportunity to liberate my secret, I panicked. I remembered that they'd argued that grabbing someone by the genitals against their wishes wasn't what they considered "sexual assault." They'd told me as much, weeks earlier when the *Access Hollywood* tape leaked.

Instead, I scratched the surface. I cried and spoke accusingly when I said, "You voted for a bully. You voted for the mean person." What I meant to say, what I wanted to say, was that they'd chosen the side of my attacker. That this was personal. That they'd voted for the dog barks and the thrusting. I felt victimized all over again. When we parted ways at the end of the night, we hugged and kissed and shared *I love yous*. I was happy we made it through a potential storm without hating one another at the end. I made a special point to walk my parents out, and I stood in the cold night air watching my breath as I asked, "Are we okay?"

They said we were. They said nothing had changed. My dad attempted to reassure me: "Remember, none of us voted for him in the primary. He wasn't our first choice. He was what we had to choose from. Make no mistake about it: nobody wanted him."

I wanted my dad's words to make me feel better. Maybe they did a little, but that small difference wasn't enough. I tapped their car with my open palm, waving and watching them back out, profound sadness and grief sitting square on my chest. Something had changed. I was split open, hemorrhaging in my brother's driveway. Maybe if I'd have chosen to bleed openly that night, or any night of the last fifteen years, I wouldn't have been dying a slow death alone right there. My truth was that despair had burrowed inside me and the decay was spreading.

It took almost a month, but a day came when I was sitting in my car alone. I'd just dropped my youngest off at his volunteer job, and I drove to a parking lot where I sat silent and still. Fear strangled me and my hands shook as I opened up the dial pad on my phone and typed in ten digits.

A voice on the other end greeted me with her name and said, "How can I help you?"

I heard a sob choke out of me. My hand betrayed me by covering my mouth and willing me not to speak.

"Ma'am," the voice said soothingly, "how can I help you?"

I was weeping. I was choking down gulps of air. "I." Pause. Deep breath in. More sobs. It was a whisper. I had to repeat it twice for her to hear. But I made up my mind that day that it didn't matter if I was different or if the tapestry that my life has woven isn't beautiful. It's the only one I've got, and it's a damn heavy thing to carry alone.

"I'd like to make an appointment to speak to a therapist, please."

Elizabeth Martin, age 45
Business owner
Cincinnati, Ohio

A Safe Shore

Death

I AM TWENTY-ONE; MY mother is dying. She has been fighting cancer for eight years but now she is tired, and I have become tired watching her die. Every day I feel as though I am fighting waves in the ocean that crash upon me, and all I want to do is stay afloat and make it to shore. Every day I am drowning. I am in the middle of the perfect storm and all I want is security.

Love

Mark is my security.

Mark has blonde hair and piercing blue eyes that cut through to my soul. He understands me and is kind to me. He offers friendship and a break from reality. He throws me a proverbial life preserver, and before I know it, I am madly in love with him.

Marriage

Angry outbursts begin six months into our marriage. At first, they are minor. He has issues with some of the shirts I wear. They expose too much of the breasts he bought and paid for. "I paid too much for those things to let anyone else get a free peek," he says.

Mark is paranoid too. He finds ways to be suspicious of nothing. Denying his claims of my cheating—it is my new pastime. Mark shoots his arrows anywhere he can find a target. According to him, I am a horrible wife. I need to worry more about my appearance. My pussy is nasty; I need to clean it up.

Pregnancy

I am twenty-two and five months pregnant. Mark has gone out drinking with coworkers. Snow has been falling for hours, and I am worried because I know Mark is driving home drunk. Relief washes over me when I hear the engine of his car roar into the driveway. But there's anxiety too. He is alive, but in what condition?

Mark stumbles through the door and walks up the stairs. I wait for him on the stairs, my scruffy bathrobe wrapped tightly around my bulging pregnant belly.

"What are you thinking, driving drunk . . . on a night like tonight, no less?" I ask.

Mark replies with an answer I don't accept. He emits a low growl and lunges at me. My back flattens against the wall, my arms pinned above my head. One hand wraps around my throat. His eyes, blue infernos burning with rage, lock with mine.

I break away and move toward the stairs. My trembling hand reaches for the banister, but it's too late. My knees crumble, and I tumble down the stairs.

I lie like a heap on the floor, my hands searching my belly, hoping for a kick, a sign of life. Above me I hear him say, "I hope you lose the baby, you stupid bitch."

My Child

Mark does not get his wish. On a mild, pleasant day four months later, I give birth to my third child, a healthy baby girl.

Married Life

Mark never lays a hand on me again, but it is too late. He laid the groundwork that night. I still see the fiery look in his eyes when he is displeased. He still towers over me. He likes to throw things too. Anything he can find. The walls of our house are pockmarked with everyday visual reminders of his barely restrained rage.

Divorce

Mark has been having an affair. Multiple affairs, in fact. The last time, I caught him red-handed. It is what I needed to finally leave. But leaving is still difficult. I am engulfed in waves of grief. I am mourning the death of what I had hoped my marriage would become so many years ago. The dreams I had for the future are all lost. The wreckage of the ship is drifting away with the waves. The carnage spreads everywhere, and I do not know where it will resurface.

Single Life

I am forty-one, and I have spent the last couple of years taking time to focus on myself. I don't have much of an interest in a relationship, but I give Josh a chance.

It's our third date and I do not feel a connection, but when he pulls into my driveway and asks if he can use the restroom, I think, *Who am I to refuse a man when nature calls?*

I lead him inside and point him in the direction of the hall bathroom. I walk to the kitchen and pull out a bottle of wine from the fridge. I think, *As soon as he leaves, I'm going to open this bad boy up and watch terrible television until I fall asleep, content and alone.*

Suddenly, a loud thud erupts from the back of the house.

I walk into the hallway. "Everything okay?" I ask to the closed door.

A moment passes before Josh opens the door. "I'm sorry. I broke it," he says.

"Broke what?" I ask, and step closer.

Josh turns to let me in, and once I am inside, he moves behind me. I feel a surge of panic.

Pins and needles on my neck. The hairs on my arms stand at attention.

I turn to look at Josh. Something shiny flashes in his hands. His arm swings down. The blade catches my skin above the elbow. I try to scream, but it's too late. His hand covers my mouth, and all at once I am being pushed down, down, down, until my cheek is pressed against the cold bathroom tiles.

Josh straddles me. His knife tears through my clothes. All at once I am naked, a blade is at my throat, and Josh is thrusting inside of me. I grow numb. It is as if I am outside my body and I can see the rape happening as if it were happening to someone else.

He leaves, and I remain curled up on the cold bathroom floor. I pull myself up and look in the mirror. I don't recognize the reflection staring back at me. I touch the mirror; yes, it's me. The waves have returned with a vengeance. The demons of the night will not give me rest. I fear this time I will not make it back to the shore.

Diagnosis

My therapist says the whole out-of-body experience was my way of dealing with the situation. The brain has remarkable defenses for coping with trauma.

I love my therapist. I found her after contacting a local place called Women Helping Women. It took me years to make that call, but I'm glad I did.

I am officially diagnosed with PTSD. My PTSD is complex. I have so many traumas that treatment is not easy. My therapist believes my first trauma was hearing at age thirteen the diagnosis of my mother's cancer. I work so hard to manage my triggers and ground myself. I am aware of some triggers, but others? Well, they just happen.

Pre-Election

I am forty-five, and the lead up to the 2016 United States presidential election causes me emotional and physical havoc. Donald Trump triggers me constantly. I see through him. I see him in the men of my past. I try to tell others, but they just shrug off my words and treat me as if I am being paranoid. Am I paranoid?

And Now

The demons of the night are visiting constantly again, but they will not find me unarmed.

I have met friends online—women who have stories similar to mine but different. In the beginning, we were there only to support one another. Not anymore. Since Trump's win, we have begun to organize. We sign petitions. We call politicians. We march. We fight. I have thousands of life preservers surrounding me, and I no longer have the fear of drowning.

It has taken years for me to find my voice; I will die before I lose it again.

Shannon M. Thielman, age 47
Registered nurse
Wausau, Wisconsin

Home

I TYPICALLY FIND IT difficult to remember what I was doing in any given year; the year 2016, however, is an exception.

In April, my husband, Darwin, died of a massive heart attack. He was only fifty-four years old. We had been married only eight years and had adopted our bright and joyful five-year-old Latino son through foster care. The three of us had recently moved from Madison to the northern part of the state to be closer to my parents, who were over the moon about having their only grandchild close enough to dote on. As it turned out, moving was a very prescient decision: in the months following Darwin's death, my parents have become indispensable.

* * *

Because I was a registered Democrat living in the battleground state of Wisconsin, Hillary's campaign approached me multiple times, asking me to volunteer, but I declined. I thought it was pointless. *She already had it in the bag,* I thought. She was running against *Donald Trump,* after all. Racist, misogynistic, unscrupulous Donald Trump, with the leering eyes and the vocabulary of a second grader. There was no way Hillary Clinton was going to lose. Why did they need me?

And anyway, on top of my new widowed status, I was experiencing health scares of my own. A cardiac workup that started before Darwin's death turned very serious as my cardiologist discovered a potentially fatal rhythm and insisted I have a defibrillator implanted immediately. "You are a high risk for sudden cardiac death," he said.

Mourning my husband and fighting my own health issues made death (and the possibility of orphaning my son) very real to me; the election campaigns, less so.

* * *

The night of the election, I sat on the couch with my son and watched the returns come in. A very sheltered six-year-old, my son knew nothing about what he was seeing on TV. But I managed to delude myself into thinking this was his introduction to democracy, and Hillary's sure victory was the cherry on top. I even planned on letting him stay up to watch her victory speech. Excitement coursed through my body; this was it: history in the making.

But as the returns came in, my excitement turned to doubt, and later, horror. I turned off the TV just before Trump's acceptance speech and then picked up my sleeping son and put him to bed.

I should have campaigned for her. I should have been more involved, I thought.

Numb, I went to my bedroom and sat on the edge of the bed, staring through tears at the collages of my husband on the wall before crawling into the sheets. My eyes would not shut despite the dark. My hand strayed to Darwin's pillow, and my tears became sobs as I yearned for him to hold me tightly and keep the world at bay. The empty space felt expanded somehow, stretching and growing in every direction—an unyielding landscape left abandoned since his death. It had been eight months; I was used to sleeping alone at this point; but that night, the acute sense of loss I had felt the first days after Darwin's death seemed to reemerge and amplify with a heavy roar.

* * *

My sense of loneliness continued into the following months. Before, I had known I was facing widowhood and the difficulties of raising a child on my own, but now I was facing something I hadn't expected: a Trump presidency and the potential demise of our democracy.

One recent morning over breakfast, my son asked me: "Mommy, why are your eyes sad?"

I didn't know how to answer. How do you explain adult fears to a child? How can I tell my son that all my previous fears have been exacerbated by our new commander in chief? How can I tell him that I alone am responsible for shepherding him through this dark and fearful time—but I am afraid: afraid of protecting him in a potential war; afraid his brown skin will not be welcome in the new era of white supremacy; afraid the country he calls home has no home for him; afraid that I am simply not enough?

* * *

My grief still seems overpowering at times. I hold my son when he cries for his daddy, and I cry with him, for him, for my husband, for myself, for our former lives, and now for our country. In the last few weeks, however, my fear has turned to anger, and my anger has turned to action.

In addition to writing letters, becoming involved in the local Democratic Party, and calling my elected officials, I have enrolled in the Emerge Wisconsin program that prepares women to run for office.

For his sake, I carry on—despite fear, despite loneliness, despite self-doubt, despite wanting to curl up in a cocoon—knowing that somewhere in me there is a core of steel. I'm trying to preserve the good inside me for better days ahead . . . *and there will be better days.* I have to believe that—for myself, for my son, and for the country we call home.

Lori Szeszycki, age 41
High school Spanish teacher
Chicago, Illinois

1,460 Days

IT'S November 8, 2016, and I'm sitting on my couch staring at the television while the Electoral College tallies turn redder. I whisper *fuck* every time Wolf Blitzer appears on CNN. "Stop with the election update prattle, Wolf!" I yell at the TV.

No dice. I stare at the screen for hours and wait for someone to appear and tell me our country is not in the process of electing a bigoted narcissist to serve as president of the United States.

And then it's all over, and Trump makes his acceptance speech. I'm wondering what I'm going to say to my high school Spanish students, most of whom are African American, and all of whom are living in challenging socioeconomic circumstances. I'm exhausted, but I know today is not the day to call in sick.

* * *

My first period class shuffles in and is more subdued than usual. I step in the front of the room and smile tentatively with a "buenos días, clase." Some of the kids meet my gaze, but most just drop their heads. I see the phones pulled from their pockets. These respectful, focused students have been in my classroom for less than a minute and already need to talk to someone outside of room 108.

I look out the window for a moment and try again, "Cariños, ¿cómo están?" The eyes stay down.

Finally, my sassy chica, Makayla, shouts out, "Miss, I'm angry! Miss, did you watch the election? Do you know what happened last night? We're all going to be sent to concentration camps or deported! Miss, what the hell happened? Miss, I'm sorry that I'm swearing in here, but seriously, what the hell happened? This is fucked up!"

Others jump in: "Miss, why did this happen? Why did those white people elect a man who hates us?"

I gaze back at them, wide-eyed and waiting for the right words to come. And then I realize white America did this. Van Jones got it right: this election was a *whitelash* against having an Ivy-league educated African American president whose "hope and change" did not bring the results they wanted.[21]

* * *

During one presidential debate, Trump argued he could clean up Chicago within a week[22] by increasing law enforcement manpower and the use of force. Chicagoans were angry our

21 "Emotional Van Jones: How do I explain this to my children? - CNN Video." CNN. Accessed February 04, 2017. http://www.cnn.com/videos/politics/2016/11/09/van-jones-emotional-election-results-sot.cnn.

22 s.n., "Donald Trump: Chicago Could Stop Violence 'In One Week,'" CBS Chicago, August 23, 2016, http://chicago.cbslocal.com/2016/08/23/donald-trump-chicago-could-stop-violence-in-one-week/.

city was called out on national television, yet the fact remains that our city is reeling from multiple lawsuits alleging police brutality, departmental cover-ups, and blatant racial profiling. Chicagoans are inundated by media telling us that "Blue Lives Matter," "All Lives Matter," and "Black Lives Matter." There doesn't appear to be any middle ground.

I listened to relatives in law enforcement complain about the public's ridiculous judgment of their job performance; the Blue Lives Matter perspective should acknowledge all of the work police officers do for the community. I watched white acquaintances preach that their All Lives Matter perspective is relevant because we need to live in a color-blind society and stop harping on old problems like, um, racism.

I argued the urgency expressed by the Black Lives Matter movement is like that of a house on fire. If a house on the block is on fire, we're not going to douse every house with water. We're going to try to stop the fire in the burning house. In the same way, all of the "houses"—nervous white people and police officers—don't need water thrown on them. We need to help stop the flames from consuming the one burning house on the street.

Just days before the election, racial tensions in Chicago escalated further when a police shooting occurred in a "nice" South Side neighborhood, Mount Greenwood. On the surface, the neighborhood appeared to be peaceful: no drive-by shootings, no gang members hanging out on the corners, a locally famous St. Patrick's Day parade, a beautiful arts education center. However, the majority of the Caucasian residents sent their children to private Catholic schools, and the majority of the minority residents sent their students to subpar Chicago public schools. The neighborhood had silently segregated itself by how and where it educated its children. And now a white

Chicago police officer had shot an African American man on his way home from a funeral.

The administration at the local Catholic high school, Marist, whose student enrollment is mostly Caucasian, learned that the local African American gang members might retaliate for the shooting by targeting white students. This threat remained unsubstantiated, but social media hysteria quickly took over. The school administrators decided to close on a Friday to let a three-day weekend cool things off.

*   *   *

Within a month of the election, posters featuring swastikas, a picture of Adolf Hitler, and the slogan *No Degeneracy, No Tolerance, Hail Victory* were removed from two locations at the University of Chicago on the south side of the city. A week later, the *Chicago Tribune* reported that a large yellow banner was hung from a business property in Libertyville, reading *Hail Trump - Unscrupulous America X - Make America White Again.*[23] Due to the owner's First Amendment rights, the police were not permitted to remove the banner, but a local business owner with ties to the property tore it down. In the comments section of the article, a gentleman accused the Democratic Party of hanging the banner in an attempt to divide the nation.[24]

*   *   *

---

23 Katherine Rosenberg-Douglas,"Pro-Trump, pro-white banner found hanging outside Libertyville building," *Chicago Tribune*, December 12, 2016, http://www.chicagotribune.com/news/local/breaking/ct-pro-trump-pro-white-banner-found-hanging-outside-libertyville-building-20161211-story.html.

24 Kenneth_M, comment on Douglas, "Pro-Trump, pro-white banner."

Recently I went on a camping trip and talked to a voter about his decision to support Trump and Pence. He said his vote was partially based on Pence's fiscal management of Indiana's budget. I agreed Pence had certainly done a better job than the crooks of Illinois. However, when I questioned Pence's position on LGBTQ rights, as well as his antiabortion, misogynistic views, my acquaintance replied, "If the people of Indiana don't like those positions, they're welcome to move to another state with legislation that aligns with their views."

I tried to protest. "We are a nation of *united* states, and one should not have to move to a different state to secure basic civil rights and medical procedures. This is why we have a Supreme Court; their verdicts must be applied to all of the states, not just those whose constituents agree with them."

A friend listening to our discussion commented that this approach would inevitably cause the states to become segregated. I agreed and added it would become a matter of "Here are the five states that grant full civil rights to LGBTQ residents. This is the state that permits abortion. These are the few states that enforce equal wages for women and men. Here is the state that mandates health insurance providers to cover birth control."

* * *

A couple of weeks after this conversation, in the lovely Lakeview neighborhood of Chicago, a racially charged incident occurred in a Michael's' craft store. A white customer ranted angrily at the African American store manager, shouting, "I voted for Trump! So there! And look who won! And look who won! And look who won!" Her thirty-minute tirade was caused by her perception that the African American employee was trying to force her to buy a reusable shopping bag. Another customer filmed her hate-filled rant, and the video was posted on social media and picked up by news outlets.

A small part of me was glad her hateful rhetoric was on video, if only so that she could not deny it had occurred. But I also knew the public shaming would not change her hatred of African Americans. Shaming does not change behavior; it changes only the manner in which the behavior occurs.

*   *   *

As I watched the election results on November 9, I took some small comfort in knowing the state of Illinois had stayed blue. In my sleep-deprived state, I reassured myself that our state was still "good" and still had "good" people who were going to hold the line against the bigots in the red states.

I was not seeking an echo chamber, but I did want reassurance that it's not okay for our country to be led by a man who brags about grabbing women by the pussy. But, instead, I kept finding myself unpleasantly surprised by the perspectives of Trump supporters. When I pointed out that Trump was a racist for saying "all Mexicans are rapists," I was told this perspective was simply a stereotype and stereotyping was not racist. When I said it was inappropriate for Trump to post statement videos online, thus avoiding questions from the press, I was told he shouldn't have to talk to the liberal media.

Illinois might have come out blue on the Electoral College map, but we are truly more of a purple state. Those of us who care about not reversing the hard-earned civil rights of minorities and women, are ridiculed as crybabies by those who voted for Trump; die-hard Trump supporters are exasperated by our unwillingness to "just get over it" or to "just give him a chance."

But there is no compromise. We have all dug in our heels. All we can hope for is not to kill one another over the next 1,460 days.

Wren A. Nicholson, age 30
Real Estate
Michigan

No Surrender

S HE LAYS ON the cold itchy carpet with borrowed blankets in a home full of other kids. Her older brothers and their friends, their sisters, her friends. The summer kids.

She is six-years-old, tiny, blonde, and shy but strong. Four times they cut her open before she could tie her own shoes. A tiny beating heart gently healed in a surgeon's hands and zipped back up again. Good as new.

She lays there with them but alone. The others sleep now, but she can't.

She knows that he's not sleeping either, and soon he'll make his way to her. The idea makes her tummy sick in a way she doesn't understand. She likes him, but for some reason, he scares her.

He is twice as old as her. He's just like her brothers but cooler, because he's not annoyed by her. He lets her hang out with them and is never mean to her.

She gets more and more nervous until he finally slinks his

way across the room through the sleeping bodies littering the floor, careful not to wake anyone on his way.

She laughs quietly under the covers as he tells a joke. Then he kisses her. He's shown her how to do this before. Said it was cool. Said it was a secret.

She doesn't know what's happening, but she knows it's wrong. He tells her not to tell anyone.

She has an amazing family—fun, loving, and safe. She's not sure why, but she knows something like this would upset them greatly. So she could never tell.

*   *   *

She is nineteen, away from home for the first time when she starts seeing a married man, her boss. He is sweet, funny, too many years older than her, and a father.

She knows it's going nowhere, she knows it's wrong, but she does it anyway.

She comes to her senses, guilt creeping in.

She tries to break it off. She tries multiple times. He isn't sweet anymore. His sense of humor is suddenly gone.

She agrees one last time to go away with him for the weekend.

She wants him to know she is done for good this time. That it has to stop.

She thinks she can make him understand.

He has other plans.

He reminds her of her brothers' friend. She recognizes the same sick feeling in the pit of her stomach.

She tries to fight him—to run. (Why did she let him bring her to this place? His place!) He has her phone. There's not another soul around for miles.

She watches his fist swing backward, then curve towards her. First, her cheekbone. Next, her jaw. Then her eyes. One after another. Over and over.

She thinks she is dying.

She is certain he's killing her. But he doesn't.

She lays there alone, blood clouding her eyes, dirt beneath her fingernails, sharp little pieces of gravel digging into her back, and tiny stones embedded into the palms of her hands.

He tosses the cell phone in her direction before he exits and leaves her lying there.

She caused this, too. So she doesn't tell.

She never wants to think about it again. So she forgets. For a while at least.

* * *

She meets a nice guy soon after. A really nice guy.

She loves him.

She gives birth to her first child, a beautiful, blue-eyed little girl. Fiercely independent and cautiously adventurous.

She loves her unconditionally. Everything is different now. A few years later, she has another daughter. An equally beautiful, empathic little daredevil.

She looks at them and sees herself at that age. They are so loving, open, and innocent. Her love for them is the best and most terrifying thing she's ever experienced.

She teaches them to think for themselves, question *everything*, and love everyone, even those who don't deserve it.

She teaches them to say no, to always tell. Always.

She makes sure they know the power they hold, and to use that power to protect themselves and others who may need it.

She is lucky enough to find an impressive example of this strength on display at a time when both her daughters are old enough to understand it.

She shares her excitement with them over the possibility of making history. She amazes at her daughter's' astute observations of the unsavory character of the history-making lady's opponent. A bully in their eyes.

She's not shocked when his true colors show. His justifications surprise her and those of the people she loves. Her father, husband, friends, and women everywhere accept his behavior as locker room talk—*boy will be boys.*

*   *   *

After the day the world went red, she doesn't sleep. The country seems much less safe for her girls now.

She sees the pain in her daughters' eyes. They are young, but aware. They know what won. They know what lost.

Eventually, she pulls herself out of the dark hole and brushes off the disappointment.

She can't stop now. She must fight. She has to teach her daughters how to fight too.

She carries on.

She speaks.

She listens.

She loves.

She will not relent.

She refuses to surrender.

Southwest

"Write with your eyes like painters, with your ears like musicians, with your feet like dancers. You are the truthsayer with quill and torch. Write with your tongues of fire. Don't let the pen banish you from yourself."[25]

—Gloria E. Anzaldúa

---

25 Anzaldúa, Gloria, and AnaLouise Keating. The Gloria Anzaldúa reader. Durham: Duke University Press, 2009.

Rachael Hellman, age 28
Copywriter
Austin, Texas

When We Mix the Pages

A
LONE AT NINETEEN in 1938 and with little more than a miniature dictionary and *Please let me off at Liberty Station* written in pencil on the back of a postcard, my grandma, then Pesia Gotman, sailed from Trochenbrod, her tiny Polish shtetl, to the United States. Barely five feet tall, barely an adult, she left her five sisters—and her parents' graves—in exploration of a rumored better life. Being "old" and unmarried never looked so good.

Her decision was driven by not being tied down, the rare score of a visa, and a mythical "Uncle Ben" to stay with until she got on her feet. The times she'd gathered around the one radio in the whole town and listened to Adolf Hitler yell about the "Juden" hardly factored into her decision. Hitler seemed manic, but not quite "murder 12 million people" manic. More like a guy with a bad mustache, a loud voice, and an impressive groupie following.

She didn't know it then, but her timing was critical. Had she delayed a day, had she stopped to smell the literal roses growing wild in the acres of forest surrounding her home, she wouldn't have made it. And I wouldn't be here. *Kristallnacht* happened while my grandma was at sea. And soon after arriving in Pittsburgh, her ultimate destination, she stopped receiving letters from her sisters. In all likelihood, they, along with their families, were lined up and shot in the woods rather than taken to a concentration camp. My aunt visited Trochenbrod in the late 90s and brought back a pinecone.

Pesia met my grandfather, Frederick, on the boat. Years later, after he served in the U.S. Army, he would stop by to visit her on his way to New York. In a rational proposal, he would ask her to marry him, not for love, but for life and their common ground of too much loss.

My grandma worked, became a citizen, started a family, built a community, volunteered for organizations she cared about, and spent her free time watching the news and writing opinionated letters to political figures. Anwar Sadat, Jimmy Carter, Hillary Clinton, and others received her letters and wrote back. Her letter to Hillary ended with a nagging plea to abandon her long hair.

Shortly before she died at 92, I asked my grandma how it made her feel when people asked her about her accent. She said, "It makes me proud. Like I know about a whole other place." I also asked her what it was like when my grandpa died. She said she sat by his bed and "mixed the pages together." When I think of her, I imagine the layered contents of her own pages: a radio, bread, sisters, a photograph, chicken soup, children, grandchildren, a trip to Paris, chairs covered in plastic, Lawrence Welk, being hit by a bus, sewing her hands to a sewing machine, catching her hair on fire, Sanka Coffee, jars of noodles, an ambivalence towards God. In the act of dying, she said she didn't know how to die.

My grandma was outspoken and unapologetic. She was a nice person, too.

On November 8, 2016, the glass ceiling was supposed to shatter. Instead, when morning came on the 78th anniversary of *Kristallnacht*, all we found were the haunting echoes of broken windows. My grandma had put up with too much, lost too much, and fought too hard for me to not take the election results personally, for myself and for the millions like my grandma who are proud to be from another place.

Call me naive, and please, call me idealistic, but should someone arrive at my doorstep with broken English and a family weary from travel and war, I will welcome them in and make them a cup of Sanka. We are the same.

Randi Vessey, age 24
Administrative assistant for
Northeastern State University
Tahlequah, OK

Hands

I LOOK DOWN AT my hands turned upward in a shaky panic-like shape of reception.

I close my eyes tightly to where I can feel every crease of every wrinkle biting down on my face.

Desperation. Hope. Clarity. Faith. Purpose. Direction.

Where are you? I am ready to receive.

My eyelids are furiously fluttering, a sign of a busy, anxious mind, a sign I know all too well.

No matter how hard I force an even breath, my eyelids will not lie.

These are hard times. You cannot blink away all of the hatred that you are facing.

You cannot pretend this isn't happening.

Silence doesn't make this go away; silence only allows the hate to linger, to grow, to normalize.

I look down at my hands, still trembling, still open. I cannot wait any longer; time is fragile and limited.

I rotate my hands, palms down; I press them fiercely into my thighs, and again I close my eyes.

These are hard times. You cannot wait for the answer. You cannot wait for someone to fix it.

You cannot pretend this isn't happening.

It's time to do the work. Who can you count on if not yourself? You are just the person you need. You are just the person this world needs.

Do not allow oppression to win again.

Bully Rule

M Y GRANDMOTHER WAS a bully, and my father was the oldest of her three sons, the golden child. They lived in China in the 1910s, and while my grandfather was away working on an archeological dig, Dorothy liked to dress up like a nurse and minister to the locals. She filled her diaries with photos of herself in a hand-sewn uniform and stories of her sacrifice and hard work. She wrote that others called her a "difficult woman" because she demanded perfection in everything, a mantle she wore with pride.

Dorothy did not allow her sons to go to the local school or interact with their Chinese servants because she believed that they were trying to poison the children. She also would not let the boys play with one another to prevent them from bonding with anyone other than her.

When I was five years old, I heard a story about my uncle, Ian, from when he was about the same age. He had found a clutch of duck eggs by a river and when they hatched they imprinted on him. One of the ducklings survived and followed Ian everywhere he went. The two secretly slept together at night.

Upon discovering her son's new friend, Dorothy killed and cooked the duckling and forced Ian to eat it in front of the rest of the family. I don't know if this story is true, but I believed it at the time. Never for a moment did I doubt my grandmother's capacity for such a harsh lesson; I only wondered which was worse: to have had a friend, as Ian did, and been forced to eat it, or never to have had one at all, like my father.

My father grew into a troubled man, and I was the youngest of his three daughters, the black sheep. My dad tried desperately to give Dorothy a male heir, but it was not to be. After two failed attempts to conceive a son, my mother was content to leave well enough alone, but Grandmother and my father insisted they try one last time. My arrival was barely acknowledged, and my grandmother never called me by name. When I needed my birth certificate to get a driver's license at 16, it was nowhere to be found. My mother remembered that she had hidden it in a shoebox along with the few photographs and mementos of me as a newborn, but years later, she couldn't recall where she had put it.

My sisters and cousins spent their childhoods locked in a complicated dance with our grandmother. She would invite them to stay in her large home filled with priceless chinoiserie and old ancestral charts. If the children were good, they could admire the treasures she kept in the globe wernicke and choose something to receive in her will. The jade goldfish and the ivory dragon were two of the most coveted objects, and each was promised and re-promised to whichever grandchild was then held in the highest favor. All, I assumed, hoped Dorothy would die at the precise moment when they held that role, and not at a time when they had been demoted for speaking up or acting out. Since I could never gain her favor, I always looked forward to my grandmother's dying. I anticipated a time when my father would be able to finally earn a little peace of mind and maybe get to know me a little too, but that was not to be either.

If anything, life became harder after Dorothy's death. The house I was born in was on a cul-de-sac surrounded by other liberal faculty families from the small college where my father taught. Unfortunately, it was not large enough to hold my grandmother's things, so my father found us a farmhouse miles away from this community, big enough to hold the grand piano, paintings, and countless boxes of paperwork he had inherited. Our new home was surrounded by blue-collar folks who wanted nothing to do with my strange, elitist family. Neighborhood kids set fire to the yard and often beat me up after school. Even some of the teachers bullied me.

"Just be nice" was the only advice my mother could offer me when I came home from battle. I'm sure she meant this small entreaty to spur enough success and popularity in me to launch myself out of that godforsaken place, but her words just made me withdraw further.

My father spent most of his time deep in his study writing and researching books on religious history, while my mother did what she could to make do. Dad had always been unpredictable, but after Dorothy's death his moods grew even more volatile. Sometimes he came out of his cave to lavish praise on one of us for some accomplishment or trait we did not possess, but more often, he'd emerge to spit abuse, which always seemed perfectly aimed at the heart. We tried to forecast his emotional weather by watching his behavior closely, but none of us ever got it right. I know we each felt relief when one of his random cloudbursts hit someone else.

"You have no idea how hard it is to be married to that man," my mother would always say whenever any of us sought comfort from her afterward. I probably heard this phrase the most, because I inspired the majority of my father's anger. After my sisters left for school, my mother tried to make an ally of me against him, which resulted in even more abuse, triggering an endless circle of cause and effect, with no real safety to be found.

Eventually, I did launch myself out of that place, but it was not because I was popular or nice. I read a lot, and that helped me get scholarships, and I chose schools far, far away. I then chose jobs and relationships as different from my upbringing as I could find, one after another.

Decades later, I'm still running from that place. I never found great success, never lived up to all my potential. There were years when it was all I could do to keep a job to pay the bills. I'm the child of bullies, you see. I balk at the slightest hint of bad management and often find myself in power struggles with anyone unfit to rule me.

Over the years, I did find things to be thankful for. I have a partner who is good to me, loving friends, and great therapy, all of which have helped me understand my young, helpless self and see my relatives through the lens of mental illness rather than inherent evil. But I still mistrust everything and everyone a little and react to threat like an inbred Border Collie. When my current therapist first met me, she asked if I might consider myself a delicate and sensitive orchid growing in a field of more hearty and indifferent dandelions. I thought for a moment, and then told her I felt more like a dandelion growing in a field of Monsanto soybeans—I was as tough as anyone, but the soil had been poisoned against me.

*   *   *

The morning of November 9, 2016, I woke up in a cold sweat. I hadn't felt such panic since I was four or five years old. My guts were full of icicles, cars all felt like they were hurtling toward me on the freeway, and even silence was excruciating. The realization that a bully was going to be our next president hit me like a physical blow—and not just any bully, either, but an emotional infant who's as unpredictable, vindictive, and textbook Cluster B/Dark Tetrad as anyone I've ever encountered. My childhood nightmare now writ large: the world governed by this deep, deep danger I know too well.

How do I live with this?

It won't be easy. Even when I was very small, I somehow knew that there were safe havens out there, for other people at least, if not for me. Not everyone had families like mine; some had homes that were easy and good. But there are no safe havens now. This new president-elect is inescapable, and every single person on the planet will be affected by his crazy whims.

How do I live with the people who support him?

That won't be easy either. I live in Texas, and while my city is pretty liberal, most of my clients are in smaller, redder areas outside of town. Until a month ago, I got along well with all of these people. I never talked politics at work, and instead concentrated on the work we were doing together. Now I have to find ways to come to terms with the fact that most of these folks think our new leader is a good idea, and I cannot fathom that. At all.

Can they really not see him as I do?

No, they can't. They really can't. They would never have voted for him if they could. All these children of safe haven homes have no experience with life under Bully Rule. They don't know about the gas lighting, power plays, and false promises. They haven't lived with the countless disappointments and betrayals. That or they're bullies themselves.

As triggered as I am by having such a man in power, I must also remember that I have an advantage that others may not: I've had time to heal from my wounds. I've learned how to decrease the harm and raise my resilience, whether the bully is my relative, boss, or elected leader. We survivors of abuse are uniquely sensitive to authoritarian coercion and know some of the most powerful countermeasures to combat it.

Here are some of the lessons I learned as a child that I believe will help me in the dark days to come:

Deny tyranny my support—non serviam. I need never uphold the actions of an authority that does not serve my needs. There will be times when I have no rebuttal or counter-action, but I will always have noncompliance, first and last.

Be grateful if I am not held in favor. The apple of the bully's eye has the most to lose.

Nowhere is safe. Any security granted to me by the bully is temporary and illusory. The things I love will eventually be threatened whether I fight or not, so I may as well fight.

Do not compete with my neighbors for scraps. They are not the enemy—the asshole who pits us against one another is.

Do not dissociate from my own pain. There may be situations in which I am forced to eat my closest friend, but the grief and shame I will feel at their loss is better than the alternative.

Do not anticipate a great liberation. The death or outster of tyrants will not wipe the slate clean. Supporters and victims alike will be damaged for generations, but something, somewhere always emerges stronger and more beautiful from the struggle.

Believe others' pain. Bullies feed on isolation. I need not validate every belief or theory that others have, but I must believe their pain. If we all make ongoing efforts to view other people's experiences with dignity, even those who are most alien and incomprehensible to us, the bully has no power.

*   *   *

There is nothing more revolutionary than this last action. I know, because years ago, someone believed me. "Sunshine is the best disinfectant," my dear friend told me, as she opened up all the closets in my soul and looked inside. I am the person I am today, with some small measure of immunity, because of what she taught me. Lately I have found the challenge of applying her lesson nearly impossible, but I know I must view the people who support this administration with love and compassion, for my own sake and as well as theirs. I must remember that they will soon be victims too and their losses will be greater than mine.

As much as it infuriates me, I have come to accept the fact that I will be ruled by bullies yet again. After spending most of my life getting clear of them, I was hoping for a nice, easy middle age, free from the constant struggle to survive and remain sane. But that is not to be.

The days to come, I'm certain, will be filled with fresh trauma for myself and countless other souls. We will be asked to harden ourselves, and it will be tempting to do so. But I plan to do the opposite. This time, when I am manipulated, coerced, and lied to, I will not comply; I will stand, I will grieve, and I will validate and dignify others. I will honor what is fragile, vulnerable, and unique in myself and in everyone around me. I've already been a victim, so I know this terrain all too well, but I know how to fight now. My weakness is now my armor.

Brooke Collins, age 42
Anesthesiologist
Albuquerque, New Mexico

How Could It Not Have Been Enough?

NOVEMBER 8, 2015 was one of the best days of my life. At the age of forty-one, I married a man who is everything I want in a partner. He is kind, considerate, intelligent, beautiful, and an amazing parent to my young children. Life was bliss.

On November 8, 2016, my husband and I decided to meet after work and go to the spot where we had our first date. We would toast to a wonderful first year of marriage and watch as our nation elected its first female president. We were confident that election night would end in a victory for the candidate we supported—how could it not? In our microcosm of Albuquerque, New Mexico, the thought of Donald Trump's having any serious contention for the presidency was farcical. And so we settled in, ordered champagne, and watched.

When we left, things looked bleak. "It's OK," said my husband. "They haven't decided Florida. The polls haven't closed in the

West." It wasn't going to be the decisive victory we'd hoped for, which was something of a disappointment. But we would still prevail. We had to.

As the night wore on, I stopped checking the polls. I stopped watching the news. I went to bed, not wanting to hear the result announced. I cried. What else could I do but cry? I felt as though that legendary ceiling *had* shattered—it had shattered from the outside, some monumental fist pounding and pounding until the whole thing came crashing inward and left all of us bloodied and blinded by great shards of glass.

Until this election, I had never considered myself to be political. I grew up in a comfortable middle class home, the daughter of a military officer. I went to college, then medical school, and began my training as an anesthesiologist. I was busy, too busy to concern myself with the nuances of political discourse. I voted most of the time, but not every time. I would tell people who asked that I was *purple*—a mix of red and blue— and held no particular affiliation with a single party. I had my head down, my nose to the grindstone, making a life for myself and my family.

In 2012, when I was thirty-eight, my first marriage was failing. Eventually, I became a single mother with three children. I decided I needed a change—a new endeavor—and I began to explore the possibility of learning more about something that had always interested me: constitutional law. While still working as an anesthesiologist, I enrolled in law school in 2015 at the age of forty and am halfway through my courses now.

Perhaps it was my newfound, fledgling understanding of constitutional law that sparked a more vigorous interest in the political process. Perhaps it was living with my new husband, who pays so much more attention to world events than I ever did. Perhaps it was the threat of a megalomaniacal despot taking office. For one or all of these reasons, I paid attention this time. I gave money. I talked to people. I argued. How could it not have been enough?

I realized, in the days after November 8, 2016, that it wasn't enough. Sure, I stood my ground once in a while, but I was not passionate. I was not furious. I was willing to agree to disagree. I wanted to maintain a sense of decorum. I let others do the talking and walking and calling. I was squarely in a blue county in a blue state. I didn't need to convince anyone.

Now I know better. Now I realize that when we all lounge comfortably in apathy, we are complying. We are tacitly allowing the degradation of the fabric of who we are as a society. I am not a black woman in Georgia, or a Muslim in Alabama. I didn't know. I wasn't paying attention. Now I know a little more. I have no excuse. I will, in the immortal words of the great Leonard Cohen, *ring the bells that still can ring.* I will, quite selfishly, fight for exposure, for tolerance. I will fight tenaciously for peace, no matter how oxymoronic that sounds. I will fight for the rights of my daughters to be treated well and fairly. I will fight for the right of my autistic son to be given opportunities for growth and for treatment. I will fight for the right of a gay man in Florida or an immigrant in Kentucky to be treated with dignity and respect and the deference all people deserve. To fight for only a few of these individuals is to fail all of them. We cannot pick and choose which persons we consider worthy of protection.

Perhaps I am overreacting. Perhaps, as a few of my more conservative friends and family posit, Mr. Trump will surprise us with a deft hand at foreign policy and a swift intellect. I hope so; I sincerely do. I hope that I am terribly wrong about his proclivities. But even if I am wrong, is it wasted time to work for something more? Never. I never again want to go to bed, as I did the night of November 8, 2016, tearfully wondering what more I could have done. So I will talk, I will work, and I will finish my law degree. And maybe then, armed with education, and understanding, and a good bit of anger, I'll throw my own hat into the ring. If 2016 has taught us one thing, it's that the landscape has changed. And though many of us, including myself, saw the election of Mr. Trump as a blow against women in positions of power and influence in our country, I now choose to look at it differently.

The 2016 election taught me that anyone *can* be president.

It may as well be me.

Chris Hicks Butzer, age 58
Mortgage banker
Cave Creek, Arizona

Blood & Fear

I HAVE A SLOW-GROWING type of leukemia called chronic lymphocytic leukemia (CLL). I think about it as little ticking time bombs floating through my bloodstream. When there are enough of those microscopic bombs, I will need medical science to stop them from going nuclear. I accept this. I understand it and have the knowledge I need to fight it, and I will fight like crazy when it's time. For now, however, the fear of my disease has been pushed into the back of my brain, as a greater, more imminent fear has taken over. That fear is about the man who will be our next president. That's why I sit here in the late hour on a rainy night in the middle of December. I wake in the night, no longer thinking about my disease. I wake and remember what happened on November 8, 2016, and dwell on the horror that is this man.

November 8 started out as a glorious day. My husband and I had watched countless hours of campaigning, debates, news coverage, and talk shows leading up to this moment. The Democrats put forth three candidates who were smart, professional, experienced, and wise. I would have been happy with any of them, but in my gut, I knew Hillary had the right stuff for the job. The thought of electing the first woman president after 240 years of male-dominated rule made my heart sing. During the primary, I considered Bernie because he is such a champion of the 99%, but her foreign policy experience and sheer strength convinced me that Hillary was the one who could guide the country through perilous times. As I watched the debates, I was even more convinced. The woman is made of steel! Even while being stalked around the stage by a crazy man-child, she never missed a beat in her message.

So on that morning, I put on my best pantsuit and then had my husband, Steve, hang our American flag outside and take my picture of me standing by my car with the Clinton–Kaine bumper sticker on it. I drove to work smiling and singing with the windows down, anticipating watching the coverage later that night at home. A bottle of champagne was chilling in the fridge, and we planned to eat in front of the TV so that we didn't miss a single return. By about four in the afternoon, I couldn't wait any longer and left work to get home and start the festivities.

A lifelong Democrat, I've watched many nights of close elections. The Gore defeat by the Supreme Court decision was one I will never forget, and I still think *what if* when I reflect on the disaster that was W and his war-mongering advisors. You can trace a line from the horrors experienced by the children of Aleppo back to the decision to invade Iraq. The Middle East hasn't been the same since that day, and neither has the entire world. The ripples can be felt everywhere in the work of ISIS and the lone-wolf misfits who take up the cause.

Steve and I settled in to watch the election coverage, knowing it could take a long time for the numbers to reach 270. As it approached eight in the evening, a couple of intelligent friends were sending me messages, discussing each state, each county, what it meant, what was happening. A dreadful feeling came over me, and also a terrible sadness that he had conned so many people. I wrapped a blanket around myself and got quieter with each state's reporting in. I couldn't speak; there were no words. We went to bed and continued to watch it unfold, hoping some kind of miracle would push Hillary to 270. But no, the Electoral College had sealed our fate. I wept in bed, holding onto my husband when I knew it was over. I wept for the strong woman who had withstood so much hate, so much prejudice, and so much ignorance. I wept for our country. And I wept for myself.

The next morning, I drove myself to work, still proudly displaying my bumper sticker. In a daze, I stared ahead at the traffic, driving in the HOV lane in my electric car. Out of nowhere, a driver next to me laid on his horn. Suddenly alert, I waited for a crash. I looked over quickly, and the driver was right there, looking at me and making an obscene gesture. My heart was pounding, and now I was pissed. There was no imminent danger. A young white dude saw my bumper sticker and was celebrating his win in true Trump fashion. With hate. With fear. With aggression towards women. All of the anger I felt exploded, and I watched as he passed me on the right.

About a half mile ahead, the traffic slowed down as it always did this time of day. As I continued in the HOV lane, I began gaining on his car. My diseased blood was boiling. I could feel those tiny time bombs accelerating along with my fear and anger. In seconds I contemplated what I should do. The mantra "When they go low, we go high" had been floating in my brain over the past month. I know it's the only way. I saw that he was waiting and watching for me. I flashed him a peace sign as if to say, "I still have love, and I will not let your hate cause me more damage."

It took everything I had to do that, not to lash out, to react against my first instinct. That is also what I want from my leaders. A cool head, a steady hand, a thoughtful approach. That is definitely not what we are getting in January. The president-elect overreacts to every slight, every insult; retaliation is in his blood. He has no restraint at all.

So now when I wake in the night, I am no longer thinking about my leukemia. Within moments, I remember and think about the world. How will we survive this man and his undeveloped personality? How will the rest of the world react to his bombastic threats? The greatest country in the world just elected the least experienced leader at one of the most dangerous times. Somehow we have to find a way. We shouldn't just be surviving; we should be thriving and progressing. Do we really elect the leaders we deserve? I can't believe that, because the popular vote went to Hillary but we were a victim of the obsolete Electoral College. But listen to some of Trump's voters and you still hear the noise of long-standing, white-male-privileged bigotry and misogyny. That noise needs to die a well-deserved death for us to move forward.

Since my diagnosis, I've thought a lot about death and dying but more about living, not just the making-it-through-the-day kind of living but really living. I don't waste time anymore. When I'm feeling good, I'm the most joyous of people. I laugh like crazy and often cry. I act the fool sometimes just to hear my husband laugh, which makes me laugh. It's not in my nature to dwell on things for too long. I prefer to deal with issues quickly and go back to the pure joy of living. But this is different. I don't want to worry about this man who will be our next president, but like my disease, he must be watched and monitored. His actions must be kept in check. So I will force myself to be vigilant against the hate. I will stand with those he intends to oppress. I will fight for our hard-won civil rights, even for the rights of those who voted for him. Because it's the only way I know how to be. It's the right way.

Imagine if everyone felt like this. That's what I imagine in the middle of the night. I will never give up hope.

Crystal Sanchez, age 34
Entrepreneur and activist
Corrales, New Mexico

I Refuse to Go Back

IT WAS FIFTH period, right after lunchtime. I had broken up with him earlier in the day. I thought I was safe inside the classroom; surely he wouldn't cause a scene in front of a teacher and all of our classmates.

The door swung open. My heart sank.

He stood at the doorway and looked toward the teacher. "I need to speak to that fucking whore right there." He turned and pointed at me. Our eyes locked.

"Bitch, get your fucking stupid ass out here now."

Shocked, everyone turned to look at me, but nobody said a word. The teacher said nothing.

My body froze, my face felt like it was on fire, and everything slowed. I sank low in my seat. The shame was overwhelming. In that moment, I had two choices: I could either sit there and continue to be belittled in front of everyone or walk out feeling ashamed for giving in to his threats. I was mortified and wanted to disappear, so I chose the latter.

After we were in the hallway, he yanked off my necklace and

threw it in the trash. He hurled me against the lockers and spit in my face.

Looking back, I don't know why the teacher didn't intervene, but I'm sure my fifteen-year-old self was relieved no one got involved. It would have only made things worse.

In those moments of humiliation, degradation, and shame, I slowly disconnected from my body. My mind became my enemy, destroying me from the inside out, while my body became an empty bag of bones.

The humiliation and psychological abuse was much worse than the physical abuse. Physical abuse is dangerous, but psychological abuse is deeply rooted. I was living inside a prison, behind thick walls of terror, shame, and dread. At times, I feared I would die there or, even worse, live there forever.

Hearing you are a whore and a slut, being told you are worthless and ugly repeatedly—you begin to lose your identity after a while. The idea of brainwashing is to destroy the old identity and replace it with a new one.

After eight long years, I finally escaped the abusive relationship at the age of twenty-two.

For years, I was numb; I hid; I chased temporary gratification in an attempt to thwart the inevitable. I'd waged war with myself, the parts that didn't want to be examined—those deep, dark hidden crevices where shame and self-hatred resided.

I gradually clawed my way out of the self-loathing abyss. I began to let go of who I wasn't, to make room for who I was becoming. I eventually found my voice and vowed never to be silenced again.

On November 9, 2016, I was fifteen-years old again. I couldn't move. The light-headedness made it difficult to see straight. My body ached; I felt like I had been hit by a bus.

The defeat was excruciating, not because my side didn't win, but because we *all* had lost. The woman who had been to hell and back. The woman who had been punished for her husband's indiscretions, who was hated *because* of her husband—yet, also was somehow hated far more than her husband. The woman who was the most qualified person to ever run for president had lost to the man with no qualifications. She was you; she was me; she was us.

Many people have told me I need to give Trump a chance, but he has already shown me who he is. He's a man who has incited racism, sexism, homophobia, and xenophobia and believes it's okay to grab women by the pussy. A man who lacks compassion and empathy and who publicly humiliates anybody who disagrees with him. A man so vindictive that he's most comfortable when he's being cruel to others.

I refuse to give him a chance. I already know who he is. *When people show you who they are, believe them.* I learned that lesson long ago.

This place is familiar; we've been here before: the sights, the sounds, the smells, the expressions of hate so profound that the hate morphs into a physical manifestation.

White men have been in power since the inception of this nation, and the fear of losing control has created a group of deranged ideologues. They are being pulled down from their thrones kicking and screaming, and they are willing to bring democracy down with them if it means staying in power for four more years.

We thought we had already done the work. No, not even close.

The sweetness of faux liberation fooled me for a little while, until I looked around and saw others still living in the bitterness of a reality many of us believed no longer existed. I failed to notice how fragile was the institution in which I placed my trust, how easily weakened the foundation could become, and how vulnerable we all are to the art of the lie. I lived in a cocoon of oblivion for almost a quarter of my life, imprisoned of my own volition. But I have woken up to a world that needs my vigilance.

This experience has been a paradigm shift. I'm no longer taking my rights and the rights of others for granted. I'm no longer trusting my fellow Americans to make laws and decisions that are in my best interests.

I'm angry, but I've learned that anger is the physiological awakening within my consciousness. It has lit a fire inside me; it has forced me to rethink my boundaries. It's shown me that complacency is not an option. Anger is the emotion that arises when we feel obligated to make necessary changes.

It is difficult to admit the dark truth revealed on November 8, 2016. But it is hopeful to know the majority of our country is on the right side of history. The majority of our country champions acceptance and inclusion.

Slight modifications, however, are no longer enough. We must demand and take part in a complete transformation of every structure and system.

I will speak up and speak out for the disenfranchised, for the invisible, and for the forgotten. I predict the glass ceiling will be shattered by a countless number of fierce women who are willing to embrace inconvenience and discomfort to make their voices heard. Silence has never protected us. We will rise. The women in this country will write, resist, dance, disrupt, rebel, create art, protest, run for office, and take up as much space in this world as possible.

We will risk it all for love and justice because we will never go back.

Jennifer Bertrand, age 40
Holistic esthetician
Austin, Texas

Combat Boots and Tattoos

MY DAD DIED suddenly when I was eighteen. At the time of his death, I had a job at a grocery store in a small Arizona town. At work I stood trapped behind a cash register in loose-fitting Dickies' work pants and extra-large band tees, the graphics covered by the shapeless navy-blue smock every female employee was provided. (Men were usually not cashiers and were only required to wear a white polo shirt.) I stood within a line of women, ranging from teenagers to retirees, and I was usually the only one not wearing makeup. Despite the crap attire, I still managed to field comments from men old enough to be my grandfather.

"Why do you have a bandaid on your face?"

"Your boyfriend said, 'Shut up,' and you thought he said, 'Put 'em up'?"

"Are those combat boots? Do you think you're tough? Because I have been in combat, and you are not tough."

"You could fit two people in those pants; want some company?"

"You'd be prettier if you smiled more and fixed yourself up a bit."

Each man smiled innocently, fully aware I was at work and completely powerless. Their wives smiled indulgently while their husbands humiliated me. Their expressions never changed regardless of whether their husbands were engaging in "flirty" (harassing) banter or suggesting it was okay if a male partner had hit me. I wondered what their lives were like. If they were willing to say such things to a stranger, what words did they use at home to the people they loved?

After my dad died, I decided no one really knew who I was, and if looking nonthreatening and feminine gave people ideas, then I wanted to challenge those thoughts. I shaved my head, and as my long, red hair fell to the floor, so did the remainder of who I thought I was trying to be.

I started going to punk rock shows the summer after I graduated, and it gave me a sense of energy and community. I related to the lyrics, a lot of them reminiscent of the more politically conscious rap I had been exposed to as a child. Some of the bands had female members, and there, in my face, feminism resonated deeply. Here were women who had not only found their passion and their voices but also were screaming those voices into a microphone. Punk shows were mostly filled with men; so when a woman was in a band (or the rare all-woman band performed), the inclusion made me feel like I could be heard too. I got a tattoo on my calf that said *fight back*, with a small version of my fist, complete with bitten-down purple-polished fingernails. I wanted a reminder to be strong and follow my own path every day.

I needed to start over, but I was afraid. I wanted to fight the idea that I had to either believe what everyone else did or shut up. I wanted to challenge my own ideas of who I was and my self-perceived limitations. As a young person away from family structure, and independent in the world, I finally started to understand what I was fighting, but I had no idea the fight was going to last my entire life.

In 1997, I moved to San Francisco. I was out of the desert for good, leaving behind a stifling town where my dad died, and I never looked back. Working at a youth hostel, I surrounded myself with people I had never encountered before. Growing up in Texas, I was somewhat afraid of true diversity. Now I met people with different gender and sexual identities and different ethnic backgrounds and immigrants from different countries. I volunteered in Berkeley and San Francisco and discovered the issues I was passionate about: sexual education and freedom. I took classes at Good Vibrations in the Mission and learned about everything from solo sex to safer sex. I educated myself about my rights, the risks women face in the world, and the role sexuality plays in a person's greater identity.

By 2007, I had two-year-old twins. The years spent focused mostly on developing my own sense of self, and being somewhat apathetic towards the world at large, were long gone. I was now worried about what kind of world my children were going to grow up in. I wanted Hillary to take office in 2008. I voted for her initially, but I wasn't willing to live with another Republican term, and ended up supporting Senator Barack Obama. I had moved back to Texas a few years earlier, and the antiwoman vibe, even in the liberal bastion of Austin, stunned me. So many people told me how similar Austin was to Berkeley, but as I drove past church after church and truck after truck with pro-gun bumper stickers, I had to disagree.

In my late twenties and early thirties, I tried to figure out what to do with my *fight back* tattoo. Was I too old for it? Sometimes I was embarrassed by it. Some people mistook it for a racist statement, while others were surprised I was the "tattoo type." One woman stopped me as I pushed my double stroller and said that despite my tattoo I "seemed like a good mom." I was learning my new role as a mother, and I wasn't sure how my past and my tattoos fit into that. *Would it embarrass my kids? Was it relevant anymore? Should I put a pair of knitting needles in the fist? An organic carrot?*

In the end, I left it as is. I was married to a man who mocked my feminism and punk-rock youth and tried to use my open-minded ideals to manipulate, demean, and control me. I had grown up watching domestic turmoil and fell right into it myself. It took years, but I was able to find the courage to leave and give my kids a better life. In the years since, we've all flourished, but sharing custody means I'm stuck in a state I have next to no love for and whose values are moving further and further away from my own.

Meanwhile, the battles for quality education and women's reproductive rights were raging on in my home state. As time passed, I found it hard to be plugged in. Living in a world with daily microaggressions and true aggression from white men in power—the news of another local politician who wanted to limit my access to birth control and abortion, or cut funding to education and Planned Parenthood, abraded my very soul. I felt like I was swallowing the hatred and negativity my elected officials had for me and my children.

When it came time for a new election, I was lukewarm about Secretary Clinton. I supported her, but the raw excitement I had felt during the first Obama election wasn't there. Being a "blue dot in a red state" was unbearable, and I found it hard to believe that a Democrat's vote in Texas mattered. As the campaign progressed, my commitment to Hillary Clinton became more and more resolute. I wanted her to win; I felt certain she would. I watched as, one by one, the awful Republican candidates were eliminated, until the most unlikely candidate of all won the Republican nomination. I watched all of the debates and followed the news with a mixture of wonder and disgust, thinking, *Do people actually agree with this stuff? It was laughable . . . right? Surely my fellow Americans saw through this?* Every single person I knew (aside from extended family and in-laws) wanted to defeat him. I was smug, cocky even.

By the time Election Day came around, I was ready. I saw a woman in a conservative part of Austin wearing head-to-toe Hillary gear, and I marched up to her and gave her a high five. All of the news stories of rape, of Republicans' threatening to pull support from Planned Parenthood, and of limiting women's rights had left me feeling hollow and helpless. We were almost safe; we were almost going to live under a president who understood what it meant to be a woman in America. Maybe not a poor woman, or a woman of color, but a woman. It was a start, a first step.

I curled up on my couch, drink in hand, waiting tensely for her to defeat Donald Trump. Nervous excitement gave way to anxious disbelief. Before Florida was called, I went to bed. My older boys had watched all the debates and followed the race with me. They were excited for Hillary to win and proud to tell me they considered themselves feminists. The morning after the election results came in, I had to walk downstairs and attempt to explain how an unqualified man had beaten a very qualified woman. I was shaken to my core but wanted to make them feel they were safe despite the fact that the man who had run his campaign on pure hatred, had won. I want them to live in a country where men in power are people they can look up to. I never imagined I would have to explain that they should always respect women, even if the president of the United States didn't.

I tried to go about my normal life, but I found it impossible.

I couldn't sleep and I cried every single day. I drove through a conservative suburb in North Austin and was shocked to see an older white man holding a poorly decorated sign: *WE DID IT, HE WON! HONK IF YOU VOTED TO SAVE AMERICA!* I regret to say that I didn't, as Michelle Obama had urged, go high. I flipped him off.

Now I live in the aftermath of the election. I joined local grassroots groups and worried about whether or not to wear a safety pin to show my support for people who may be targeted for hate crimes. I watched the news of hate crimes sharply increase as our then president-elect gleefully engaged America on social media; I asked myself if I was actually part of the problem.

Some days, numbness is inescapable. I've joined a project to knit hats for women marching in Washington, DC, on the day after the inauguration. As I knit the fuchsia yarn, I'm connected— to myself, my punk rock/DIY past, my community, the women who will be marching and wearing the very hats I am creating. I plan to march locally and involve my older children. First we will attend a rally to protest the bill that would require burying fetal remains from miscarriages or abortions performed in a hospital, and then a rally to protest this administration's seeking to erase the progress we have made. I hope to volunteer with a few different local grassroots organizations because working locally makes the most sense to me.

I've tried hard to not let the results of the election render me joyless in my personal life. On days I feel most hopeless, I gain strength by focusing my energy outward instead of in. I wallowed; I did. But now I'm ready to fight back. At forty years old, I finally found my voice, and I'm going to use it to defend those in my community and in my country who may be marginalized. The confidence that had eluded me my entire life is finally here.

Two things have helped me during these uncertain times: journaling and rage-scream-crying the lyrics to my favorite old songs. I've found so much comfort in the music I've listened to my whole life. I thought I was too old for it, but it turns out, the lyrics are more relevant than ever.

My *fight back* tattoo is permanent.

Kari Pottinger, age 42
Editor
Austin, Texas

Grabbing Back

NOVEMBER 8, 2016, 9:30 p.m. I knew it was over. Knew it like I knew when my stepbrother would hold my hand and put it under the covers. Knew it like when he would call me into his room late at night. Knew that Trump, the other "pussy grabber," would win.

I muttered something to my husband, no idea what, and went upstairs. I buried myself under the covers, the way I'd done since I was six, when it had all started for me, and now, thirty-five years later, here I was again. But now my nightmare was going to run the entire country. A man who had made rape culture normal, made it all just "locker room" talk.

Two days. That's how long it took for my dad to call me. I think he was both scared and waiting for the dust to settle around his headstrong liberal daughter. He was a conservative Christian minister, after all, and I went and married the Jew. My father had the gall to tell me he didn't vote for Trump, and left a question hanging there, then what did he do? I'd heard him call Hillary a "bitch" way back in the early 2000s, around when the first gay Episcopalian bishop was elected. He gave me a canned speech about how the pendulum of politics swings; how checks and balances worked; and that Trump couldn't do anything "that bad," a sad but somewhat sweet attempt to keep his daughter from feeling any worse. He, after all, didn't know about the stepbrother, his wife's son.

I think I nodded . . . a lot; muttered, "Yeah," a few times; and then hung up after an "I love you, Dad." We'd go back to talking about the weather and movies next go-round. When my stepmother texted me the next day to say she wasn't coming to Thanksgiving—because there might be "political talk" among the mostly liberal crowd, except for her and my dad—my husband's advice was "Call her."

"Dammit. That's hard. Can't I just text back, *I understand, but we'll miss you?*"

"*Call her.* She's got what? A good ten or fifteen years left in her? Do you want to see her again?"

I waited thirty seconds.

"Well?" he asked.

"I'm still thinking."

"Babe!"

"Okay, fine, grrr, I'll call her."

"And remember . . . she's a narcissist. Diagnosed. You won't ever be good enough for her."

"Thanks, hon."

"Just a reminder of what thousands of dollars in therapy has taught you."

My heart was beating like crazy, but I picked up the phone and began pacing my bedroom. My stepmother didn't know about her son's past proclivities. That was an added worry.

She picked up my call with a frog in her throat or a rattle of fear. Her thin "hello" made my stomach drop. The woman scares the shit out of me to this day. I imagined her sitting on their crisp white duvet cover, fresh tulips on the bedside table. She'd be getting ready for her "hair frosting" appointment before lunch at the club with Sarah.

"Um, hi," I said.

"You just caught me. I'm heading to get my nails done."

Close.

"Well, I got your text, and I'm really sorry that you're not comfortable coming to Thanksgiving."

"I just think it's best. I'm not good at political discussions and with me voting for

Trump . . . I mean, you know I did that while grimacing, don't you? I mean, he can be so crass, but I just couldn't vote for *that woman.*"

The bile in my stomach rose up and my head started to spin. "But what about his appointment of Bannon? The guy who runs the white supremacist website? The anti-Semite? I mean . . . my husband, my family?"

"I need to do my research on that, but we really need to give Trump a chance. He's our president now." She sounded as if she were reading from a fax she'd received from Fox News earlier that day.

I ran to the bathroom and dry heaved. Then again.

Silence on the other end of the phone.

"Are you back?" she asked.

"Yes."

"We went through eight years of Obama. I mean, when he said, America is no longer a white Christian country, my heart just broke."

Oh my God. Did she just say that?

"Did you just say that?"

"And we respected him as our president."

"Do you really think Christians are under attack?"

"I know we are. Your father was going to be forced to marry gay people."

"When? I didn't know that."

"It was headed that way."

I rolled my eyes and wished I was video calling.

"He did vote for Trump, by the way," she said. "Your father."

I bit my lip and started to cry. *Daddy.*

"What do you tell the girls where you volunteer?" I blurted out, wanting to hurt her. "Those girls who've escaped from their pimps, and have finally found a sanctuary . . ." I felt my heart begin to flutter and my body almost levitate. What was I about to do?

"What do you tell them about what Donald Trump said? About grabbing a woman's pussy? What do you tell them? WHAT DO YOU TELL THEM?" I screamed this. I'd never raised my voice to her before, and I was afraid, almost dropping the phone.

Silence.

"What do you tell the girl who you're talking with on the phone who's been molested? What do you tell her about Donald Trump?" I said, standing taller and looking at my puffy eyes in the bedroom mirror.

"Are you talking about yourself?" she whispered.

I was quiet for a moment. *This is it. No turning back.* "Yes. Me."

"I tell her it's not okay."

I fell to the floor, sobbing. "Thank you . . . thank you."

There were a few seconds of quiet, but she offered nothing more. "So a woman at the church makes brownies in the shape of turkeys. They're precious. I'll be sending a dozen with your father for Thanksgiving. My treat."

"Thank you," I repeated, my heart breaking. I nodded and repeated myself again before hanging up.

I'm so glad we had a chance to talk.

2016 is over. So there's that.

Elisabeth L. Sanchez, age 39
Writer
Las Cruces, New Mexico

I Will Not Let Them Turn Me into Something I'm Not

I FINISHED MY THIRD glass of wine and turned off the TV. It was close to midnight, but instead of heading upstairs to bed, I found myself in the kitchen, rummaging around in the freezer for my husband's cigarettes. He claimed the subzero temperatures kept the cancer sticks from going stale, which was a common problem. Carlos smoked only when he went drinking with his friends, and between his job, our three kids, and myself, social hour didn't happen often.

Cigarette in hand, I wobbled to the front door and stepped outside. A black November sky hung over the dimly lit streets of my neighborhood. A dog barked in the distance. Daytime brought the children and their laughter, the rat-tat-tat of footsteps running along the pavement and tumbling along the rocks of our desert lawns. Only at night did the well-maintained streets of adobe and stucco houses take on a quiet stillness. Usually I felt calmed by its mute inertia. But tonight felt eerie, as if the children had not just simply disappeared into their homes but had disappeared from the world altogether.

I walked down the steps to the lawn and took a seat on the wood bench. I lit the cigarette and smoked it down to the filter. Only after I had exhaled the last cloud of smoke did I allow myself to lean down and let out the first of what would be many loud sobs that shook my entire body.

* * *

My America exists in a tiny southwestern corridor of the country, a humble desert sprawl sandwiched between the Doña Ana and Organ mountains. My America is not much, but it is all I have. And so it is everything.

I had many reasons for being afraid of Trump and what his presidency meant for the people I love; my uncle Cliff was one of those people. He and his life partner, John, practically raised me while my ultraconservative father was busy drinking and doing drugs. John and my uncle had been together for thirty-five years and were the happiest, most functional couple you could ever meet. John lost his battle with pancreatic cancer in 2012, just before he and Cliff would have been able to legally marry. Cliff still resides in the home they shared together. He is doing well, but some days are tougher than others. During the campaign, he and I would often speak about Trump's shenanigans and shake our heads at the ridiculousness and terror of his campaign.

* * *

I went with my eldest daughter Katrina to vote on the day of the election. At eighteen, she was voting for the first time, and she had a dog in the fight more than anyone else I knew. She is a quarter Hispanic, a quarter African American, and bisexual to boot. On top of all that, she was set to join the navy in May.

That evening, I poured my first glass of Cabernet and turned on the news just as the polls in the northeast were beginning to close. The kids had already had dinner, and by 6:30 p.m., Brinda was rubbing her big blue eyes and looking sleepy.

"Ba ba, maaa!" she demanded.

I scooped her up. Her curly brown hair tickled my nose as I kissed her little neck. I laid her gently in her crib before tiptoeing back downstairs to watch the results, my heart pounding with excitement. Carlos was opting to stay upstairs and watch a movie with our son, Hunter.

"Keep me updated!" he yelled when I passed him in the hallway.

*   *   *

Warm water flowed from the kitchen faucet, rinsing the soap from my hands. I ripped off a paper towel and dried my skin and then picked up my phone and drunkenly texted one of my husband's Trump-supporting cousins: *Michael, thank you and f*** you for your vote—the next four years will ruin our country.*

I stumbled up the stairs to my bedroom and crawled into the sheets, pushing myself against Carlos, suddenly ravenous for his warmth. He reached for my hand and held it.

"That horrible man is going to win," I said in a half hysterical whisper.

Carlos sat straight up in bed. "Are you serious? What the hell is wrong with everybody?"

I didn't answer. He reached over and held me. I felt him draw in a very deep breath and then slowly let it out. "It will be okay. It will. I love you," he said.

*   *   *

Brinda woke up just after five in the morning. I heard her cooing and stirring in her crib through the monitor. "Baby. Baby baby. Ma ma ma ma. Maaaaaaaaaa! Baby!"

I slowly forced myself out of bed, releasing the air from my lungs and stifling my tears as I dragged my feet down the hall and into her room.

"Good morning, Princess!" I said, forcing a smile. She jumped up and down, holding tightly to the railing of her cherry wood crib. I laid her gently on the queen-sized bed in her room and changed her while singing her favorite good morning song (to the tune of "Happy Birthday"): "Good morning to you! Good morning to you. . . ."

I carried Brinda downstairs, placed her in her high chair, and started cooking breakfast. In robot-mode, I took out the ingredients for my famous breakfast burritos—green chile, bacon, egg, and cheese. I could hear Carlos upstairs getting his clothes out of the closet, putting on his heavy leather belt and pushing his feet into his clunky size-13.5 black steel-toed boots. My baby girl was watching me intently from her high chair, devouring strawberries.

I felt like a zombie. I was just going through the motions. Part of that fog was definitely because of the wine; the other part was my consciousness not wanting to fully awaken or become aware of the country in which I had awoken. I was dreading turning on the TV or looking at my phone. I could already imagine what all of the Trump supporters were posting. I wanted to vomit, and the urge had nothing to do with the wine from the night before.

"Well?" Carlos asked, walking into the kitchen.

"I can't," I said, and my eyes welled up with more tears.

Carlos picked up the remote and turned on CNN. And there he was: this person who had called Mexicans rapists and criminals, mocked a reporter who is disabled, and bragged about being able to sexually assault women because he was famous—this man the KKK supported was our president-elect. My husband quickly changed the TV to our local news so that he could catch the weather report, and I went to shower before he left.

* * *

I was in the middle of bawling my eyes out and combing my braid out with my fingers, staring blankly past my reflection and into nothingness, when Hunter came around the corner. My son rubbed his tired blue eyes.

"She won, right, Mommy?" he asked with a hopeful smile.

I turned to him and looked down. "No, sweetie; I'm sorry. She didn't."

He looked at me in complete disbelief, and my crying escalated. My arms reached around him, pulling him into a tight embrace. I told him his daddy and I would never let anything bad happen to him. I told him that I didn't want him to be sad and that everything would be okay (although the last part, I wasn't too sure about).

The rest of the day felt like the day after a close relative dies. I cried off and on. At midday, I went online to see how the rest of the world was dealing. I signed into social media and checked my online liberal women's group. I started commenting on others' posts, and they began replying to me—comforting me, sharing my fears and sadness. I began feeling better and very cautiously started sending friend requests to some of the women. At the same time, I began unfollowing many of my husband's family members, including the cousin I had drunk-texted the night before.

* * *

As the days passed, my new friends posted ideas, petitions (I signed them all), and actions we could take to make us feel like we were standing up against Trump's America. I wrote letters and postcards and made calls to elected officials, but I still had this emptiness inside of me—this sense of dread. I knew I could not go out and fix the country's brokenness on my own, so I kept communicating with my new friends: listening, commenting, sharing laughs as well as tears. I still felt I needed to do something else.

I was scrolling through my feed a few weeks later and came across a post from one of my new friends. She was devastated—her bank account was overdrawn, and there was no hope of being able to afford Christmas gifts for her kids. I private-messaged her, asking for her email address. An hour later, I sent her a gift card. I can't explain how much better reaching out and helping a specific individual who really needed it, made me feel. That statement sounds silly because my help was just a gift card, but the gesture was also more than that. My action was a way of showing solidarity. So if you have the chance to help someone, do it. Sometimes you can help with a meal or a kind word, or even just by listening. You never know how much even a small action helps someone.

I have had the opportunity to help others since then, and I have acted each time. Doing so has actually saved my sanity. It has reminded me that no matter what challenges we are facing—no matter what Trump tries to destroy—Trump and the people who support him cannot change who I am or what I stand for.

I've learned that the most important thing to do is to stay involved. Since the election, I have felt as if basic human decency is on the line. Many people are in situations different from mine, who will be much more adversely affected by his win. I will be okay—not as okay as I would be if I were a man, but okay nonetheless. I fear for those who are now being openly harassed, those who are at risk for deportation, those who are in fear simply because of their religion or whom they love. That is why I pay attention when I am in public. I want people to know I will stand up for them against this hate. The best thing I can do is to stay who I am—kind, compassionate, and accepting. This is my response: for all of their ugliness, I will do something beautiful for those who stand against them—whether it's for a friend I know only from the Internet or one of my friends I see often who are as bewildered and frightened as I. My small efforts seem like not much, but if everyone does a little, through those combined efforts we can change the world for the better. I won't give up, I won't stop fighting, and I will not let *them* turn me into something I'm not.

Tina Mougouris, age 50
Sociology professor
Houston, Texas

They Didn't Know
We Were Seeds

I TOOK A DEEP breath and walked into my classroom. It was packed. Every student was in attendance, which is the norm for exam day. But today was not a test day. Their faces said it all. Disbelief, shock, disappointment. I guess they were expecting me, their professor, to say something, to make sense of it, but I could not. I lectured but struggled through it. I still needed to process what happened the night before. On November 8, 2016, we elected a man to the highest office in our country, who, only two weeks prior, had been caught on tape boasting of sexual assault. A man who mocked a disabled reporter. A man who referred to Mexicans, a demographic that comprises most of my class, as rapists and alleged that they were bringing drugs into our country. A man who talked about creating a registry for Muslims. A man who saw Blacks as a homogeneous group, all living in poverty. A man who was not endorsed by any of the country's major newspapers but supported by the KKK. A man who was not even supported by his own party and denounced by most of their leaders. How could this be?

I have been a teacher at a community college for twenty years. My school is in Pasadena, which is a suburb of Houston, Texas. I have seen a demographic shift in the time I have worked here. It was a predominately white, working class area when I started working here in the mid 1990s. Pasadena was a honky-tonk town. *Urban Cowboy* was filmed here in the early 1980s, solidifying that reputation. It also had a Klan presence. Many of them have since gone underground, but it's still here. Many of the residents were transplants from the Rust Belt who came down to find jobs in the oil and gas industry. They were employed by many of the surrounding petrochemical plants. Now I find that when I look at my roll sheets, I see *Gonzalez, Ramirez,* and *Garcia*—Hispanic names. My colleagues and I were also excited when in the past year, two Vietnamese restaurants opened near the campus. This clearly reflected a demographic shift—one that I embraced wholeheartedly as a professor of minority studies.

"What scares me more than Trump is Pence," stated one of my students later that week. "He believes in gay conversion therapy. We deal with a lot of shit being gay. Families who don't accept their gay son or daughter can sign them up for this." Others spoke about their fears of being deported or having family members deported. As an instructor, I know this fear is real. I organize a trip to the Harris County Jail every year. Since a valid state-issued ID is required to attend, some students have been unable to go since they do not have the required documentation. Some will confide in me as to why; others come up with excuses.

That every student was present in my class on November 9, is no surprise to me. They wanted to be with others while they struggled to understand what happened the night before. I remember seeing the same expressions on students' faces days after the Oklahoma City bombing and the September 11 attacks. They wanted to be with others who could make sense of what happened. This feeling wasn't limited to my students. Many in our country tried to understand the outcome of the election. We sought each other out on Facebook and Twitter. Lifelong Democrats, such as myself, gained hundreds of new friends daily. We all wanted to make sense of this. We started organizing protests and marches. There was even a discussion of a "blackout" on Inauguration Day.

Through my friends, both old and new, I see that we are all doing what we can to deal with this election. I am trying to combat prejudice and discrimination through education. I have invited guest speakers to talk to my classes. These guest speakers represent the marginalized groups that Trump mocked—a trans woman; a disability rights advocate; a professor of African-American studies who specializes in the Civil Rights Movement; and the executive director of CAIR, the Council of American Islamic Relations. I want my students to see the people whose lives will be impacted by the policies of the Trump administration. I hope that my students will take their stories and tell their friends and family about what they learned.

There is a proverb that has been circulating in social media: "They tried to bury us. They didn't know we were seeds." I believe that through education, we can undermine and combat the hate that has been unleashed by this election. We will not be buried. Our voices will be heard.

Valerie Fulton, age 56
Freelance writer and community college professor
Austin, Texas (and the Blue Hill Peninsula, Maine)

Permission to Speak

SHORTLY AFTER A quarrel with my ex-husband in the newer of the two Mueller Starbucks˙ coffee shops, I bought a 27-acre historic homestead on the coast of Maine. I know: it seems like a strange reaction. It happened very fast. I boarded a flight from Austin and conducted the brief house hunting process with an efficiency I didn't realize I possessed. Finally, I plopped down in a chair before the large stone fireplace in the great room of the smaller of the two houses and announced, "I'm going to buy this place." It was the most thrilling moment of my life. Now that the tender grass around the buildings has been ransacked by my neighbor's backhoe in order to make way for a new septic system, I have a more jaded view of things. But at the time, birds were singing, and the air was full of raw energy. I saw myself wearing warm pajamas and a robe, with a steaming mug of tea, sitting down to write.

* * *

I grew up in suburban Massachusetts during a period of social transformation that I watched through the sanitized filter of television programs like *The Brady Bunch* and church group outings to Boston, during which we saw Black people wearing Afros and combat gear in our hushed walk through the Common. My parents embraced a thoroughly conventional life. At Christmas, Connie Francis and Perry Como sang while we opened the exact same toys our friends were opening beneath their own glittery trees. We ate meals inspired by the pages of *Redbook*. I slept in a canopy bed with lilac flounces and did my hair in curlers to look like Dorothy Hamill.

For my mother, "being normal" was a way to escape the chaos of her childhood, that place where my grandmother came home from work to get drunk in her bedroom, and my grandfather stayed out looking for a dame with money. Things would be different for us. There would be no secrets. The house would stay clean. On family drives home from Sunday dinner at my grandmother's duplex in Watertown, my mother pointed out scenes from her youth. This is where the mafia hung out. Here is the place she walked home doubled over with pain from a ruptured appendix. I looked through the window of our Rambler˙ sedan and saw streets glazed with ice, in which the fractured glow of a stoplight shone too brightly. It was hard to imagine my mother sashaying down the block, gangsters' eyes passing over her. It was hard to imagine my mother ebullient or scared. Such was the force of her will to power.

Like most people who don't know they are pretending, she took things a bit too far. The house was more than clean; it had to be spotless. She searched my room, reading my journals and the stories I wrote for school. She went through my handbag. My body was her clay to mold. When I was sick, she came into my room spraying choking clouds of Lysol˙ spray. When I suffered from constipation, she held me down on the bathroom floor so that my grandmother, a practical nurse, could administer an enema. Years later, as a teenager, I sat on the toilet of the same bathroom, submitting to the painful ritual of blackhead removal. Her disgust at my imperfections sent a clear message: *unlike her, I wasn't normal.* Of course, in time I learned to mock her dire conventionality. Being the perfect housewife was hardly my idea of a successful life. But inside, I felt ashamed.

A couple years ago, visiting my parents, I opened a box of high school memorabilia. There were the usual cards, autographed playbills, and photographs. Neatly grouped, profoundly unrevealing, nothing about these documents spoke to the kind of girl I'd been. No hopes or dreams. No vestiges of madness or bitchery or plain old despair. Emotionally, the box was empty. That's what happens when you're groomed to be a prop in someone else's story. The person you might have been, your authentic self, goes into hiding. You leave behind no clues.

When I think about the effect that Donald Trump's election has on me—the visceral effect—I think about this desperate need to shape reality, how the illusion of reality can be more seductive and tempting than cold hard facts. I watched the primary debates unravel one by one as Trump refused to acknowledge any reality outside his own. The economy was of no importance compared to the size of his hands or the deals he had made. His opponents were sucked into this world of lies and endless subjectivity. The stronger their grasp of economics and political reality, the easier it was for him to pick them off. Their outrage at his shamelessness, their refusal to lower the discourse, their stammering contempt, and finally their inauthentic schoolyard jibes, made them losers in the eyes of Americans accustomed to the lens of reality television, where being the last person standing is the only thing that matters.

* * *

The quarrel with my ex took place because he wanted me to move to California. He'd been offered a prestigious directorship position, and he was mulling it over. If that was asking too much, he felt sure I would remain in Austin until our daughter graduated high school. That way, the ex could visit his girlfriend and daughter at the same time. He thought he would keep the house as a *pied-à-terre* in the city. He was being practical.

"If you leave Austin," I said, "I'm moving back to New England. Why would I stay here when I don't have to anymore?"

I didn't expect my ex to react to this announcement by storming out of Starbucks in a huff. My response was not really unpredictable. We'd fought about it often. "Mommy hates Austin," he used to tell our daughter. The fact that he reneged on our agreement to leave Texas once he got established in his career is one of the main reasons we divorced. He'd slapped a geographic restriction on the divorce decree because of the flight risk I represented. The only explanation I can come up with for his outrage is that he never actually saw me as capable of exerting a separate will—in the same way that my mother couldn't see my destiny as separate from her own. Though I never thought they were alike—and in fact, they can't stand each other—I realized they both objectified people, fitting them into their preconceived scripts. They didn't see this thinking as causing confusion or pain. They felt justified. More than justified—when others didn't agree, they felt attacked. They fought back righteously in any way they could, as if their lives depended on it. Insults. Court orders. Threats.

*   *   *

One portrait of the Trump family continues to haunts me. Taken in the penthouse of the Trump Tower, with the lights of Manhattan glimmering in the background like jewels in an opium dream, the photo shows Donald seated in a golden,

Baroque-inspired armchair with Melania, coiffed and waxed, standing next to him. Her posture would be regal were it not for the strange dissociative expression on her face. Wind from an unseen source blows the batwing sleeve of her gown at an unnatural angle, such as one sees in fashion spreads. The child, seated on a large stuffed lion he is much too old to play with, has the same look of uncomfortable detachment. Trump himself is grinning broadly. His expression invites the viewer to see this is a real photograph, a real family, and that is perhaps the most disturbing thing about the shot.

Trump's dynastic narrative has me deeply troubled about his ascendency into the geopolitical arena. That narrative is squarely at odds with the principles of our democracy. He cannot have the kind of power he wants without violating trade agreements and peace treaties. He cannot have the society he wants without violating our constitutional rights. In fact, much has been written about the political threat he and his followers pose to democracy for precisely these reasons.

I also worry about something slightly different. How can we continue to speak authentically, as the diverse citizens of a nation, when our reality is under siege?

*   *   *

My own personal reality shifted that day at Starbucks. Watching my ex leave the coffee shop and get into his car, I felt a remarkable sense of freedom and clear-headedness. It was something I thought I would never experience: a defining moment. I realized I been waiting for a permission that would never come, the permission to be myself. How ridiculous. I remembered wandering the aisles of an upscale grocery store near my house, gripped with anxiety, tears streaming down my face, because the seafood department didn't have fresh mahi-mahi, and my ex needed it to make his signature dish for colleagues whom he had invited to the house for dinner that night. The same afternoon, I called a real estate agent in Maine.

I now own a two-house compound with a lovely barn, a three-acre meadow, twenty acres of mixed woods, and a giant blueberry field. The larger of the two houses was built in 1812 by the son of one of the original settlers. The more reasonably sized Adirondack-style cabin in the back, constructed to house overflow guests of the family from whom I bought the place, I am converting into a four-season property to live in once my daughter graduates from high school. There are deer in the woods, and at night I've heard the call of loons. For the better part of June, the meadow is full of blooming lupine. I can hardly wait to watch the first snow of the season fall on the moss that surrounds the cabin.

For a long time, I was uncertain about what to do with the larger house. Should I simply rent it out as a vacation property? Take in boarders? Cater weddings? I was so sure that Clinton would win the election that one of my ideas, to run a summer enrichment program for girls, seemed frivolous; our new president would speak for girls.

However, the idea of a summer program came back to me with clarity as soon as I learned that Trump would be our next president and a backlash against women was all but inevitable. Like moms across the United States, I sat on my bed sobbing with my daughter as the election results came in. Although she wanted "the girl to win," my thirteen-year-old cried largely because I was so upset. I cried because I knew we had failed an entire generation of girls. Collectively, our votes said that both misogyny and a lifetime of work on behalf of women's rights could be overlooked and trivialized.

In the aftermath, I continue to watch as the narrative shifts from women to the white working class, from a latent conversation about patriarchy to a rebuke that Democrats failed to take white men seriously enough. I'd like to show first-generation college-bound girls how to succeed in a university environment. But more than that, I want to build a space where girls learn to value their unique stories as women and future leaders. In order to speak authentically, one must know it is okay to follow one's own path without asking permission. I want to share that gift of insight.

West

"The children of the revolution are always ungrateful, and the revolution must be grateful that it is so."[26]

—Ursula Le Guin

26 K., Le Guin Ursula. The Day before the revolution. New York: UPD Publishing Corporation, 1974.

Marie Ellis, age 40
Telecom technician
Denver, Colorado

I'll Be Here When You're Gone

I GOT OUT OF my truck, opened the side panel to access my tools, and announced my arrival. I felt someone watching me—eyes I could sense had a preconceived idea about me and my abilities. My core pulsed. I put on my game face that showed this Frank *you don't intimidate me.*

I've met many Franks. *Frank* is the name I give to customers who bully and tell *me* how to do *my* job. Here, Frank was a white older man closer to his seventies. He answered his front door with an imposing grin. "It's not a phone man. It's a phone woman! They sent you to fix my trouble? And good looking too!"

Jesus Fucking Christ, here we go. I shoved that pulsing into my tool belt. "My looks have nothing to do with how well I do my job."

He quickly backpedaled. No apology.

Frank was convinced the issue lay up the street on a random fucking pole, because four years ago, that was how the "guy" fixed it then. *Oh, please send me on a wild goose chase up a pole where your problem* isn't! "Maybe the problem is on a pole up the street, but I have to determine that by testing at the telecom interface on your house. Can I please get in your backyard?"

Frank led me out to what I requested, but he had a bunch of stuff piled up in front of it. *Great.* He broke a flowerpot in the process of making room and began throwing things in a passive-aggressive way so as to make me feel guilty. I rolled my eyes at the hilarity of the situation, but Frank still hadn't reached I-gotta-tell-the-guys-this status.

Instead of moving out of the way and allowing me in, he began telling me how the interface works, equipment I've worked on six to eight times a day for decades. "Why don't you let me in there so I can actually do what I came here to do?"

Frank had found a way in to observe closely. He was breathing my air. *Gross.* He instructed, "You have to unplug that little plug," and pointed to an isolating jack. *I know very well what this plug does, and I will unplug it at the exact moment I want it unplugged.* When I unplugged it, Frank exclaimed, "Atta, girl!"

"I *do* know what I'm doing after twenty years in the industry, but this will take me a while. If you'd like to go inside and wait, I can let you know when I'm done."

He got the point, hustled to go inside, and slammed the back door.

When I fixed the problem, it wasn't on the pole up the street. I told him he was up and running. He replied, "I'll be darned! It is working!" *Of course it is, dick!*

Another Frank, a former coworker I dub "Office Frank," noticed I was wearing a pair of waterproof camouflage pants I kept after leaving the military. He said, "Did you actually serve in the military, or do you just like to wear things like that?"

What the fuck? I felt the room begin to spin and said, "I was in the military! These were—"

He interrupted, "I think it's offensive when people wear stuff like that and didn't actually serve." *Franks love to backpedal and explain in such a way to suggest I offended them.*

Another coworker stopped Office Frank's elitist rant to defend me, and I blurted out: "You're so concerned my camouflage pants are offensive to veterans but fail to realize *you* just insulted one!"

Nearly Naked Frank, another mid-sixties white man, wore nothing but boxer shorts. That he didn't see the need to put on more, bothered me, but I was in his home. I stood in Frank's living room impatiently listening to his vexation. Frank started to sweat. I knew the install would go smoothly, but the longer he talked, the longer he'd be without service. I interrupted and asked if I could get started in his backyard. I laid my tools out and began making connections. Through a window, he asked if he should call the other provider and complain. I replied, "Sure. You can do that."

"How am I supposed to call? I don't have a phone, you fucking bitch!"

I marched through Frank's house and out Frank's front door. I heard him ask me where I was going, but I'm not losing sleep that he didn't get an answer out of me. He still had no phone.

* * *

The first time I voted I registered as a Republican at eighteen. I knew it was my right to vote even if I had no idea what I was doing. Mom suggested she and I go together. Looking back, it makes sense Dad wasn't there; I wondered why he wasn't but didn't ask. While who and what I voted for was a blur, I remember the experience.

A few years later while enlisted in the military, I paid little attention to politics. Then after climbing poles for a few years, I became a union steward. As with the desire I have now, back then I wanted to be more active in improving the lives of those around me. I learned Democrats were for the working people and unions by fighting for living wages, healthcare, and overtime regulations. During contract negotiation time, I organized teams of strikers, made picket signs, and motivated coworkers. I even took my young son to the union hall. He recalls helping make the picket signs and sleeping in the back of my car when organization efforts went late. I felt it was important for him to be there and see what his mom worked so hard for.

When Obama won in 2008 and 2012, I cried both times when confetti and balloons fell signifying Obama's win, and because . . . maybe . . . racism was dying. Anyone following Obama has large shoes to fill. Any person with emotional intelligence would want to take a bath after observing Donald Trump's behavior. His "circle talk" insults the average intellectual. Interruptions, insults, and gaslighting—every time he speaks. He is a bully. He is a *Frank*.

This year, voting was very basic: an ink pen, circles to fill in, and my kitchen counter.

My eighteen-year-old son's first time voting rang familiar. Because of my political involvement and the Internet, he was more aware than I was at that age. He read the proposals and asked questions on items he found confusing—I am proud of him! Once he dropped our ballots off at the library, he confided in me he voted for *her*.

The day after Hillary's loss felt unnatural and off-balance. I texted my boss, hoping to skip work for the day, but she encouraged me to come in, knowing I needed supportive familiar faces. So did she. On the drive to work, I called my mom, tears trying to stream, but they had all been washed down my shower drain. She's a registered Republican and never liked Trump. We had watched all three debates in disgust and disbelief. We had been convinced he wasn't fooling anyone. It's terrifying how wrong we were. Mom offered the most comforting words I've heard since November 8. When I told her I felt so betrayed, she said my dad, Bob, hated Trump so much he had made it a point to register and vote for Hillary prior to his weeklong hunting trip. He had registered for this election just so that he could vote for us. Bob stood by us when it mattered most.

*   *   *

My first customer interaction after the election was significant, and I like to think of it as a sign of friendships yet to be made. I noticed Alabama license plates in the driveway. *Oh hell. I am NOT ready for this bullshit. Not today.* My game face was misplaced somewhere between snotty tissues and steel-toed boots. I climbed the pathway to the house, but never did I feel Frank-eyes watching me. Something was different—I smelled marijuana. Conservatives from Alabama don't relocate to Colorado to smoke weed.

A younger woman opened the door and smiled while letting me in. Her smile was genuine; *she* was genuine. While I worked on her lines, she and I casually talked about why she was in Colorado. Then she blurted out, "I'm just glad I'm here and not in Alabama around my family. They're all excited that he won." *Shut the fuck up!* I nearly lost it. I looked up at her as I knelt on the floor and could feel tears well up in my eyes. She had tears too. I stood up and threw my arms around her. We both sobbed for a solid couple of minutes. When we gathered our composure, I told her: "It's good you're here. Colorado stood by us. You're in the right place." People like her make it worthwhile to face Franks every day.

It's important to me to not raise a Frank. My son was a year old when I started working in the telecom industry. He has seen me work endless hours of overtime, obtain a degree, buy a house, and work in a male-dominated industry—all as a single mom. I've wanted two things for him: to be a compassionate, open-minded individual and to stand up for humanity. I want him to face his fears and be resilient. He's even corrected me on occasion when I'm out of line. So I can proudly say that I raised anything but a Frank: I've raised a Bob.

It's taken twenty years of working to face sexist remarks and aggression head-on. I encounter it in every corner of my life. Since I expect it's not going to diminish with this election, I have a responsibility to myself and all women to educate those who make sexist remarks. Donald Trump and the Franks of this world are insecure and view women as inferior. This thinking is intolerable. Women need men to stand with us and beside us in solidarity in our lives and at the polls.

If you see a woman in a traditionally masculine job, don't say, "It's so nice to see a woman doing this line of work." And for the love, don't ask me how long I've been doing my job. You're questioning my abilities. But if you do ask, you better believe my answer will be exactly what I told a former coworker: "I was here when you got here; I'll be here when you're gone." Your notion of me says everything about you and won't change who I am. You won't shake me. This fight is mine, and I will persevere.

Tamica Sears, age 38
Senior Human Resources Business Partner
Phoenix, Arizona

He Brought Out the Ugly and Called It Beautiful

I DON'T UNDERSTAND WHY no one listened to me when I said that Donald Trump was a shoo-in. I had so many well-meaning friends say that with all the hate he spewed, it would never happen. "Hate will never win," they said. I don't think they thought about all of the hate in recent history. I had siblings born before the Voting Rights Act in 1965. There are people alive today who grew up thinking interracial relationships are an abomination. Fifty years is not enough time to change the culture of an entire country. And from my point of view, there were so many White people who hated Obama. Not because of anything he did or did not do, but because he was Black and he had more than they have. Poor White people can be really fucked up. They want someone to blame—"Fuck those Mexicans for taking our jobs!" Because, of course, they were lining up to pick fruit and those damn Mexicans were chosen instead . . . So someone comes along and says *yes, you have a reason to be upset. You are laying the blame in the right place. Before all of this "political correctness" (read the need to treat people equally), America was great.*

So let's roll back the clocks. Do you remember when you could come home, beat your wife, fuck your slave, and then do it all over again the next day? Well, I don't either, but it sounds like a helluva good time. We are going to build a wall to make sure that the White majority stays the majority. We can't have all those Brown folk getting together and realizing that if they all come together as one, they CAN demand equality and there is nothing that White people will be able to do about it.

Leading up to the election I overheard horrible things in the workplace. There was a lot of "uppity nigger" talk. Obama? Uppity nigger. Me? Uppity nigger. All of us were going to be put back into our places when Trump got elected. Now I know that he wasn't there for the conversations, but I am real hard-pressed to think that Donald Trump was not at all aware of the hate speech being done in his name. It is always hard for those at the top to have a clear idea of what those at the bottom are thinking and doing, but what was being said and done in his presence at his rallies was a clear indication he knew and was complicit. He didn't put an end to it. He encouraged it. He stirred it up. He played on the emotions and fears in our society. He brought out the ugly and called it beautiful.

And now he's won. Just like I said he would. And there is no plan. Everyone is crying in a corner, weeping because Hillary didn't win. Well, no shit. No way she was ever going to win. It wasn't a presidential race. It was a popularity contest, and let's face it: she sits at the lunch table by herself. So what are people doing? Pointing fingers. Getting pissed off at their friends who didn't vote for her. It's silly. I think she was a horrible candidate. I did not want her to be my president. I wasn't "with her." I was against him.

So what's happened since the election? I've seen a lot more Confederate flags. I live in Arizona, so it was a bit of a thing before, but I see them a lot more now. I've had conversations with people who say I am stupid for thinking the Confederate flag represents racism or a proslavery stance of any kind. But when I ask what it does represent, I get the same answer: Southern pride, our history. Well, what part of that history are you proud of? The rebellious act of fighting to secede from the country because owning people was so important? Losing that fight? Was that when America was great? I'm confused . . .

I've had the uncomfortable conversations where people say that the people who refuse to perform at the inauguration are just as bad as the people who refused to bake a cake for a gay wedding and that if I thought they should have to bake a cake and not be discriminatory, I can't have it both ways. What do you not get? Refusing to perform a service for someone who has clearly made their vile, disgusting point of view widely known has nothing to do with a company that is refusing to perform a service because they disagree with your sexual preference. That's like saying that refusing to bake a cake for the Jewish man who murdered your child is the same as refusing to bake a cake for Jewish people in general. Two very different things. But what seems obvious to me is clearly not obvious to others.

I had a long and frustrating Facebook battle with a White man who told me using the word *nigga* was perfectly appropriate and anyone could do it because it had a totally different meaning than *nigger* and I just wasn't up to date with what was trendy. This was on a thread where a very wonderful White woman talked about speaking out against racism because someone advised her to stay away from Costco on the 1st and the 15th, because that is when the *niggers* come out. My hero of a friend admonished her and let her know that her language was reprehensible. My friend encouraged other White people to speak up on behalf of those who do not have a voice in Trump's America. And on this wonderful post, someone found room in their heart to school me, a Black woman, on the use of the word *nigger*. I don't care how you spell it, I don't care how you say it, you just shouldn't. My personal point of view: you can try to take the power away from it and use it yourself, but people fought and died so Black people would never have to be called a nigger. Don't do it voluntarily. And you as a White person, don't you dare try to tell me that it is trendy.

I'm tired. I'm tired of being on edge. I'm tired of waiting for the other shoe to drop. I'm tired of trying to explain White privilege exists and that White people's denying its existence is, in fact, a form of White privilege in itself. I'm a moderately successful middle-aged Black woman. I was raised in a lower-class neighborhood, and I had a child when I was eighteen. People point to my upbringing and say, "Well, how can you say White privilege exists? You made it; look at you now!" I'm tired of hearing that! I'm tired of people telling me I'm surprisingly articulate. I'm tired of people asking me what I'm mixed with. I'm tired of people making it seem like I have to be some sort of something else because I "made it" and got out of the ghetto. In Trump's America, all Black people live in the inner city and cash a welfare check. That isn't reality. THAT is White privilege; White people can go their entire lives thinking Trump's America is reality.

You don't get to know people of color, you don't care about people of color, you mock people of color, and sometimes you even fear people of color. And for you to accept them, they have to be Whitewashed. I straighten my hair, I enunciate, I choose my words carefully. I understand the game that needs to be played, and I play it. But I'm tired. So many people are tired. If I wore braids to work, people would look at me like I had straight up lost my mind. But if a White woman does it, she would be praised for her uniqueness. You can't have it both ways. Well, I guess I can't say that, because right now you do have it both ways. Equality seems like it is getting to be a distant dream. People shouldn't have to look like you to get the same treatment as you.

My crystal ball is a bit cloudy, but I see segregation. Not just based on color but also based on class, gender, etc. And the sooner poor people realize that hating other poor people just helps the rich get richer, the sooner poor people can stop struggling on their own. I see more and more people acting like crabs in a barrel, stepping on others to try to get to the top, pulling people down to try to get ahead.

Compassion, collaboration, community—those things seem almost a distant memory. I'm at a loss as to what I can do personally to help bring those things back. I feel overwhelmed by the hate, greed, and selfishness of Trump's America. By the need to build a wall to keep people out. By the inability of people to have open and honest conversations. By the stagnation and eventual regression of cultural advancement. By the lack of acceptance of people who don't look or act like you.

Here's what I don't get. Just because a problem hasn't happened to you, does that mean the problem doesn't exist? If you or a loved one has never been murdered, does that mean murder isn't a problem? If you have never been raped on a college campus, does that mean rape isn't a "thing"? Sounds pretty ridiculous when you put it that way, doesn't it? So when your privilege has allowed you to not see the ugly face of racism, does that mean racism doesn't exist? So many people have said Obama divided the country. "I mean, really, what do all these people of color want; you got your Black president. Simmer down, folk!" We want equality. We want a president with more than the ability to tan well, to not be an anomaly. We want to make the same amount of money, to be given the same opportunities, to not have someone call the police on us because they think we don't belong in the neighborhood. I want to be able to ring someone's doorbell in the middle of the night to ask for help if I've been in an accident without worrying about them shooting me when they see me, an unknown Black face. I want to be able to take it for granted that if someone is mean to me, they are just being an asshole, not a racist. I want to wake up in a world where a White person would be perfectly fine waking up in a Black body. And that is not going to happen in Trump's America.

April M. Padilla, age 42
Paralegal
Antioch, California

Turning Point

I VISITED WASHINGTON, DC, in 1982, when I was eight years old. It wasn't the first time, but it's the first of the DC trips I can remember. We didn't go inside the White House, but my mom has a lot of pictures of us outside—including one of me strolling along the fence. In the photo, I look like I'm daydreaming, but it certainly wasn't about being president one day. I wanted to be Nancy Drew. I was a smart kid: I started reading at age three. I could recite books from memory and won a prize for spontaneously being able to spell *Czechoslovakia* in the first grade. (I guess I'd seen it somewhere.) I was put in gifted classes, and it seemed like people were always using the word *potential* when they talked to me. But the thing was—no one ever, *ever*, told me I could become president someday.

Fast-forward ten years. In 1992, I was turning eighteen and excited there was a presidential election that same year. I was in my second year of college, and everyone in my small hometown knew about the girl who had gone off to New York City to be educated. Most of my former teachers would ask my mother what I was studying and how I liked college, and people who had known me since I was a baby would stop me in the grocery store and tell me how they expected a big and bright future for me. They thought I might become a lawyer, or a writer, or a psychologist. The word *president* was never mentioned.

My mother was from Arkansas, so we were a Clinton household, at least when it came to Bill. I didn't know much about Hillary until the media started turning on her. They vilified her. She wasn't pretty enough, not sweet enough; butter would melt in her smart mouth.

But the more I learned about Hillary, the more I liked her. She was educated and not afraid to own it. She had a career and didn't stay home baking cookies and having teas. She was a badass, and I needed a little of that in my life. I voted for Bill, but part of that vote was for Hillary Rodham.

In 1995, Hillary made history in Beijing by declaring that *women's rights are human rights.* I missed the whole thing. I was in college and in a fight for my life with depression and anxiety. I wasn't paying attention to what was going on in the world because I could barely get out of bed. I was living about a dozen miles away from the White House, but I had lost the ability to dream of any sort of future for myself.

I managed to make it to my graduation—1996, University of Maryland at College Park. Our guest speaker was none other than the first lady herself. Hillary spoke about the age of possibilities, about progressive politics in the new millennium. She assured us she didn't believe GenXers were apathetic and made a joke about her hair. It was a high point in my life. The family who had gathered to watch me walk in my blue cap and gown told me how proud they were of me, how smart I was to have accomplished this goal, and how I would do great things in the future. They didn't suggest that maybe I could be president.

I wish I could say that the commencement address was a turning point in my life, but things are rarely that simple outside of the movies. I took a year off after college because I didn't know what to do with myself and spent it sitting on my mother's sofa, paralyzed with self-doubt. Then I went to law school because people told me I could, and I didn't have any better ideas. I got in, and then out of, an abusive relationship that derailed my career plans. I'm sometimes ashamed to admit it, but that experience still messes with my mind today. I moved cross-country when I was twenty-eight and got married almost five years later. By the time I was forty, I had accepted I was never going to have children. Along the way, I settled into my new life and made some excellent friends. Time passed.

The year 2008 came, and Hillary ran for president. That was a huge moment. For the first time, it felt real that we might have a woman holding the highest office in the land during my lifetime. My heart was broken when she lost in the primaries, but I learned to love President Obama. And deep down, I knew Hillary would run again. My faith in her kept me going, even when I sometimes wanted to give up. If she wasn't giving up, then neither could I.

I grew older and started to pack away some of my insecurities. I found a job in which people valued my skills and let me use my brain. I started to feel like a whole human being for the first time since I was a little girl. Love won, nationwide. I finally sought some help for my anxiety and depression, and it seemed like maybe everything wasn't actually terrible all of the time. When it was time for Hillary to run for president again, it just felt so right—like everything was coming together for the best, in the best of all possible ways. I let go of my natural cynicism and allowed myself to believe everything was going to be okay. No, not just okay; it was going to be great.

I poured my heart and soul into the election—at least, it felt that way. I mean, I lived in California; how much did I really have to do? I put up signs and stickers, wore my T-shirts and buttons, and posted every positive Hillary story I could find. I became a great keyboard warrior against Trump; I was absolutely certain he would not win. I took out a map and showed my coworkers why Florida, my birthplace, was going to come through for us this time. I have general anxiety disorder, social anxiety disorder, and chronic severe depression, y'all. Combine those with a natural cynicism about people and I am rarely optimistic. But this time I believed.

Why? Because I believed in *her*. Hillary Rodham Clinton had been my hero for two dozen years, and now she was going to be my president. I was dancing with excitement on the morning of November 8. I'd taken a pass on early voting so that I could go to the polls on *the* day and savor the experience. My husband and stepson came with me, and we took a group photo I entitled "A Nasty Woman and Her Two Bad Hombres." The champagne was on ice and I was ready.

Then the glass ceiling came crashing down right on my

head. Devastation. Utter and complete devastation. I took an "emergency" pill and curled up in the fetal position in my bed, hoping for oblivion. Unfortunately, when I woke up on November 9, it was still true. I spent the day in my pajamas with my phone tuned to a *support* group for Hillary supporters. Millions of other women and men were pouring out their agony and grief. We cried together; we got angry together; we held one another's hands. It was cathartic and consoling.

But as much as I appreciated this commiseration, I couldn't shake the grief. Beyond the horror of a Trump administration, was pain: something I had wanted so intensely was never going to happen. And beyond myself, there was the sorrow I felt for Hillary. I couldn't imagine giving so much of yourself for so long to so many—standing up to bullies everywhere you turn, shrugging off insults, and hiding your tears—just to lose the most important battle of your life. I couldn't imagine the depth of her disappointment, while I wallowed in my own despair.

And then things started to change. As I continued to read the stories of other women and men who were finding ways through their sorrow, my depression began turning into determination and my anger into action. I realized more people were going through the same emotions as I had, more than I ever would have realized. During those dark days, I connected with almost four million women and men who have collectively said we are stronger together. We have resolved that we can do more, we can work harder, and we will. The year 1996 hadn't been my turning point, but 2016 was.

I have pushed past the anxiety because it's time to put my words into motion and be the goddamn change. Hillary would expect it of me. I'll never get over the fact that she won't be my president. But she will always be my hero, and I refuse to let her down. It's 2017 and Hillary Rodham Clinton has shown us the way—we just have to find the courage to follow.

Amanda Larson, age 51
Chemist working in the oil industry
Anchorage, Alaska

Bystander to
Engaged Citizen

I AM A CHEMIST living in deep, red Alaska, whose economy relies on oil production. I work in the industry and love my job. When I was eighteen, I first registered as a Republican. A fiscal conservative and a social liberal, I'm libertarian at heart. A decade ago, I left the GOP and changed my registration to Green Party, due to the rising influence of conservative evangelicals. For me, small government means thoughtful regulation, not regulating women's uteri while eliminating the Safe Drinking Water Act. My voting choices are pragmatic and issue-based.

This year, during the primaries, Trump insulted and bullied his opponents. It was appalling behavior; my employer would have fired any employee who made those comments. How can that behavior be acceptable to the GOP membership? Do they have standards for conduct? One particular moment of conduct during a debate—boasting about one's sexual prowess—was a disgrace. When Trump earned the nomination, I was astonished to see my fellow Americans' values laid bare.

Many voters supported him because they wanted more conservative Supreme Court judge; they were worried about gun control issues. Or they wanted stronger policies for border control. Or because they thought he'd be better for business. I may not concur, but I could respect those reasons. What I could not accept was the behavior Trump supporters were willing to tolerate for their priorities. No transgression was too great to break this deal. My fellow citizens left me feeling betrayed by their unspoken justification: *a narcissistic sociopath is acceptable as long as he is* my *narcissistic sociopath.*

*   *   *

I'm older, no longer a slender woman. But when I was both young and slender, I wore elegant business attire. At one conference in Phoenix, I was riding up the elevator with a man I'd been talking with for the evening. He grabbed and forcibly kissed me. I was horrified and so ashamed. I was there as a professional woman. What if my colleagues saw and thought I'd wanted it? I was terrified that this incident would damage my career with my peers' thinking I was a floozy, unworthy of intellectual respect. I shoved him off and didn't get off at my floor. I didn't want him following me to my room and forcing his way in. My only option seemed to be to carry on and hope for the best. Recent outcomes of horrifying rape cases clearly illustrate that few predatory men suffer consequences from their actions.

Some men think their desires override others' autonomy. They feel entitled to what they want, even if it's at someone else's expense. These men don't have to pay bills if they don't wish to. They find ways to avoid taxes. They sexually assault women. Trump's infamous grab-'em-by-the-pussy tape was shocking and confirmed my opinion of his character. He is a man capable of committing sexual assault and likely has done so repeatedly. Trump's character was appalling and so consistent with narcissistic personality disorder that I could only believe this diagnosis was the case. I hoped desperately that the analysis by political science professor Allan Lichtman, whom I've always followed and who believed Trump would win, was wrong. Surely enough American voters would prevent this unstable, dangerous man from gaining the Oval Office.

Because I had been voting in Alaska since 1987, I knew the drill. The poll worker asked for my ID. While a typo had been in my registration for close to thirty years, I never saw it as an issue. Suddenly, it was an issue on Election Day in 2016. I was going to be denied a ballot. I dug through my wallet and found what I needed: my official voter registration card, complete with the typo. The roster, voter ID, and driver's license all had the same address and first and last name. What were the odds that Amanda D. Larson, registered voter at a certain address lives with Amanda P. Larson at that same address, and suddenly, Amanda P., instead of registering to vote, decides to impersonate Amanda D.? Thank goodness we averted the crime of the century.

Alaska has had several proposed bills to require a photo ID for voters, and so far, they have not been enacted. Alaska is a state with a large rural population who have no need for photo IDs unless they want to travel by airplane, which few rural residents can afford. Most of those communities have no facility that could provide an official state ID. It upsets me that suffrage, so easily taken for granted, can be placed out of reach for fellow citizens with only a few strokes of the pen. And I am utterly impotent to protect their voices.

After casting my ballot, I left completely disheartened. I did not feel good voting for Clinton. While she clearly was the most qualified candidate, I was not confident she would win. Worse, I had to face the ugly fact that fellow citizens supported a man who spewed vitriol and who engaged in behavior far worse than anything I'd seen in a fraternity house, much less the White House. On election night, I knew what the risks were. Though I was stunned to see Trump win all of the borderline swing states, I felt gutted. I was accustomed to supporting candidates who lost. This time I felt as if every shred of security was being stripped away. Knowing Speaker Ryan's agenda to target Medicare and Social Security, I feared *everything* I have been working for my entire adult life is at stake.

I watched the returns and drank a whiskey. I never drink on a work night. I had a second one. The numbness allowed me to keep breathing. *Inhale. Exhale.* I always knew this could happen. It did. I didn't want to go to work the next day. Heck, I didn't want to live in my country anymore. It's not because Hillary lost. I was okay with her losing the Electoral College. It was because the most divisive candidate I have ever seen, a con man, convinced people he would look out for them.

I forced myself to head to work. If I had headed to my desk braless and in a hospital gown with my fanny hanging out, I would not have felt more raw and vulnerable. I logged onto my computer, and a colleague commented, "You'll notice I'm wearing black today." I started sobbing. I didn't cry when a cat I loved and spent half my life with was put to sleep just before his twentieth birthday. However, I cried on the morning after the election.

*   *   *

In more than thirty years of voting, I have only on one occasion contacted an assemblyman regarding a bill he drafted. Since November 8, I have begun contacting my two senators, my representative, and senate committees—I write, call, and

I encourage friends and family to do likewise. I attend town hall meetings, ask questions, and present my concerns. The meetings provide opportunities for access to the lawmakers, for them to fathom the full weight of our concerns. Our elected representatives have one paramount priority—remaining in office—if they hear over and over how critical it is to preserve Social Security, they will realize their job hinges on it. I feel as if I've discovered a subterranean sea that I'm learning to navigate and ride, reading the currents that tell me what to do and who to call. Transitioning from a political bystander to a changemaker, is empowering.

To stay on top of legislative developments, I keep track of the bills under consideration in the House of Representatives. If I notice an item of significance, I contact my representative to help him see that this issue matters to constituents and that we are involved and aware. The odds that I will influence any actions are slim. I will not, however, allow my representative the comfortable ignorance of the impact his actions have on me.

Since we need grassroots involvement, I pass information along to others who need it. I wrote my nonpartisan Civic Information Committee at work about our state assembly website's legislative search tool and suggested it as a brown-bag luncheon topic, which garnered an enthusiastic response. That information will help many more concerned voters know how to engage. Citizens can have a bigger impact on their state legislators than ones in Congress, but engaging representatives at every level is important.

My activism emerged in other ways. Christmas is always a turning point; this year was no different. As cold, dark days begin to become longer and brighter, we bring evergreen trees into our houses; even the coldest winter days hold life and promise for a better future. My gifts to family were donations in their names to charities already fighting for that better future:

the Southern Poverty Law Center, the American Civil Liberties Union, Planned Parenthood, and Reading With Conviction. We don't need stuff. We need freedom; it's more important than new possessions. For my family, those donations were perfect gifts, more meaningful to my loved ones than a music download or gift card.

We are indeed stronger together. Pooling our resources into established freedom fighters protects our future. Though I've been a political bystander for most of my life, I've learned from this experience that paying attention requires sustained effort. Acting even more. But the risk to my future is too great to sit by without making my voice heard. The opposition's brand is intimidation. Standing up, speaking out, and protecting one another, we march forward.

Sandra Jense-Forgach, age 42
Nurse practitioner
Layton, Utah

Reflection: What Can I Do?

THE MORNING OF November 10, 2016, I woke up with eyes swollen from a night of crying.

The man who had just been elected president represented in every way men who had treated me poorly my whole life. Men who had abused me, physically and emotionally. Men who had sexually mistreated me. Men who saw me as nothing more than a "dumb cunt," whose opinion on politics, religion, science, and medicine didn't count.

I went online to see how most of my friends and family were faring and to block the ones who were celebrating. I was greeted by a memory from November 9, 2013—a photo of my husband holding our then six-day-old daughter. The two were regarding each other with pure love, and the reason behind my fear, sadness, and anger made itself clear to me then.

I shared that picture again on my Facebook page, with the following caption: "This sweet baby is going to grow up, for the next four years at least, in a country run by a man who will tell her that how she looks is more important than what she thinks.

That a man can 'grab her' as long as he's rich enough, and she can't say anything about it."

"I don't even know how to cope with that reality. I only hope we can shelter her from his rhetoric and raise her to know she is just as valuable as her brothers, in every aspect of her life."

While reflecting on my post from that day, I realized people who support Trump have developed the rhetoric that those who are mourning the outcome of this election are "special snowflakes," weak-willed people who don't have the strength to admit defeat and carry on. That hardly describes me. I am a fierce woman, a warrior. I have overcome many things in my life—poverty, mental illness, abuse—to advance my education and my place in the world. Professionally, I have devoted myself to caring for persons who are marginalized. I am a primary care provider for elderly and chronically ill persons. I make myself available to my patients and their caregivers 24–7, with the goal of avoiding hospital admissions. This kind of work doesn't bring glory or fame. I can't complain about my salary but when I add up the hours I spend coordinating their care, I am decidedly not making a fortune. I do what I do professionally because I am passionate about meeting my patient's individual needs. Medicine shouldn't have a cookie-cutter approach, and it takes time to outline the right medical plan for one person.

I have dedicated myself to raising kind and empathetic children who think before they speak and place other people's lives on equal footing with their own. I teach my sons to do their own chores and not assume that anything that needs to be done is linked to one's gender. I teach my daughter that anything she wants to do is within her reach. I teach all three of them to be compassionate and that the choices they make—where they shop, what they say—can affect other people. My oldest son already gravitates towards books that expand his world, rather than collapse it (he has read *Nickel and Dimed* three times). In 2012, my children decided we would no longer eat at Chick-fil-Aˑ, even though it was one of their favorite fast-food restaurants. They made that choice because they didn't want to contribute to a company that didn't support equal marriage rights. The day they told me their decision I hugged them tight and cried, realizing "there's a light somewhere. It may not be much light but it beats the darkness."[27]

On the morning of November 9, encased in grief and fear, I saw two choices for myself going forward: (1) I could suffer without doing. I could continue to cry. I could wish things would get better in two or four years. Along the way, I could post angry memes and avoid anyone who thought differently from how I do. Or (2) I could continue to fight the way I had my whole life. I could channel my anger and fear into a constructive effort.

I have never been an organizer or been politically involved (other than as a voter), but I have always been a fighter. I'm smart. I have learned over the years to identify bacteria, to knit a prize-winning shawl, to put a central line in a patient. But my biggest accomplishment was learning to talk with patients and their loved ones about death and dying and making plans in the face of terminal illness. I have been told I do this with grace, humility, and empathy. That kind of discussion, fraught with such intense emotions, makes political wrangling look like schoolyard taunting.

Facing Donald Trump with eloquence and intelligence, failed this past fall. But if we all raise our voices and strive to be heard, we will not be overpowered. I have faith in this belief. Serious conversation is an art, whether in a hospital room with

---

27 Charles Bukowski, "The Laughing Heart," *Betting on the Muse: Poems and Stories*, Santa Rosa: Black Sparrow Press, 1996.

a grieving family or in a public arena with a grieving nation. In reflecting on what I could do to help our cause, I have determined that I can teach people this art, just as I have taught medical residents and nurses how to elicit medical goals from someone who has heard they have heart failure or end-stage liver disease.

I don't pretend to think this will be easy. I don't have a platform for delivery. I have never set up an educational forum on my own. But I know I have sisters (and brothers) who have. I know I have help. I know I can fight. I know we can win.

Barbara Barrette Parsons, age 53
College English professor
Tacoma, Washington

The Nasty Professor

"I FEEL SO DISCRIMINATED against!" Kendra's eyes were full of tears as we sat in my office in late September 2016. "Everyone assumes that because I am going to vote for him, I am racist. I'm not! My professors talk about the election all the time; even my math professor did last week. He knew better. But when I raised my hand and asked what this had to do with calculus, he just stared at me. Another student, the one who always reeks of pot, turned around and gave me such a dirty look; then he hissed, 'Bigot!'"

I knew I was that professor. I taught English, not math, but for a solid year, I had been using the presidential election as a teaching tool. In composition classes, I had had students analyze speeches, examine rhetorical appeals, and identify the fallacies in the policies detailed on seventeen Republican candidates' websites. I had forced them to select a candidate as their audience and write to persuade John Kasich that women should have a right to choose or Ben Carson to campaign that Black Lives Matter. Some students found this approach annoying. Others loved it. This quarter, with the election down to only Clinton or Trump, I had let go of the protocol every professor attempts to follow: *keep political comments neutral.* This was no longer possible. I had to focus on facts, and those facts betrayed my bias.

In my understanding-teacher voice, I said to Kendra: "That must be hard. Tell me, what makes you want to stand up for this candidate?"

"I know him!" Kendra cried. "I've been watching him on TV my whole life, and I know he isn't racist! He has really good ideas."

My head spun as I tried to decide how much to say. Should I say, *Reality TV doesn't actually represent reality, you know*? or *How many of your pleasant associations are because you watched him on TV with your family as a kid, and how many from understanding his agenda?*

I settled on "Do you think he understands the way our government works well enough to run it?"

She sucked in her breath and let it out fast. "Yes. Yes, I do! He will stir things up. He will make the government shrink. Plus, the alternative is so bad. I mean, Clinton is really corrupt!"

This reaction was new to me. In the previous year, students had sometimes favored a Republican candidate, but they had based their choices on issues. At this rural Washington community college, one of two where I teach, the students are 90% white and largely high school students from evangelical families who are earning college credits early. Many of them believe gun ownership is a threatened right, disapprove of homosexuality, and consider abortion a sin. They think Trump is posed to protect those values. By stating that Clinton was corrupt, this student had shared a viewpoint that was not grounded in any reality—but in September 2016, I had not yet wrapped my head around the problem of fake news.

The other college where I teach is an inner-city institution full of employed adults, single moms, LGBTQ students, and homeless folks allowed to take classes tuition free when there is space. So the population of scholars is completely different, and my teaching must be different, too. There, before the election, students were worried about their personal safety. We joked about the attacks on Clinton's emails. We discussed her flip-flop on gay rights and concluded her change in position mirrored that of most of the people in the United States during those same years. In my evening city college class, whenever the serious discussion picked apart Clinton's stance on fracking or international trade, a student in the back row would say mournfully in his deep voice, "But, people, the alternative . . . !" And we would all laugh.

On November 8, 2016, I showed up in class at the country college wearing my $1.99 thrift-store pantsuit. "Wow, professor, you look so professional!" a strawberry blonde sixteen-year-old said. I thanked her and explained why many women professors would be wearing pantsuits that day. Today, looking back at my confidence early that morning, I see only shocking naïveté. "If things don't go the way the polls suggest, don't be surprised if I cancel class tomorrow," I warned my early class. "I may need to take a mental health day!" We all smiled.

In a later class, with slightly older students, I asked how many of them were qualified to vote. Perhaps three-quarters of the class of twenty raised their hands. Then I asked how many had already sent in their ballots, and I counted four hands.

"I wanted Bernie!" someone volunteered in response to my exaggerated shocked face. A few others murmured agreement. Even then, I didn't get it. I didn't understand that many young people in this election cycle might just check out or might follow their parents' politics, not seeing unavoidable generational differences in culture and the role of government.

That evening at the city college, we sat at computers pretending to do research, but really keeping tabs on early election results. I wanted to be at home, eating pizza with my boyfriend and daughter. I had put champagne on ice to chill, anticipating Clinton's certain victory. "We are going to dismiss at 6:30," I said, which was 9:30 p.m. Eastern. "I think we all want to be with our families tonight."

"It doesn't look good," one student said. "He's winning."

"It's early," I reassured. We broke at 6:00, and I hurried home.

The rest of the evening was a blur of my family members' dour pessimism and my testy optimism as the election results rolled in. I went to bed angry before any concession, and I woke up, angry, to the final results. Sitting up in bed, I tried to picture a world in which the United States was not a leader, not a voice of reason and guidance. A burden drifted onto my shoulders as I considered how to frame this version of America for my college students. After sitting numbly for an hour, I shook myself. I was damned if I would cancel class and let those students smirk.

NPR was broadcasting Clinton's concession speech, and I listened as I drove to campus. She finished her notes of encouragement just as I pulled into a parking spot. In my early English 101 class, my students didn't know where to look. I had dressed in all black that day. (Many of us professors did.) They were embarrassed for me, I realized. I sat on the edge of my desk and looked at them, silent for a minute. "Should we talk about this?" I asked, finally. They were reticent. "Is anyone feeling really great this morning? This is the outcome you were hoping for?" Three students raised their hands. Probing, I got them to explain their reasoning. One wanted Pacific Northwest forest logging to start up again, which I saw as a reasonable basis for a vote against regulation. Another was excited about what the new president-elect had said in his speech.

"I didn't see it," I said, not mentioning that I had determined I could never watch another speech he made. "What stood out?"

"You know," the student began, "he'll make America great again. He talked about infrastructure. He's going to fix the infrastructure."

"What, roads and things?" I asked.

"Yeah, I think."

* * *

A day later, I was relieved to teach students at the city college. I was still miserable, but these students would share my bewilderment at the election results and my outrage that no one seemed to be doing anything substantial to delegitimize them. Again, propped on my desk edge, I talked with these students about the violence against minorities already playing out in our cities and the Seattle protest some of them had participated in the night before.

One black student, an evangelical in recovery (as she had once described herself), spoke up, "You folks finally seem to get it. That's great. This is what we have always been up against in America. This racism isn't anything new. It was always there. You didn't like Black Lives Matter. You wouldn't get 100% behind it. You call us African Americans. Did anyone ever ask us whether we like being identified that way? Well, we hate it. But we don't even say anything, because it's such a small issue compared to the rest of the bias. Yeah, we're going to have a horrible four years, but is it really going to be any different? I don't think so."

* * *

I've thought a lot about what that student said and what it will mean to be a good American in the immediate future. I think it comes down to truth in teaching. My actions in the classroom must clearly lead students to understand what is real in the world around them. Since the day the students spoke up, I've refocused my teaching of writing to concentrate on identifying legitimate sources, sound evidence, clear logical trails, and real news. My critiques have become harsher. Over and over, I demonstrate how we judge authenticity in sources and use facts to support our own conclusions. Some students get it. Some do not, and at the end of the term, their grades reflect that. In the class with the three confessed Trumpers, one wrote a final paper about rape culture that was well researched and persuasive. She was apparently able to compartmentalize the sexual assault allegations against her candidate. Another student wrote about the evils of illegal immigration, an essay full of general statements about what *they* take away from *us*. Three times, without evidence, he claimed that "illegals" collect welfare. Two times in the margins, I asked for evidence; the third time, I just told him they don't. The third student never turned in his final essay about the climate crisis, but in conference, he had told me the evidence was clear that human impact on climate change was a ruse.

"Then why are the polar ice caps melting?" I asked. "What will be the impact? What about the polar bears?"

"What about them?" he asked.

"I think evidence shows they can't adapt to the changes taking place. They will go extinct. What's your research show?"

He shrugged.

*   *   *

I don't look forward to teaching students to think critically, when we have a government composed of people who have chosen to ignore analysis, logic, and fact. I don't know how I will respond when a student claims *ethos* because his invalid position is also the one the president of the United States has supported. I am concerned that this administration will convince some of my students that *The New York Times* is a failing, lying newspaper or that observations about a woman's appearance or a judge's racial background are relevant to a serious discussion of issues.

Most of all, I dread being at the front of the classroom as my less worldly students gradually discover the world of hate and injustice that is rolling out. I anticipate incredulous tears when a young woman student realizes she won't be allowed to abort an early pregnancy and her future is about to be curtailed. My LGBTQ students haven't known a time when there weren't posters on campus walls announcing in big letters that students have the right to use any bathroom, but they soon may know that time. When the NRA gets this Congress to pass national laws allowing guns be sold to domestic violence perpetrators, I dread the absences from class that will follow someone's mom being shot by her ex-boyfriend, right here in liberal Western Washington.

Conservatives at Turning Point USA have begun compiling an internet list of professors whose lessons don't align with those conservatives' perception of American values. This is modern McCarthyism, of course, as are other changes we have begun to see in government and the private sector. These movements may trickle down. Job security may be affected. Nevertheless, my proper response to these developments is clear. As we all face the hard lessons that are coming in human rights, the environment, and world relations, I hope I have the courage, wisdom, and character necessary to teach students how to see truth—because when these lists of liberal professors' names grow on internet blacklists, I want mine to be there. Nice professors don't end up on blacklists because they have compared the elected president of the United States to other historical fascists, because nice professors don't say those things. But nasty professors do. In the coming years, it will take gumption for me to maintain my insistence on facts, but I will try. I hope I am soon identified as a "nasty professor."

Chris Kelly, age 53
Mother, writer, speaker, entrepreneur
San Diego, California

Dear Daughter

IN 2008, AT almost forty-five, and after already having two sons, I gave birth to a daughter. She is not the same race as my sons or myself. Her father is African American. My sons and their father, like me, are Caucasian and Jewish. Religiously,

I have been just about everything. But I've recently settled on being a Christian, and I raise my daughter with faith. (More on that later.)

My daughter, born the year of the first Obama election, was a proud face for the Democratic party on the little Pacific Northwest island where we lived. She was actually on a poster in the office, the face of the future—her little brown face and bald head wearing an Obama button, a tiny American flag tucked into her stroller and a fist pump of support. As her parents, we were proud to see change in our government. We believed in hope. We trusted that our country was moving forward and would continue to do so.

Fast forward eight years: the Obama years were nearing their end. It was time again to place someone in the most powerful leadership role for our country. Although several candidates vied for the position, in the end it came down to two, and one was a clown, a clown in the most feared sense of the word and picture. He is a laughing stock, a narcissist, a heathen—the descriptive words are never ending. There was no way he could win. There was no way the people of the United States of America could vote this poor excuse for a man into the office of president of the United States. You could see it in the polls: there was no way the people would buy his bullshit and support his lies, racism, sexism, fraud, thievery, and disgusting behavior.

The polls lied, it turns out. Facebook told the truth. During the election season, I kept seeing his supporters asking the question of their friends: "Who are you voting for?" and the answers of "Trump" piling up. Were these people kidding me? Why were these women—mothers and grandmothers—voting for a man who stands for everything that disempowers women? What was wrong with them?

I don't have television. I don't watch the news. I read online. I protect my daughter, the only child left at home, from the hate and hideousness of the media. I don't promote hate or unkind words in our home or life. She doesn't have Facebook; she is eight. She watches silly videos about cats. We didn't talk about the vile candidate. Yet on election day, she walked into the voting precinct and announced, "We are here to vote for Hillary Clinton." We believed. She believed. She chose her candidate. *We* voted. We went home. We had dinner. We believed. I watched the polls online. I tucked her in bed. I heard her say her prayers: "Dear Jesus, please let Hillary Clinton be the new president. In Jesus' name, amen." She went to sleep. I watched polls. My watching quickly turned into horror. I began private messaging a Facebook friend at 7:08, p.m. (PST), who has been a long-time political analyst, Democrat, and Hillary supporter—first asking her to explain the electoral votes and *then* asking if at that point we were doomed. She assured me, "We are still ok."

At 8:36 p.m., I asked, "Do we still have any hope?"

Her reply, "Yes, we do. But it's getting scary."

The last exchange was when I told her that my daughter was praying out loud, and my friend's reply was, "Bless her."

Less than two hours later, it happened. Hillary didn't win. He did. This country voted against all odds.

I had to face my daughter in the morning with the results. But first I had to write a letter, to her and to the other little girls and women in the United States.

"Dear Daughter, While You Were Sleeping and Dreaming, the Man Who 'Grabs Them by the Pussy' Won. I Am Sorry."

Dear Daughter,

I am so sorry. While you were sleeping and I was up worrying and praying, something terribly wrong happened. The man you have heard about who thinks it's okay to grab a woman by what we call "your privates" and he publicly calls "your pussy," has been chosen by half of the people of our country to be the leader.

I am sorry that the progress you have seen in your short life will be erased. It breaks my heart to think that the rights so many women in our history have fought for will soon disappear. I wish I could explain how so many people could decide that a man who has placed his personal gain ahead of humanity over and over again could be the winner. I am so sorry that the man who protected himself financially while destroying lives is the leader of the "free world."

I am sorry that this country of which I have spent a lifetime being proud to be part of is now the laughing stock of the world. I am sorry that you will hear the question over and over again from the rest of the world, "What made Americans elect a man with no political experience, no morals, and no values?"

Your inheritance? I hope there is something left for you after the stock market crashes. I pray for your African American side of the family. I pray for your Mexican cousins. I pray for my ability to go high when they go low.

I am sorry, my sweet daughter, that you have to live in a country riddled with hate. You are strong because I am strong. I will not show you that my heart is broken. I will show you that we will overcome. I will continue to teach you that love wins. The journey assuredly will be more challenging with what happened while you were sleeping. While you were dreaming of a brighter future and becoming anything you want to become, my job just became harder.

With each person I meet, it will be difficult not to wonder if they were one who chose misogyny and narcissism and evil over love and forward progress. It will be hard but I will continue to believe in my rose-colored lenses so you do not see me become the skeptics who chose this road.

I promise you I will be your rock today and every day as I

always have been, but I am doubling down on that for the next four years. It has been said before by the woman who became so hated by half of our country that it takes a village to raise a child. I will lean on those who are that village. I will find those people for you, for us, and we will overcome.

I will not let you see my tears as I reflect on this political tragedy. I will not bury my face in my pillow. I will be your hero and together we will win. I am sorry I don't know how to explain this to your innocent sweet heart and face.

I am sorry that I don't have the answers for your brothers.

Dear daughter: You are worthy, you are respected, you are important, you matter, you can do anything, and you will. This man will not stop us.

But I am still so sorry.

*   *   *

Before midnight on November 8, 2016, this letter was published by *The Huffington Post*.

I stayed awake until 3:00 a.m., messaging with a friend in utter disbelief, attempting to reassure her that we would be okay. She and her Jewish daughters, me and my children, the people we love—we would all be okay. I slept.

As I woke up, I heard my sweet daughter in the other room. I heard her speaking into her tablet: "Siri, who won president of the United States?" In a panicked moment I called out her name. I could not let my daughter hear this devastating news from a mobile device and some nonhuman voice recognition software. When my daughter came into my room, I had collected my tears, swallowed hard, and grasped for every ounce of courage I have ever had. I pulled her face close to mine and said, "Theresa, Donald Trump is president."

My daughter gasped and threw her body on mine, crying. Her first words were "What are we going to do now?"

I answered, "We are going to be strong, we are going to be courageous, we are going to be kind and loving as we always have been. We are not going to allow this decision to change who we are."

The next few days were a nauseated blur. The so-called Christians and their boasting made me reconsider my personal claim of that title. Many Facebook friends blindsided me with "Neener neener neener get over it" and were immediately unfriended. The news reports and photos showing swastikas, the KKK, and hate toward people of color, horrified me. Fellow parents of biracial children called and emailed me in desperate fear. I did my best to calm them.

I received messages from Christian women: "I don't know how a Christian could vote for Killary." Another Christian woman called me a liar and bigot when I asked her to be sympathetic towards others in reference to her boasting. I was being attacked by women who call themselves Christian while name-calling and being hypocrites, just like the candidate they voted for.

I became paralyzed. My mind was mush. My heart broken. My soul felt shattered. The beauty of humanity no longer existing. The promise of a better future, of progress and hope for my children, gone. I couldn't write. I couldn't think. I couldn't believe it.

Just days before the election, I had been added to an online group that consisted of other liberal, like-minded women. The stories posted after the election—stories of hate repeated one after the other—deepened my sadness.

As days turned into weeks, however, the stories began to shift to strength and courage and standing up for one another.

Not long after the election, I attended a baby party for a family who is Muslim and wore a safety pin. I was asked by an arrogant white (only one of five of us present) male attorney if he could have my safety pin so he could use it to pop my daughter's balloon.

"No," I replied, and to my daughter, I said, "He is not to be trusted."

No one may take my safety pin. No one can stop me from being the voice for the underdog. No one will be allowed to squash the dreams of my children. No one will be getting away with vile behavior to me or my loved ones on my watch.

I will shine the light upon your darkness. I will continue to empower women. I will teach and model strength and courage. I will not be stopped. I will not act in hate but in love. I will not call names, but I will share the truth. I will do my part to make this world and this country a better place in spite of the people who are too ignorant to begin to understand what they have created. As for being a Christian, I will continue to be a believer. I will continue to discern with a heightened sense whom I associate with, and I will continue to be a mom who in my child's eyes is a superhero. (Don't tell her differently.)

L.M. Carroll, age 32
Photographer and rental property owner
Sacramento, California

A War Is Formed

Not from the outside . . . but from the inside.
It starts at dinner tables, and with faceless cowards on the internet.
It starts with a "harmless joke" and lack of accountability.

A war is formed with whispers behind closed doors,
Until those whispers become words,
Those words become shouts,
Those shouts become laws,
And those laws become truth.

When will we as a nation, founded on the blood, sweat, and tears of immigrants,
STAND UP as a country united, and no longer divided?
When will we become more civically engaged?
When it's too late?

A war is formed when good people are complacent,
When our truth loses its laws,
When those laws are no longer shouts,
and those shouts dwindle into whispers.

Darlene Jacobson, age 49
Independent sales representative
Kalispell, Montana

Winter

I T WAS WINTER.
    She has always lived with fear in her bones but felt it most in the darkest days of winter.

She had lived with fear and anxiety the way some people live with scars. Her scars were hidden. Etched into her cells. Hieroglyphs on the surface of her DNA.

Some of her earliest memories are of her six-year-old self in a white nightgown, of words made from sharp edges and broken glass, and of large greedy hands that had the power to make her disappear. If one were to follow those hands like a map, traced them upwards past wrists and elbows, past shoulders and collarbone, along the neck and past the Adam's apple, they would arrive at the face of a narcissistic, authoritarian patriarch and pedophile, who taught the "word of God" to her while he used his hands and body to emphasize the more advanced points.

Her six-year-old mind reordered itself in the wake of his lessons, which came one after another after another over a period of seven years. She became accustomed to watching for danger. Looking around corners. Keeping her eyes on the bedroom door and her ears in the hallway. Her grandfather, after all, taught her that monsters were real. His hands reshaped her view of who she was. They habituated her to the objectification of herself. Accustomed her to abuse, to violation, to silence. And so it was that she moved forward into the world, always on the lookout for danger, her nervous system hypervigilant, overresponsive, easily startled. But no matter how she looked ahead, she could never seem to see the true dangers before they were already, quite literally, on top of her. She also didn't know that for most of her years, this was because she was asleep.

It took cancer to wake her up.

At age forty-four, she sat on the edge of an ER bed in a nightgown much like the one she wore when she was six. The flickering fluorescent lights tried to beat back the darkness of December, and she watched in silence as the doctor told her without fanfare that she had far too many errant B-cells swimming through the river of her blood. One moment she didn't have cancer, and the next moment she did. One moment she was immortal, and the next her mortality screamed out at her with a voice raw from years of going unheard.

It happened, she thought, *much as it had for Saul in the book of Acts:* "And immediately there fell from [her] eyes as it had been scales: and [she] received sight forthwith, and arose, and was baptized."[28]

She arose and was baptized into the truth of who she was, into her voice and her story, into the inner workings of the culture she was surrounded by. Suddenly, she could see. The sexism, the injustice, the inequality. It had all been there before, but now, baptized, she could see it. She could see how religion

---

28 9 Acts 18 Jesus appears to Saul.

had been used to manipulate her into believing she wasn't wholly human. How God was a man and his son was a man and they spoke to men who had written down the words to be read by other men, who could then disseminate those words to their property and their wives. She could see that *submissive* was another word for *obey* and *be quiet*. And once she saw that truth in her own life, it was like the inner light cracked her open and spilled out so that she could see that truth the whole world over.

She owned the word *feminist* and saw that its meaning was intersectional and that even she had power and privilege she hadn't realized she carried with the color of her skin. She could hear that her voice—which had always been chastised as too loud, too opinionated, and too much for a woman—was actually just right. That it was beautiful precisely how it was. And oh, that voice was powerful. It could change things. It could alter the course of history just by being used.

It took a death sentence for her to realize she was worth loving. It took the face-to-face confrontation with her mortality to realize she would miss the hell out of herself if she were gone.

And after that, the scales continued to fall. She enrolled in a graduate program for Women's Spirituality. She joined her local American Association of University Women and found like-minded "nasty women" who were as strong and sure and as opinionated as she was. She established Women's Spirituality Circles, sacred spaces where women could come and, often for the very first time, hear their own voices and tell their own stories. She marveled at what transpired, the way women came to the conclusion that they were powerful and beautiful and had stories worth sharing and that by doing so, they could change the world.

And then Trump.

When she heard Trump speak, all the old pathways of fear

and anxiety were reanimated; the dormant hieroglyphs flared back to life, exerting a power over her she had no control of. She turned off the television, but the sentiment was everywhere. Those who had previously hid their hate-filled views began crawling out into public and vomiting that hate out for all to see. She wanted to withdraw from all of it, but she knew the situation was much too important, the consequences much too dire to hide from. Trump's mannerisms, his actions, his demeanor, and his voice were the same as those of her grandfather, of the predatory men who had sexually assaulted her, of all the men who had belittled her opinion, and of the men in the church who told her she would be banished if she were to speak out about her grandfather's actions.

So instead, she pulled in a deep breath and got to work. She realized that the vulnerability and fear she felt on election night was a call to action. That the trauma she had endured as a child had created a well of resilience inside of her that could stand up to what was coming. She recognized that she is a nasty woman, that nasty women have autonomy and power to influence the world and make it a better place, and that nasty women together are unstoppable.

On January 7, she will stand alongside hundreds, just ten minutes down the road from her house, at the Love Not Hate rally in Whitefish, MT. She will use her presence to stand against the injustice that has so publically reared its head in her small corner of the world. Anti-Semitism powered by Richard Spencer, the Trump-fueled neo-Nazi who founded the National Policy Institute and who also lives in Whitefish, will not be tolerated. Like-minded humans will stand together in arctic temperatures to support the one hundred plus Jewish families and business owners who are being targeted by Spencer and his ilk.

Yes, it is winter. And although she has always lived with fear inside her bones, the darkest days of winter call for the brightest torches of light. When held side by side, those individual torches become as brilliant as the sun, illuminating what is broken and protecting those who are mistreated, marginalized, and oppressed. Yes, she still has fear in her bones, but she was made for days like these.

Julie Tyers, age 65
Gypsy
Portland, Oregon

Welcome Home

IN 2016, I did not know what America had become.
I did not know children could be shot dead in a park, or men be shot in a car or on the street, by police officers who would not face many consequences other than suspensions from work. I did not know our country ousted foreign dictators not to promote democracy or to put an end to atrocities but rather to benefit the businesses that would rebuild the devastated nations after our intervention.

Then there are the children without mothers and mothers without children. There was a time I did not think much about the suffering children. I am *ashamed* to say, to admit, I did not think about the suffering children. In 2016, there were far too many things I did not know. Far too many. *I should have known.*

I have always loved my country. I remember knowing we were the greatest country in the world, I remember pledging allegiance standing proudly at my desk. Being an American meant something. My father was on the anticommunist squad of the FBI in New York City when I was born in Queens, in

1951. I was to learn early that he hated communists and he unquestionably hated them because he loved his country. He lived at stakeout sites, watching alleged communists come and go from their New York apartments. Later in my life, he told me the KGB was so good at infiltrating and spying that there was a spy on the Harlem Globetrotters' team. He also hated the Beatles—he was convinced they were trained by the KGB and sent to America to subvert the young.

Later in my life, my father also told me this: He quit the FBI ultimately because the wrong people go to prison. He told me the Rosenbergs didn't have any secret atomic information. Everyone "ratted" on them, they "ratted" on no one, and they professed their innocence until the day they died. Mrs. Rosenberg's brother implicated them and then later confessed to providing nuclear secrets. He was imprisoned for ten years. The Rosenbergs were convicted in 1951, executed in 1953. My father told me they were used in order to send a message that the United States was serious about espionage. They were American citizens, allegedly members of the Young Communist League, and parents to two young boys.

I did not know until much later that my father also was a racist. I brought home a black boyfriend from college. It was the second of two times my father nearly hit me. I'm not sure he knew he was a racist. I think he thought he just loved his country, albeit the white one.

Fortunately, when it was time for me to leave home for good, I wanted little to do with my parents and their beliefs. They weren't religious, but they were afraid of so many things. My mother was forever afraid I would be lured into becoming a lesbian, or worse, a gypsy. Their beliefs didn't offer much meaning in my life, so I became a fundamental Christian, thinking maybe God would. I reluctantly married a man God wanted me to marry. I wore dowdy clothes and grew my hair long because God wanted me to. I so wanted to be a woman of God; however, I did not submit well enough. At my small evangelical church on an island in the Northwest, it became a church goal to get Julie to submit. When I was twenty-five, after five years of a miserable marriage, I realized I did not believe in original sin and thus was not a true fundamentalist.

After I filed for divorce, the church organized a statewide prayer vigil to cast the demons out of me. Several men came to my door to announce I was a harlot and would be damned, would be cast out of the kingdom of God, and would probably die soon. One forced his way into my home and managed to pin me to the floor. I knew this man. It was as if he had simply chosen the straw to be the man to rape me. It happened so fast, but as he was suddenly on top of me, I simply said, "Fred, you don't want to do this." Suddenly completely limp, he started to cry, got off of me, and quietly left.

Now I knew something about Christian hate.

I learned they could hate me because they loved Jesus and needed so desperately to be right, to be the ones who knew what God wanted and what God thought. That was 1976.

In 2016, I learned far too many things. I did not know what America had become. By 2016, I still did not know about racism in America. Institutional racism. Serious, deadly racism.

Years ago, I read a biography of Sojourner Truth, *Sojourner Truth: A Life, a Symbol,* by Nell Irvin Painter. Born into slavery in New York state, according to this biography, Sojourner was part of the first wave of the emancipation. Some accounts say she escaped with her infant child a year before the first emancipation, for which she would have qualified. This account says she bought her own son out of slavery; bought her own home; and became a preacher, speaker, abolitionist, and forerunner of the suffragist movement. Towering at a commanding six feet tall and possessing a powerful singing voice with which she delivered her sermons, she is most notably known for her famous speech "Ain't I a Woman?" However, one day at a heated abolitionist meeting, she stood up and asked a question perhaps more deeply profound: "Why"—and I can imagine a powerful pause here—"does the white man hate the black man so much?" She then sat down. I am certain the room was quiet for some time.

I am ashamed to admit I did not think much about how much the white man hates the black man until I witnessed the Donald Trump campaign, until I saw the T-shirts on his supporters and heard their comments captured on video. Men and women with passionate hate in the name of passionate love for their country.

I should have known. Love for your country is evidently a dangerous thing. I had witnessed it before.

In February 2016, I went to Israel as part of a small group to lead an international prayer vigil at the Syrian border. The effort was organized by author and peace activist James Twyman, from Portland, Oregon. Twyman's original vision was to gather members of the three Abrahamic faiths in Jerusalem, and he had hoped to enter Syria for the vigil. That, he learned, was out of the question. The vigil was not approved by the State Department and was roundly mocked on air by Bill Maher.

On the morning of the vigil, ten of us from the United States boarded a bus headed to the Golan Heights. Along the way we added Palestinians, Jews, Muslims, and Christians from East Jerusalem and various checkpoints along the way. An incident had occurred at one of the checkpoints, and Muslim women and children joining the vigil had to wait for several hours and walk for several more to reach the bus. I was struck with how easy it had been for us to walk out of the ancient hotel inside the gates of old Jerusalem and find a seat on the bus. We picked up clerics from all faiths and a man who tended camels in the desert. We crossed the Jordan River, and we were greeted by a

Druze guide in Majdal Shams, a Syrian town on the Israeli side of the Golan Heights.

The day before, we had been hosted by a Muslim philanthropist who lived at the top of the Mount of Olives. The details about our destination were known by only one man, a Jewish friend of both our lunch host and of James Twyman. That night, there ran among us the tiniest question about the secrecy of our destination and the proximity to the Syrian border. We joked about the Last Supper. I thought about my grandchildren and wondered if I was doing the right thing. I wondered only slightly about trusting the unknown.

In the town of Majdal Shams, we were twenty feet from the security fence between Israel and Syria. A bombed-out building sat not far up the hill from the fence. We were told not to venture any closer to the fence, as there were land mines on either side.

We arrived at our vigil place high in the Golan Heights, overlooking Syria in the valley below. That valley was inexplicably beautiful, with rolling hills leading toward the snowcapped peaks in the far distance. We could hear the howls of wolves not far below us and bombs far to our left.

We started the vigil at exactly 5:00 p.m., together with the thousands of others joining in prayer from locations around the world. As we became silent and I could hear the bombs, I cried for the children. My sadness was overwhelming. I imagined at that moment a blanket of white golden light, almost like molten gold and marshmallow, flowing gently and completely over the valley below, all the way to the mountains and as far as I could see. As I cried for the children, I wished for the blanket to protect them and that they would be safe and not alone. Later, I spoke with a woman who had the same vision. I feel tears welling now as I remember that moment.

I met no hate there. I met only a clear and present desire for humanity to embrace peace, and a shared conviction that the focused minds, hearts, and intentions of many thousands around the world could and would make a difference. Making that difference could take a long time, but we trusted that effecting a change might take only an instant. *We must not give up.*

I returned to the United States after only four days in Israel.

The more the campaigns began to unfold, I started to hate so many things: war for profit; prisons for profit; regime change for profit; destroying the earth, the air around her, the living things on her (and in her) for profit; fracking for profit; undrinkable water for profit; suffering children for profit—results of years and years of the status quo.

I did not know I was a hater.

Only Bernie Sanders was taking the strong stance I believe we so desperately needed. But his nomination was not meant to be.

So now we are left with the inconceivable idea of Donald Trump as the leader of the free world. He is armed with his loyal band of old businessmen in every cabinet position and social media posts about the ratings of *The Apprentice* with Arnold Schwarzenegger. And we now suspect he did not win legitimately.

I hate it.

So now is the moment I must change. I remember who I truly am. I am not a hater.

If we live long enough we might get to see the turning points in our lives. My father hated Communists until he saw the faces of a man and a woman, who loved their two young sons, and shared hopes and dreams for their future, just like him. My mother told me my father cried for the Rosenbergs many times throughout his life. We are told Jesus stood on the Mount of Olives, exactly where I stood, and cried for Jerusalem. I have cried for the children of Syria and for all the wars and regime changes in the world. And I have cried for the children who will grow up idolizing parents who hate for the sake of the love of their country.

This is something I have also come to learn in 2016: Home is not where we live, but how we live. I'm ready to live what I love and ready to choose the one thing I will focus on and not let it die. This moment will make a difference. I'm ready once again to be home.

Dominique Christina
Writer and poet
Colorado

The Things We Do After

THE YEAR 2016 was calamitous. We lost David Bowie and Prince, for God's sake. But 2016 was the year we would elect the first woman president of the United States, and that was something. We lost so many icons, but we were about to iconize Hillary Clinton. And once it was clear that she would be running against Donald Trump, I was more than ready to do that. I was not in love with her, but I have never been in love with *any* politician. I don't know how to be. Politics are in, so many ways, antithetical to what I do as a poet. Politicians distort the truth. Poets emphasize it.

I remember when I met Obama. I was a part of educational programming for the State Department, and he was a junior Senator. I liked him. A lot. His charm and toothy grin grabbed me. And so I couldn't understand why someone who seemed to be so genuine and intact would want to occupy a position that would likely challenge all that is good in an individual. How can you be head of a superpower and be moral at the same time? But I gave up on the idea that politicians could be messianic when

I learned that those cut from that cloth were often assassinated. I digress.

Hillary Clinton. A woman who had been a career politician and who, for all intents and purposes, had done some extraordinary things, precedent-setting things, the most obvious of which being when she became the first woman to be nominated as the presidential candidate by a major political party in the United States. Every feminist bone in my body was edified.

I watched both conventions: Republican and Democratic. I even took copious notes. I made my children watch everything with me, every one of the debates. Sitting in the living room with a seven-year-old child and fifteen-year-old twins, I watched the literal performance of toxic masculinity and bullying play out on a national stage. We saw the lynch mob pantomime in the "Lock her up!" chants that rang through the Republican convention. We saw the chauvinism, the egomania, and the gaslighting. My kids learned these terms. They were seeing the performance of it all; they just didn't know how to language it. We discussed everything. By the third debate, my second grader had more political acumen than the Republican nominee.

My daughter, who was in an Honors American Government class, was becoming increasingly flummoxed by it all. She understood. The was the first woman to be officially nominated to represent a major party in a presidential election had to be overqualified, while her opponent only needed to be a wealthy reality TV star with a predilection for posting on social media insults in the middle of the night, whose "political career" essentially started when he led the call for our first African American president to prove he was in fact American by presenting his birth certificate.

We heard the reports about Donald Trump's lawsuits, his affairs, and his refusal to provide his tax returns. We saw the

Access Hollywood tapes in which Trump declaratively affirms his right to kiss women without consent and to "grab 'em by the pussy," and we heard his detailed description about the time he tried to have sex with a married woman just months after he himself had gotten married to Melania. Yeah, we heard it all and felt confident that, while his nomination was despicable and certainly proof of why we need more Women Studies departments in schools, he would not win.

I was performing at Gettysburg College on election night. The students in attendance were nervous about the outcome. I reassured them: Hillary would win. We'd all write editorials about the culture of fear and loathing that Trump amplified and normalized, and then we could get down to the business of healing from the lunacy of it all. Sure, I was in a state of perpetual chagrin and outrage leading up to the election, but I was cautiously hopeful too.

But Hillary did not win. The womanizer did. The bully did. My daughter was almost catatonic from it. My seven-year-old son cried. My partner's cynicism grew. My mother felt betrayed. All of us were glad my grandparents, Civil Rights activists, were not alive to witness it. I went numb. I boarded a plane home the day after the elections and encountered frat boys in *Make America Great Again* hats screaming Trump's name into the faces of every person entering the aircraft. Flight attendants looked bewildered, but they tolerated it. When I got to my seat, I wept. I wept the whole way home.

Listen. I come from mighty people, powerful, supernatural, impossible people. My grandfather fought in a segregated army in World War II. He experienced liberating a Nazi camp with other Black soldiers and then being forced to give their seats up on a bus to Nazi war criminals because despite being heroic they were still black. My aunt Carlotta was one of nine students to desegregate Central High School in Little Rock, Arkansas, under the loose protection of federal marshals and decades later received the Congressional Gold Medal from Hillary's husband, President Bill Clinton. My grandmother taught elementary school for forty years. My mama is still a professor of Africana Studies at Metropolitan State University of Denver. My partner is an environmental engineer. Our children are brilliant and capable, and they believe they have a right to the world. I am an Afro-Latina woman writer with two master's degrees, three published books, and five national poetry championships. My God, the privilege in all of that. . . .

But Trump is president now, and in the wake of that reality, I have never interrogated my privilege more and examined what it means. Trump is president. The man who talked about bringing Stop and Frisk back on a national scale is president, and despite my degrees and accomplishments, I am still a Black woman and, therefore, not a member of a protected class. My children do not belong to a protected class. Nor does my partner. He and my sons fit "the profile." You know, the ones who during routine traffic stops die. The ones who, in death, become hashtags and a means for activists to shout even louder about police brutality.

What I know for sure is that everything in me that was rebellious, feels more amplified now. Every part of my identity feels more urgent. My womanness feels more dangerous, more necessary. The election radicalized me in a wider way. I have always been an agitator, always been brash and outspoken and a bit irreverent. Well, Donald J Trump, the man who bragged about how easy it is to sexually assault women if you're famous, is president, so now I'm fucking unapologetic. I have committed myself, as a woman, as a mother, and as an artist to interrupting the culture of violence, and violence is linguistic as much as literal. More even. When Trump declared Hillary a "nasty woman," I thought, *Well, this is oddly perfect.* Nasty woman *is an eponym for feminist, for the unconquered woman,*

the indomitable woman, the one whose blood we borrow from in
order to keep our names.

And on the subject of blood, I do have a lot of it in my eyes, but there are stars there too. I plan to keep all this fight I got and all this light I got. If my daughter inherits anything from me, let it be that. Let her make a world where this can't happen again, because we're smarter and braver and wiser . . . and nasty as we want to be . . . and free. Damn free.

Kerrie Houston Reightley, age 57
Writer
Bainbridge Island, Washington

By the Absolute Tips
of Our Fingers

THE STATE OF women's rights in America—exacerbated by the results of the 2016 presidential election—recalls a science-fiction scenario from Ray Bradbury's 1951 short story "The Other Foot." This masterpiece, one of many contained within Bradbury's award-winning *Illustrated Man*, is set in the 1950s. All African-Americans have settled on Mars after centuries of unspeakable cruelty on Earth. Twenty years have passed since the exodus, and Earth is now caught in the throes of World War III's nuclear ruin. One white man travels to Mars to beg forgiveness and requests that the remaining whites be allowed to take refuge on Mars. The elders first want to exact their revenge, but ultimately decide to allow the refugees to settle and live as equals.

Perhaps the "moral majority" will someday arrive at the same conclusion after being brought to understand their horrid treatment of women and minorities. Perhaps they will beg for forgiveness. One can only hope.

Fighting for women's rights for virtually her entire life is Christine Charbonneau, 56, chief executive officer of Planned Parenthood of the Great Northwest and Hawaiian Islands (PPGNHI). PPGNHI is a 500-employee not-for-profit organization with revenues of $51 million per year, serving more than 100,000 clients in twenty-eight health care sites across Washington, Idaho, Alaska, and Hawaii. Planned Parenthood is devoted to providing all aspects of reproductive health services, including sexual education and cancer screenings. According to Planned Parenthood's own statistics, three percent of the organization's services involve abortion—what, as Charbonneau put it, is "the most private decision a woman, and partner, will ever make."

Charbonneau began her inspired (and inspiring) career path with Seattle's Planned Parenthood in 1982, at age twenty-two, but her journey to protect women's rights was set in motion at age 11.

In 1971, her father, an international banker, moved his family to Zurich, Switzerland, to run Seattle's former Old National Bank. At the time, a debate was raging regarding whether Swiss women should have the right to vote. "I remember asking my mother why grocery and department store bags everywhere had imprinted on them: '*Frauen Wahlrecht ja*' [Women's Right to Vote: Yes!]," Charbonneau said. "It was embarrassing to the country, because the U.S. had the 19th Amendment and other places in the world had settled it. But, Swiss women still couldn't vote in federal elections. And they had to fix it, because it had turned into human rights abuses, and so every major store was in on the campaign."

"I kept asking my mother, 'What does this mean?'" Charbonneau continued. "I realized I was living in a place where women couldn't vote. It would be akin to growing up in the 1900s in the U.S. and suddenly it was as if we're having a debate if women had souls or not. I realized that women get—and hang on to—our rights by the absolute tips of our fingers," she said. "There is no time anyone will hand women anything, and there is no time when you can't be vigilant about it."

In due course, while studying history and political science at the University of Washington, Charbonneau gained a first-hand look at the plight of Seattle's inner-city Planned Parenthood clinic. For one Tuesday a week, she volunteered between four and six hours per day to help people access contraception. "I was absolutely clear that if women didn't have contraception, they couldn't finish their academic goals," she said. "You, in fact, could not control your destiny, and your body would not be your own."

Her memories of the old clinic stand in contrast to the new and improved Planned Parenthood of the Great Northwest and Hawaiian Islands. The previous location, now in a gentrified Seattle neighborhood, is just one block away from PPGNHI's current, beautifully appointed office building, made possible by the community's eighteen-month, $7 million capital campaign. "It was an old Albertsons, an A-shaped place with windows only in front, and burnt-orange and olive-colored furniture and countertops, [favored] in the 60s and 70s," she said. Still, it was a "vast improvement" from their variety of former storefronts and makeshift locations. "Before my time, they would set up a clinic so women and volunteer doctors would show up," she said, "and they'd set up curtains and people would get served one after the other. But I don't think any privacy would have met our standards today."

With fewer legal requirements and methods, she said, it was less complicated back then, because the organization mainly only offered diaphragms and pills. However, women had to "qualify" for tubal ligations—if enough money existed for one. One-month counseling sessions were commonplace. "We wanted to separate the movement from any exploitation that had gone on in the past, where women were sterilized in mental institutions and hospitals," she said. "We wanted to differentiate ourselves from that, and ensure that women were doing this on their own free will."

Charbonneau said she never imagined that women would have to fight an everyday battle for *Roe v. Wade*, a 1973 landmark decision by the United States Supreme Court, that ruled a right to privacy under the Due Process Clause of the 14th Amendment extended to a woman's right to have an abortion. "I was very young, thirteen, when it passed, so I didn't have personal experience with women dying, but I sure heard of women's experiences," she said. "There was a 40-year-old woman with an unimaginable circumstance, and the solution, because abortion was illegal, she was given a hysterectomy, and I remember thinking there was so much wrong with that."

Before *Roe v. Wade*, as is well-documented, clandestine abortions were the norm, resulting in women seeking self-induced, or dangerous, illegal procedures—often leading to death. The death rates were staggering. For wealthy women, however, the scenario was different. According to Charbonneau, in 1969, a Seattle travel company would every Friday fill a chartered 747 with women and fly to Tokyo, where abortions were legal.

"They'd go to Tokyo, have abortions by doctors, go to a few Shinto shrines, pick up some souvenirs, and pretend they did a weekend jaunt to Japan, for fun," Charbonneau said. "It cost $1,700, which was a truckload of money back then. That's how the rich women did it. Poor women did scarier stuff."

The scarier stuff, according to Charbonneau, often resulted in "septic abortions" that accounted for 40% of U.S. hospital admissions. *The New England Journal of Medicine* describes septic abortion as "an abortion associated with infection and complicated by fever, endometritis, and parametritis." It remains one of the most serious threats to women's health worldwide.

Charbonneau holds vivid memories, as a young adult, marching alongside "Emergency Room Physicians for Choice," who witnessed that dark period in U.S. history. "They put themselves out there," she said. "They were all doctors who were first line when people came in, and they were talking about women bleeding to death in their hands, and how completely unacceptable that was. They were all men who were at the top of their careers prior to *Roe*. They were the ones called in and asked 'Can you save her?' and sometimes they could, but a lot of times they couldn't. The physicians said they never want to go back to that."

The legalization of abortion, according to Charbonneau, started with an outbreak of German Measles (otherwise known as Rubella) in the United States in the early-to-mid 1960s. Mothers infected with the disease often passed it to their unborn fetus, rendering the child likely to die in utero, or to be born with any of a number of serious physical and mental disabilities. "You were stuck as a family," Charbonneau said. "If things went wrong with a pregnancy, and you had a dead fetus inside of you, you could have [it] for months, while it slowly killed you." After the right to abortion was recognized by the Supreme Court, everyone involved thought the fight was over. But, then the "Right to Life" movement was born. "At first they did ineffective things," Charbonneau said, "but then they came up with smarter ways to make it more difficult for women to get care."

Along those lines, however, the United States Supreme Court, in *Whole Woman's Health v. Hellerstedt*, recently overturned Texas laws that would have had the effect of limiting women's right to an abortion. If the laws had instead been upheld, states would be able to pass laws requiring physicians who perform abortions to have hospital admitting privileges, live within a certain radius of a hospital, and require abortion clinics to have facilities comparable to an ambulatory surgical center. The case became a "political nightmare," according to Charbonneau, and, before it was overturned, similar laws had been used in places, like Mississippi, where everyone could be easily pressured never to grant admitting privileges.

"There were things like mandatory twelve-foot hallways," she said. "The conditions had to be good enough for neurosurgery, even if you were just handing patients pills. We saw mandatory ultrasounds, even though your doctor doesn't think you need one, but the legislature does," she continued. "It was absolutely invasive, outrageous things that were decided so they could punish women if they decided they needed an abortion."

Charbonneau believes that the attempted restrictions on abortion posed in *Hellerstedt* stems from a long line of that kind of thinking. "There are people who are really angry with women who dare to determine [their] own reproductive choices, let alone run for president," she said. "It's the old double standard," she continued. "Hillary is responsible for Bill's affairs; he is not." At the same time, she said, the entire "Right to Life" movement—which she calls the "Anti-choice Movement"— refuses to support sexuality education. "There is much less chance of an unintended pregnancy if you know what your risks are, and a way to think through your plan in a situation like that," she said. "I think that, weirdly, if you were interested in avoiding unintended pregnancy, you would want people to have education, and highly effective contraception methods."

As an example of exemplary sexuality education, Charbonneau commended the "wonderfully open, progressive" state of Hawaii. PPGNHI was instrumental in passing a sexual education bill that provides medically accurate sexuality education for every student in Hawaii. "If parents don't want their children in the program," Charbonneau said, "they don't have to opt them in, they have to opt them out."

For this generation, Charbonneau hopes they'll have a better understanding of the most personal issues that people deal with—without the fear and trepidation that come with fundamental life issues.

"There is a place where nothing is quite like somebody who cares, in helping in some real way, whatever form that takes to help you know what to do next," she said. "I'd like Planned Parenthood to end up with a real combination of every smart thing that makes us super-efficient and technological, coupled with the warmest, kindest approach to what is frightening that we can muster."

Back in her early days of volunteering, Charbonneau recalls, "We were like everybody's oldest sister that you needed to know." She doesn't want that lost. "In women's reproductive care," she continued, "where you're naked, undressed and vulnerable— and things like death and dying, or for some people, handling money—it's places like that, where it's about survival and your identity that need to be handled delicately. Keep humanity, so everyone has access. We have to make sure we cover things women need. At the end of the day, we're a community of people together. We want to take care of each other."

Elizabeth Blakesley, age 47
Librarian and Artist
Pullman, Washington

We Thought We'd Come
a Long Way, Baby

I ACTUALLY WENT TO bed fairly early on election night because I was exhausted and I felt sick. I never even got around to mixing drinks. I watched those results stone cold sober and sat there with paper and pen working the math, reality sinking in long before anyone else seemed willing to admit what was happening.

I think the reason I was relatively numb was that, no matter who won, during this election cycle the country had shown its true colors and that, in some ways, the outcome didn't matter. If you didn't know you were living in a racist country, I don't know where you've been. Yes, we had made some strides. Certain things were illegal everywhere, and enough people were on board to make them rare occurrences instead of the norm. But the Internet's vitriol and hatred about President Obama for the last eight years is stunning, and not in a good way. People who want to "take our country back" or "make it great again" have come out of the woodwork and risen up, and no matter who won in 2016, those people had become loud.

Immediately after Trump's win, instances of hate crimes, personal attacks, racist graffiti, and hate speeches rose. I find myself recalling the racism I grew up around in Kokomo, Indiana, in the 1970s and 1980s—the presence of a KKK chapter and the existence of a sundown town nearby. I recall people's believing that Catholics weren't Christians. Saying you were Catholic was the easiest way to get the Jehovah's Witnesses off the porch, fleeing as if you'd told them you were devil worshippers. And I could write a whole different essay on the homophobia tied to the Ryan White case. When I see the press's coverage of words and images spray-painted on walls and of some people's hateful behaviors, it is as if the progress I've witnessed in the last twenty-five years has been erased overnight.

Before the election results were tallied, reports of harassment were surfacing. In my library, on a university campus in eastern Washington state, we had two incidents of hate graffiti. One targeted African Americans and included the words *Trump 2016*; the other was directed toward Asian Americans.

I used social media to show my outrage, publicize our new security cameras (which unfortunately did not capture either event), and generally make it clear: not in our library. My equally outraged colleagues sprung into action to remove the offending graffiti and have since incorporated checking for graffiti into existing walk-around procedures.

While a lack of racial justice and a reemergence of xenophobic policy-making may be hallmarks of the Trump presidency, misogyny is at the core of the issues that led to Clinton's technical defeat via the Electoral College. Patton Oswalt said it best on Twitter˙ on election night. To paraphrase, he indicated that Americans are more misogynistic than racist, and that's saying a lot, given how racist we are.[29] Election Day itself was an interesting day. Many of us women felt particularly empowered, dressed in our pantsuits, our bright blue jackets, or our white suffragette-honoring garb. It was a bit surreal then when, on Election Day, I found myself faced with a male colleague's trying to force me to apologize for communicating about a work issue via email to a group of people who had been impacted. I was apparently supposed to have phoned him privately to handle the matter. He even tried to shame me for having expressed some anger and frustration in my communiqué. If it hadn't been Election Day, if issues of feminism and equality hadn't been so heavy on my mind, perhaps the situation wouldn't have struck me as anything more than a run-of-the-mill interdepartmental misunderstanding or conflict over programming that I deal with routinely.

It's the little things like that incident, even in this day and age, that pile up and weigh us women down. Many of the big problems may be solved, but the casual slights, the small indignities, and the careless omissions continue. And because the big ones are solved—*hey, come on, we let you vote and wear pants to work!*—the little ones are so often brushed aside or dismissed.

Those of us who believed Clinton could, should, and would win relied on people being good, or at least reasonable. We thought being on the side of fairness, equality, and love was enough, even though every day the news headlines reminded us the world is not filled with those things. Yet, we hoped.

And so, there can still be hope. But it is difficult to remember

---

29 Patton Oswalt, Twitter post, November 8, 2016, 5:23 p.m., https://twitter.com/pattonoswalt/status/796176331377516544?lang=en

that truth on days like November 9, December 19, and January 20, when the events crystallizing the opposite of hope play out on television screens ad nauseum. For the past eight years, those of us who were holding signs back in 1989 that urged our country to *Divest from South Africa* and who were wearing red ribbons finally had a president whose values and policies reflected the world we wanted to live in. Now the guy who in 1989 blasted the newly syndicated Rush Limbaugh radio show and who soaked up Breitbart in more recent times has a president to represent him.

For the last eight years, the right has obstructed President Obama and his party's policies and nominees for the courts, as well as made racially charged comments about him and his family. Now, as people protest the policies, executive orders, cabinet, and court selections of Trump, his supporters want us to "get over it," to "move on," and to "respect" Trump. It is startling how so many conservatives have no memory of their reactions on election nights in 2008 and 2012. It is amazing how people who have spent the last eight years refusing to accept the legitimacy of the elected president are now chiding others for not immediately getting on board with their guy. Others hated Obama for no reason other than his skin color, and they were not even subtle about it.

Worst of all is the *now you know how we felt* rhetoric, which highlights another issue beyond race. Leadership of the nation has devolved into a sports rivalry, with the presidency's being the equivalent of the Old Oaken Bucket or the Territorial Cup, a trophy to be flaunted. But what can we expect from a society where sports and reality television have become so embedded in our culture that an entertainer with absolutely no experience with public office can be taken seriously as a candidate and is now installed in the Oval Office?

I have an icon on my wall of Mary Harris "Mother" Jones

proclaiming her battle cry: "Pray for the dead, but fight like hell for the living."[30] The Republicans' zealotry for repealing the Affordable Care Act, even though many of their voters didn't realize they were benefitting from it due to their confusion with the "Obamacare" nickname,[31] certainly highlights the first fight to the death we may face.

When I finally worked up the nerve to watch the video of Clinton's concession speech on November 10, the moment I heard her implore us to "never stop believing that fighting for what's right is worth it"[32] was when I finally broke down and cried. I cried for all that I knew we had lost in that moment, and I cried in anticipation of the exhaustion we would feel with the impending endless fight for what's right.

Zora Neale Hurston once wrote that "there are years that ask questions and years that answer."[33] It may be difficult to see clear answers for a few years, but we must keep asking questions, all of the questions, bringing the disinfectant of sunlight to the gaslighting, and keep fighting for what is right.

---

30 Elliott J. Gorn, "Mother Jones: The Woman," *Mother Jones* (May/June 2001): http://www.motherjones.com/politics/2001/05/mother-jones-woman

31 See, for example, Hillary Busis, "Way Too Many People Think Obamacare and the Affordable Care Act Are Different Things," *Vanity Fair* (January 10, 2017): http://www.vanityfair.com/hollywood/2017/01/obamacare-affordable-care-act-jimmy-kimmel

32 "Hillary Clinton's concession speech (full text)." CNN. Accessed February 05, 2017. http://www.cnn.com/2016/11/09/politics/hillary-clinton-concession-speech/index.html.

33 Zora Neale Hurston, *Their Eyes Were Watching God* (New York: Lippincott, 1937), 21.

C. Elisheva Offenbacher, age 37
Writer/editor
Seattle, Washington

The Huddled Masses

I HAVE A PRETTY extensive trauma history, but I'm resilient as fuck, and have erected scaffolding around my heart to protect myself from spiraling into the abyss. But ten days after Donald Trump's *grab them by the pussy* tape came out, I called a crisis hotline four times, saw a therapist twice, and met with a domestic violence advocate. I was a mess.

Survivors get mocked by Trump supporters for being "snowflakes" because they think we're fragile, but here's something I know firsthand: trauma leaves an indelible mark on one's person that is hard to navigate around. People who haven't been touched by trauma often can't comprehend the severity of its symptoms. They don't know what it's like to be catapulted into thoughts of suicide and self-harm after being triggered by something as innocuous as a smell or sound. They don't understand the phenomenon of getting so lost in a memory that one can't talk themselves out of it or convince their mind and body that they are safe.

Some Trump supporters show no compassion—they've

turned harassment into a sport. They antagonize and berate people who have already survived hell and back, without any thought for what that might do to a "snowflake's" already damaged psyche. Trauma victims often kill themselves because they can't cope with severe symptoms of PTSD, or the abject despair that often comes with it. They don't need the extra help from Trump supporters to push them over the edge.

Even though my anxiety never diminished, I became pro-active about the election as a way to cope with Trump's nomination. I began phone banking for Hillary Clinton every day, routinely engaged in public discourse, and gave what money I could afford to the people in red states knocking on doors. It alleviated some of my hand-wringing, but I was still nervous about Trump. I've learned not to underestimate the population's ability to do something misguided at any given time. I wasn't entertaining the idea that he might actually win. Trump couldn't *really* beat the most qualified candidate we've ever had for president, could he? I would have a lot to lose if he did.

I'm disabled, and because I fell ill with degenerative conditions in the middle of my university education, I lack the credentials needed to work in my field. I now depend on Social Security and state and city-based social services to stay marginally afloat. I also rely on the Affordable Care Act, Medicare, and Medicaid to keep me somewhat functional, and a housing grant to keep a roof over my head. If Trump won and followed through with his promise to eliminate or drastically neuter these social programs, I'd be screwed.

* * *

We all know how the final count turned out. History had definitely been made, but in the wrong direction.

I watched the election day coverage on a TV at a diner where

I was having dinner with friends. As the unexpected results became clear, some of my friends left, some cried, some seethed; others were enraged. I was one of the criers.

The tears kept flowing all night and into the early morning as I waited on hold for a crisis line counsellor for four and half hours. Yes, *four and a half hours*. During the election, calls to rape crisis lines increased dramatically across the country. After Trump won, the backlog became even worse. After hours of not getting through, I finally cried myself to sleep around 4:00 a.m.

The next morning, I went to a coffee shop—not for coffee or to work, but because I didn't want to be alone. My friends who worked there saw me and ran over, putting their arms around me as I cried against their chests. (I'm not a public crier, but I couldn't help myself.) Throughout the day, tears kept streaming unabated down my face while I worked. My friends kept bringing over coffee and pastries. They clearly did not know how to ease my pain, but their concern reassured me that we were in this mess together.

When I walked out of the coffee shop, cops were pulling up out front and I could hear protesters chanting in the distance, "Fuck Donald Trump! Fuck Donald Trump!"

The plan to go home and seek peaceful refuge evaporated like water in a frying pan. I joined the protest.

In Seattle, marching and protesting for social liberation movements are a matter of culture and pride. This wasn't the first protest I'd participated in, but it was the first in which I felt the true power of a unified whole. No one was distracting from our message with violence. No one was antagonizing the police as they directed traffic around the protest. Many of us even took the time to thank them for their protection, and the cops were incredibly respectful of our right to protest—some even looked like they wished they could join in. People streamed out of buildings, some mixing in with marchers, some staying on sidewalks and raising their fists in solidarity with the chanting, "Not my president!" We continued marching for over thirty miles.

I'd never been in such a large protest, with 1,200 people marching in unison. It filled me with pride to be a part of it. I went home and slept better than I had since mid-summer.

* * *

During the month of January, I slept little, consumed as many innocuous forms of media as possible, swam almost compulsively, and tried to avoid any anxiety-unleashing social media platforms. I was exhausted, but moderately functional.

On January 20, 2017, I slept as long as humanly possible. I couldn't bear to watch the Inauguration. I kept reminding myself: one more day 'til the Women's March on Washington, just one more day.

My friends and I had plans to march together. I waited downtown for the protest to reach the city. I needed crutches to walk safely and I knew there was no way I'd be able to march the entire length. The feeling in Seattle was electric and all the coffee shops were full, people filling up the sidewalks like they were waiting for a Super Bowl Parade. If you can imagine it, somewhere between 175,000 and 220,000 residents, most of whom will never feel the brunt of Trump's actions (thanks to our city's predominantly blue politics), participated in the protest march. Everyone was friendly, chatty, and buzzing to join the march when it went by. It took hours for it to reach us, and then four more hours to make it across the Central Business District, but it was worth it—to be surrounded by the beautiful pink mass of pussy hats, the witty signs, the anti-trump shirts and hoodies. The march wasn't angry. It was compassionate, forgiving, and determined—but not angry.

That feeling of hope and unity was reinforced the following

week when we went out en masse to march against Trump and his ban on Muslims. The rally was attended by city leadership, state representatives, our governor, and around 3,000 citizens (the same amount had gone to the airport the night before to protest).

The next day, our state Attorney General announced he was filing a lawsuit against the Trump administration, Trump himself, and his top aides, in a bid to avoid implementing any part of the executive order banning migrants and travelers from predominantly Muslim countries.

Washington is taking a stand against this administration and standing up for its citizens in a way that is not only empowering, but that unifies us as well. Trump will not divide us. He will not destroy us. We've seen this game before and we're going to fight him every step of the way. We'll comb through executive orders, along with House and Senate Bills, looking for even a hint of unconstitutionality. We'll relentlessly call our representatives and demand they acquiesce to our values of equality and freedom. We'll put our names on any Muslim registry created. We'll don hijabs to show Muslim women that they're not alone. We'll file as many lawsuits as necessary to protect our sanctuary cities and their residents. Then we'll march on behalf of whichever group he decides to marginalize next!

We're tired of Trump wrongly claiming that Mexicans are rapists and drug traffickers, insinuating that people of color and the impoverished are all criminals. We're fed up with being told that women only dissent if they're on their periods. We are sick of corporate interests taking precedence over the interests of everyday citizens. The reason this Republic is called the *United* States of America is because, though we suffer from "affluenza" that occasionally makes us forget what's going on outside our privileged bubble, we're generally good and principled people who share similar values.

The world needs to remember that more than seventy-four million people in America voted against Trump; his main competitor won the popular vote by three million. Despite a sometimes-checkered history, we've worked hard over the last fifty years to become a country that values all of her citizens and residents, not just the native-born, not just the top earners, certainly not just reality TV tyrants. We still want your huddled masses. We want them so badly that we have become a huddled mass again ourselves, and we won't rest until our country looks the way it is supposed to: free and equal.

Melissa Bobula Miotke, age 36
Business owner
Mesa, Arizona

The Blame Is on Us All

A T FIRST TRUMP'S campaign for president seemed like a joke. I almost hoped he would win the primaries, because I figured his nomination as the Republican Party's presidential candidate would mean a sure victory for Clinton. The year leading up to the election had been an eye-opener. Donald Trump made it socially acceptable to act hateful, racist, and judgmental, and his supporters followed his lead.

*   *   *

I was a Republican for most of my life, raised to believe that most people shouldn't need help in the land of opportunity. I was fed lies about people living in the projects, who didn't work, yet somehow owned boats and always had plenty of cigarettes. Those lazy people whom I had never met, and whose existence I never bothered to question, were proof that government assistance encouraged laziness. Anyone truly enterprising could get ahead and improve their lot in life.

Through the years I moved further and further to the left.

Living on my own, I saw firsthand how difficult the world could be. It came as a surprise. I was from a two-parent household, with a stay-at-home mom and a dad who earned six figures. Growing up, I went to private schools in a city frequently rated as the number one place to raise a family. My whole life was steeped in white privilege, and I never knew it.

I now live in one of the most conservative neighborhoods in one of the most conservative cities in the conservative state of Arizona. As the election approached, the racism and hate continued to seep from the pores of people I knew and loved. I found myself engaging in fights daily, online and offline. I posted inflammatory memes promoting old-fashioned sentiments like *equality for all*. I shared articles on history, statistics, and morality. When racist comments appeared under my posts, I didn't let them go unchecked.

The public spats with friends had a double agenda. My husband and I came to the conclusion that the fights weren't simply to prove our friends wrong, but to showcase our views to those silently watching, still undecided. Our hope was to sway them. I received reassurance that these tactics were working on multiple occasions when, those on the sidelines reached out privately and told me they agreed 100%. Having their support made me feel less alone, but I didn't understand why they wouldn't publicly denounce hate. Now I have to admit that I resent those who shared the same views but kept silent.

*   *   *

I've been screaming into the wind. My voice gets carried away, lost and small. Still, I keep putting myself out there until I'm hoarse, and it comes back battered and bruised. I speak up because, as a parent, I don't have the luxury to stay silent. Silence is an action, and that action is acceptance. I can't tell my children they are free to be themselves, while tacitly accepting the fact that others are not. I can't teach them to let others in, while we build a wall to keep others out.

When I was a child, I learned about the various atrocities throughout history. I thought whenever a child read Anne Frank's diary, they fancied themselves to be the one who would have hidden her in the attic. That when we read about the underground railroad, we knew we would have had enough courage to offer protection to black runaways, at the risk of our own lives. I suppose it's easy to flatter ourselves in this manner when we don't believe we'll ever be tested. The 2016 presidential election was a surprise test. We failed miserably, but that failure did open our eyes.

Once my eyes were fully opened, I realized I would never be able to forgive myself if I didn't live up to my childhood ideal and fight inequality. I wasn't letting racism go unchecked and was trying to spread awareness, but those efforts just weren't enough. I started seeking out groups that promote equality, such as the United Front, and I bought a *Black Lives Matter* T-shirt. None of those actions seemed like enough, and so I got involved in the creation of a post-election march. Trump scares me, as a woman, but he scares me even more so on behalf of minorities. And they have always been the focus of what I'm fighting for.

* * *

The morning after the election, I volunteered as a teacher's assistant at the school my older daughter attends. As I filed away the kids' "About Me" papers, I noticed the question *What am I curious about?*

The lilting sound of the children's voices dimmed into a low hum as I found myself reading their answers, the pages crisp between my fingers. For a moment, the world stopped as I enjoyed a few minutes in the minds of the young. My daughter had written that she wondered how people began. Another girl had said that she wanted to know what she would be someday. As I slowly became aware again of the sound of innocent chatter, a hot rage began at my cheeks and spread through my body. I felt dizzy, and my stomach started to turn at the thought of what we as a country had done only the day before. Those beautiful inquisitive minds are ripe to be shaped by the world around them. We tell them every day that when they grow up, they can be anything. What are we telling them now about their value, and how have we adversely affected their futures?

Had things turned out differently in this election, we could have easily slipped into complacency, believing others would try to make our world a better place. Now we have no such illusions. I've learned that oftentimes what initially seems catastrophic turns out to be a blessing in disguise. The blessing here is that recent events have spurred so many of us to action. We will unite. We will fix corruption. We will fight for the lives of refugees, as well as for true equality for women, black people, gay people, all people.

At the end of the day, who I am matters more to me than who stands next to me. I am willing to be alone, rather than sink into the muck with those I thought I loved. I don't care if we're both liberal or have the same last name; if you don't care about human rights and equality for all, then it's my intention to fight you, with strong spirited daughters at my side. But if you fight for equality for all, I will stand beside you as a sister.

Because the blame is on us all, we must stand together to correct our wrongs. We *can* fight for the redemption of our generation, our country, and our souls.

Jennifer Tyree, age 30
College student and mom
Phoenix, Arizona

Now Is the Time to
Make History

I'M A THIRTY-YEAR-OLD white woman married to a black man. We have a daughter together and a son, who is part Puerto Rican, part white, from a previous relationship of mine. My husband and I have been together since 2004, and married since 2008. We live outside of Phoenix, Arizona.

I had never followed politics until this election. During my growing-up years, my mom walked the line between conservative and liberal. My stepdad was pretty conservative. His parents were Republicans, and he grew up in a predominantly white town. My dad never explicitly said I couldn't date or marry someone of another race, but he didn't exactly encourage it either. Rather, I'd get passive-aggressive remarks that tried to push me into the direction of "someone of my same color."

I grew up in a very diverse area of northern Ohio. In high school, I didn't really date. I was a senior in high school by the time I started seriously considering dating someone. I began dating a tall, dark, and handsome Puerto Rican man. Our age difference—he was twenty-three; I was seventeen—didn't matter to me. In fact, I thought it was cool (and it gave me bragging rights with my friends). Now that I know better, I realize he was a predator. He didn't exactly pressure me into sex, but I certainly felt like I *had* to. We ended up doing it in his van. (Classy, right?) A few minutes in, I told him I wasn't comfortable and wanted to stop, and he listened. But not soon enough, because the next thing I knew, I was pregnant.

At that time in my life, abortion wasn't an option, and I certainly wasn't comfortable with giving the baby up for adoption. I knew what I needed to do: grow up and be a good mom (something I swore I wouldn't be until I was at least thirty). I wasn't going to let the baby keep me from going to college in Arizona, however. And I told my boyfriend this. He didn't seem to mind. He was excited to make the change and move with us.

I was eight months pregnant when I graduated from high school. Not too long after, my boyfriend and his parents approached me, asking me not to go. I said no because I knew myself; if I didn't do it then, I wouldn't do it at all. I'd mastered the art of procrastination.

My son was born, and the boyfriend was around very little. I broke up with him before moving to Arizona when it was clear he didn't want to be a part of our lives.

* * *

As a teenage single mother, I had a hard time exuding confidence when I went out. I tried holding my head high, but unfortunately, I couldn't deafen my ears to the criticism. I definitely wasn't old enough to have a child. My son had dark skin at birth, but by a few months old, his skin became lighter. I guess my genes took over and he turned into a fair-skinned, blonde-haired, blue-eyed boy. He looked *just* like me.

My husband and I met after I moved to Arizona. He was also from Ohio and had been living in Tucson for five years when I moved to Phoenix. We had an online relationship at first; then it progressed to visits on the weekends and on breaks from school. Eventually, my son and I moved to Tucson to live with him. A few years later, we married, and eventually we expanded our family when I got pregnant with our daughter. My son was now a big brother.

My husband claims he doesn't pay attention to people's reactions when we are out in public. I, on the other hand, can't help but notice the dirty looks from white people (and sometimes people of color). I guess they don't like seeing a little white boy call a black man *Daddy*, or maybe they assume I'm cheating.

Prejudice rears its ugly head in other ways. For instance, if my husband and I go to the furniture store, nine times out of ten, the salesperson will come up to me and ask me, "Can I help you with anything?" assuming I'm the one making the purchase.

*   *   *

A couple years ago, a death in my husband's family required we drive back to Ohio for the funeral. While my husband stayed at the house with our kids, I went with some of his family to pick out a headstone and select a suitable inscription. Driving home from the cemetery, my father-in-law was going a little too fast. None of us in the car saw the speed limit signs, and I don't think any of us realized how fast we were going. Then we saw the cop on the side of the road. Immediately, he pulled out behind us, and we saw the lights. He hadn't turned on the siren, as we pulled over immediately. Instantly, the air in the car felt tight.

My father-in-law had his window already rolled down. The policeman asked my father-in-law for his driver's license and registration. After my father-in-law showed him the requested documents, the cop went on to ask, "Why are you in town?"

I flinched. What kind of question was that? I had been pulled over plenty of times before in towns where I wasn't a resident, and a cop had never asked me that question.

"We're here for a funeral," my father-in-law explained. "We're staying with my parents."

The policeman stared hard at my father-in-law for a long second, contemplating the authenticity of his statement. Finally the officer said, "Hold tight." He went to his car and came back with a slip of paper. "I'm giving a warning this time," he said. "People who live on the street have been complaining lately because many cars just speed through here."

* * *

When I first heard Trump was running for president, I thought it was hilarious. Then he talked about Mexicans like they were horrible people. Little did I know, he was just getting started. *Oh. My. God. Did he say that? Whoa, he said that too? Please let this be a joke.* I knew instantly that, here in Arizona at least, there would be unrest. As a white person, I had an uneasy feeling.

On election night, I printed cheat sheets. I was ready to mark off all the Democrat squares. Then, suddenly, it felt like I was being shown the wrong news feed. Trump was ahead. I started to get nervous. My heart was racing. I started to sweat. I jokingly told my husband: "I feel like this must be what menopause will feel like." I felt ill, as if I was going to vomit. I flipped the channel to *Law & Order: SVU*, which was much less depressing. Later, I came back to ABC, and Trump was still ahead. My husband went to bed because he had to work early in the morning. "No matter what the results are, please don't wake me up," he said. He knew if I was happy, I would talk his head off as he tried to sleep. Same for if I was mad. He just wanted to get enough sleep for work the next day. His outlook was that life would still go on no matter who won.

When it was a sure bet Trump would win, I began sobbing. I didn't stop for hours. The next day was just as bad. I avoided the news, radio, social media, and any talk about politics.

*   *   *

Weeks after the election, my family and I went shopping. Right as we were ready to check out, my husband and son walked away to use the restroom. At that moment, an elderly white woman, who had been staring at us while we shopped, walked up to me. "Why aren't you with your son's white father?" she asked.

I was horrified, but also grateful that my husband and son had walked away, so they weren't in earshot. "The child's birth father is not white, and the man I'm with *is* his father," I explained, even though she sure as hell didn't deserve an explanation. "He stepped in when he didn't have to when my son was only three months old."

The woman appeared a bit stunned and backed away.

I couldn't believe I had even responded. It was, in fact, the first time I *had* responded to someone's racist remarks—at least in person. (Unless commenting on online posts written by racist cowards, counts. But that's a different story for another day.)

Since that time, I've decided to speak out more—not just to the people who stare or make snide remarks about my family but also whenever I see or hear discrimination in any form. If I see a call to action to write letters to lawmakers, I will. If I see someone of color being harassed, I'll speak up. If I see my brothers and sisters of any race or religion being harassed, I'll step in.

I'll help my fellow humans in any way I can. We must prove we are better than the racist bigot who sits on the iron throne. We must rally. Now is the time to make history.

Kelly Lomeland, age 44
Fire safety national account representative
Rancho Santa Margarita, California

Bravery in the Bones

W HAT DO YOU do when you're terrified of the current nightmare?

Terrified is second nature to me; I came screaming into the world, riddled with debilitating fear. Because of birthmarks that cause people to stare, I knew I was different from everyone else; the fear of others kept me hiding from the world.

On election night, I sat in the hotel ballroom to watch the election coverage. When it became clear Trump would win, absolute terror settled into me. My hands were shaking, a cold sweat came over me, I started freaking out inside, and this feeling came over me like I couldn't grieve by myself. I was in a social networking group online, and I started sending out friend requests like someone else was in control of my mind and fingers. I got in my car, started driving, broke down, and cried like I had just lost a family member. The crying brought on a gnarly migraine, so I took days off at home, shut off from the world. I kept thinking, *I have to do something. Am*

I capable of moving forward? How do I look at people? Maybe
if I sleep, the horrible events will just have been a nightmare.
Can the universe reset that day? . . . So I sit. And I think what
can I do and reflect back to where I go to find strength and
courage.

*   *   *

I grew up in a family who are proud of our ancestors and their
legacy of service. My great-great-great-great grandfather was
John Brown, the slave abolitionist.

Hearing and learning from my grandfather about John
Brown was inspiring to us. He inspired me to think about what
I can do too. Then my grandpa would share stories of when
my grandparents were politically active, working with Robert
Kennedy or Cesar Chavez. During my grandma's time, the
Democratic Party sent a letter to her work requesting that she
be allowed off to serve and be the party's convention secretary.
We still have the letter, which is the coolest thing. The phone
company allowed her time off to serve.

Those years were painful: we lost leaders who had given us
hope. The night of Robert Kennedy's speech at the Ambassador
Hotel, my grandparents were invited to be in his room with
others waiting for the victory party. My mom was downstairs
still with everyone else when he was assassinated. The chaos
was devastating, and my mom still to this day can't talk about
it without crying. Most of the time, she can't talk about it at
all. The pain they felt kind of reminds me of how we felt on
the night of November 8, 2016. My grandma officially dropped
out of being politically active; she said the assassinations of
John Kennedy, Martin Luther King, and then Robert Kennedy
became too much for her. I know she always voted, but losing
the three leaders who brought hope to everyone—and those
deaths' being so close in time—had such an impact that changed

the directions of a lot of wounded people. They felt that hope was now a fleeting memory.

Hearing my grandpa talk about the deaths, pained me made me think that if my grandparents could endure that pain and keep fighting, then I should find my voice and fight. My grandpa talked about his time working with Cesar Chavez and Dorothy Huerta and inspired me to always be on the firing line. How did my family always get back up, knock off the dirty mud, and push on? They have always been my heroes, showing the way, not just giving lip service. I know I can endure anything if I keep them close to my heart and find that spot in my family's legacy of service to take their strength with me.

I watched my sister work with senators representing California, and campaign to elect Bill Clinton. Growing up and knowing the history of why Harvey Milk and Mayor George Moscone were killed in a city where it's supposedly safe to be who you are, I knew the risks.

I kept thinking, *It won't matter if I get involved, people are shitty, and can I handle the letdown?* The 2016 election was different. I worked the phone banks and spoke out about my support. So then why did my internal system keep screaming at me like a hollering monkey? My opinions about my friends were changing, and the respect I had for them, drastically shrinking. How did they get past my approval stage? I don't have any room for racists in my life, and they revealed themselves.

I started to go numb so that I could remain friends with them. But why did I allow this? *Maybe it's only a nightmare, and I will wake up. . . .*

Nope. Social media was killing my respect of people— watching them post conspiracy theories, one after another, exhausted me. I thought, *How did we become so dumbed down that we can't see the path of hate and we deny its potential to overpower everyday people?* I decided I was sitting in a tsunami of fears that were getting stronger every day. Soon I feared I wouldn't be able to function. I needed to get some sort of stable ground under me or I would shut completely down.

I don't want to fear being bullied for being gay, and I can't be shoved back into the closet. Anger and depression come from being forced into the closet for fear of violence where I live; job security means survival. I can tolerate being yelled at and called "dyke" from far away—maybe one day they will hear me laughing at what is considered an insult. Here I am terrified we're going to lose the right to marry, and bringing back conversion therapy to "cure this evil" scares me. I feel lucky that I live in California, as the state government already put in place laws that protect the LGBTQ community. The new federal administration is not going to be able to sway California's state leaders. But I fear the teaching of Christianity will become a requirement in public schools. I fear such a law because history shows the church to be highly against my community, terrified we are contagious. People who think that whole "it's a choice or lifestyle" view have no idea the consequences of these words. If it's a choice, then be gay for a month, just one, and then tell me it's a choice. The pain of these politically correct words does more damage to the LGBTQ community, as we're not entitled to be like everyone else—we get special words that make us stand out more.

To know you're different and not understand because you hear it's wrong, is soul crushing. Soul crushing. But you're dying inside from rage and the confusion of wondering, *Why am I different,* and *why me?* Great. Those thoughts spiral: *Now that I have more to fear, I am depressed. How do I find* me?

The moment I finally found my people and was embraced by drag queens, dykes, and fags, I finally breathed a sigh of relief. I felt normal and accepted. I could ask them all of my questions too.

The hardest part was outing myself officially to my family—who already knew, of course—but it was scary. *Would they disown me like others were doing?* I know I'm lucky in that regard and in many ways. After I found myself, the rage lessened; I was not so angry all the time. The drag queens who stood up at the Stonewall Inn, in the heart of New York made me realize that I need to be active for my community.

In the days following the election, two of my sisters tried to ease my fears about the likelihood of my rights' being stripped again. I understood what my sisters were doing, but their words overwhelmed me. Flashes of past memories pierced my heart. I adore them for trying to show me that Trump couldn't strip our rights. Their effort to try to ease my fears reminds me how loved I am and accepted for who I am.

In contrast, I live in a Republican county where too many people love to flaunt their new money. My response to the snooty, is living louder, so I wear my queerness for all to see. I will not be forced to feel like I'm a disease and to be depressed or angry about who I am. Oh, no—I'm going to be confident and live in the love that I've been surrounded with my whole life. Nothing pisses the haters off more than someone's living a happy life.

* * *

Since the election, I've decided that no matter how many times I was needed, I must step out of my comfort zone. I wanted to be a friendly face. I decided to empower myself and volunteered to be secretary of my local Canyon Democratic Party Club. My goal is to attend the city council meetings and report back to my community to keep local politicians accountable. I will not back down for four years. I will *not* accept this administration as the people's choice. This presidency was stolen from the people, and the keys were handed to the most dangerous people, who are not even qualified to hand out tissues to millions of people weeping. I never thought the citizens of the United States would hand over their freedom for a price. I've never been this scared for the people of the world. We have been duped and have fallen for the snake oil salesman. So I'm not willing to be mute until we have endured four years—instead it's time for me, and others, to live loud and proud. It's time for me to make men uncomfortable by being a self-confident woman who will speak up no matter what.

I'm going to be in the face of hate, wearing it down as I stand on the firing line and take shot after shot so that people can feel safe. I want to be a thorn in hate's path. Love will win. It always does, and its recipe is *us*. We need to get on our soapboxes and keep shouting back. When they go low, we go high. The hatemongers just woke up a sleeping giant. They have no idea how fucked they just got. For the first time, I will not honor the office of the president. I have no respect for an office bought using a foreign power's help; the traitor was rewarded. And no one on the Republican side cared. They are enemies on domestic land, who need to be arrested. We need to "clean house" of the traitors willing to sell America so that a woman doesn't become president. Shame on them, and I hope they rot in hell. I have watched the sleeping giant awaken, and it is pissed and is a force to reckon with.

My goals are to help get America back in the hands of sane people who won't get offended and start World War III. History will not be kind to this time period. We'll be the people who are considered as the dumbed-down version of what we once was.

So I stand on the firing line ready and gaining strength. If you need help, come see me. I've got your back and will give hugs first—then we fight the haters!

Signed

A pissed-off American who is proud to be gay and liberal and to be a human who welcomes love as the answer. *Love harder.*

Erika P., age 39
Nurse educator
Hillsboro, Oregon

Who Am I?

WHO AM I? I am the descendant of a Revolutionary War soldier who lost his arm in battle while hoping to make this country independent.

Who am I? I am a relative of John Adams, a Founding Father and second president of the United States, who said, "Government is instituted for the common good; for the protection, safety, prosperity, and happiness of the people; and not for profit, honor, or private interest of any one man, family, or class of men."[34]

Who am I? I am the descendant of immigrants from Ireland, Sweden, and England.

Who am I? I am the descendant of a Union soldier who, after immigrating to this country to seek a better life, fought for the civil rights of others.

---

34 Mass. Const. Part I. Art. VII. https://malegislature.gov/Laws/
Constitution#partTheFirst.

Who am I? I am a woman from rural Alaska, a "red" state, with parents who always instilled in me a sense of the necessity to fight for what is right, to stand up for the civil rights of others.

Who am I? I am white female with a graduate degree and professional career living in Oregon, a consistently blue state. Demographically, I fit the description of a Hillary Clinton supporter and voter.

Who am I? I, like too many others, am a survivor of sexual abuse. While my history of sexual abuse does not define me, my history—all of my history—shapes who I am.

This is who I am, and this is my story.

When Trump initially announced his candidacy, I laughed. I laughed even harder when he started winning primaries. What were people thinking? When he won the Republican Party nomination, I was sure Hillary had the election in the bag. There was no way someone who had said such hateful and hurtful things could possibly be voted into office. I took his candidacy as a joke. But this was no joke.

In early October 2016, the infamous *Entertainment Tonight* tape with Trump's saying "Grab them by the pussy" was released. Many GOP leaders, once again, tried to distance themselves from the GOP presidential nominee, the man who had made these disgusting remarks. This incident brought the issue of sexual abuse to the forefront of the campaign. It invoked feelings in many women who were survivors of sexual harassment or sexual abuse. The dialogues that arose from the tape opened the eyes of many people and allowed us to recognize the extent of misogyny in our country. It also made many of us realize that our previous situations were sexually abusive. We declared ourselves, stating, "It happened to me. This is real."

I am one of those women. While I had known that the relationship I was in prior to the one with my husband, was abusive, I never fully examined the extent of my abuse. Honestly,

I was happy to have left the relationship behind me and move on. I was proud of my growth and of the fact that I had moved past the pain of my previous relationship. The events of this election, Trump's remarks, and the discussions surrounding the infamous tape all brought the negative memories and feelings from the abuse flooding back. Women who accused the candidate of sexual assault or harassment were told they were lying. They were told they should let go of things that happened decades ago. Survivors were told their sexual assault experiences weren't that big of a deal. But to us, to survivors, sexual trauma is a big deal. Hearing Trump speak in the video, listening to the dialogue the video brought about, listening to so many women speak up about their own experiences with sexual abuse, harassment, and rape all led to my realization that not only had I been a victim of sexual abuse but I had also been the victim of rape. *I am a rape survivor.*

In 2003, I was living outside of Portland, Oregon, and started dating a man. We seemed to have a lot in common. But having things in common does not prevent sexual abuse. It does not stop a man from being a predator. A man who was supposed to care about me forced himself on me. I said no. He did not listen. He raped me. Multiple times.

Looking back, I see that it should have been the end of the relationship. As happens in so many abusive relationships, I did not leave. The abuse continued. At the time, I blamed myself. I felt vulnerable. I thought he cared about me and must be attracted to me. I did not want to acknowledge what was happening: *This could not be happening to me. This only happened to weak people, and I wasn't weak. I was a self-proclaimed strong, independent woman. I was educated. I was a professional. Sexual abuse "doesn't happen to people like me."* But it did. The abuse continued until wonderful, supportive friends helped me understand I needed to end the relationship. They helped me see it for what it was, though I never fully told them the extent of what he did to me. They simply saw the emotional toll the relationship was taking on me.

I have moved on and now have an amazing, supportive husband and two beautiful boys. With the introspection sparked by this campaign, I realized that if rape and abuse can happen to me—someone who considers herself a strong, independent woman—it can happen to anyone. This realization has made fighting for women's rights a visceral urge, a calling. I have to fight for the rights of all women.

As October continued, for the first time in my life I went to my local Democratic Party office and purchased campaign signs for my yard. I had to *do* something. I wanted to do something even more tangible. I volunteered at the phone banks. I donated to Hillary's campaign. I thought I might make a difference. Even though I thought there was no way Hillary could lose to a person focused on fighting social media wars and putting down anyone who said anything that went against him, a little voice inside my head made me tremble with fear: *What if the polls aren't right?*

Fear coursed through my veins as I realized Trump supporters were believing the fake news spewed about Hillary Clinton. It became clear they weren't looking at credible sources or fact-checking. As I heard them speak, I fully recognized the extent to which misogynistic, xenophobic, racist, and homophobic undertones were saturating our society. It was no longer a "what if": it was reality. I was shaken to my core: a bomb had dropped and an entirely new and horrifying world was exposed.

Eleven days before the election, James Comey, the director of the FBI, sent out a letter about looking into Hillary Clinton's emails again. I thought, *Oh, shit! He just handed the election to Trump!* I looked up the Hatch Act, something I'd never heard of before. The Hatch Act prevents employees of the executive branch of the federal government, with the exception of the president, vice president, and certain other designated officials, from engaging in political campaign activities with the intent to interfere with the results of an election.[35] And here we were, looking into how Director Comey, a known GOP supporter, was interfering in a United States presidential election. Despite this, polls were still strongly in Hillary's favor. I thought, *Thank God: people still know how bad Trump is.*

On the day of the election, I put on my pantsuit and wore it proudly. I took a photo of my two young boys in front of my Hillary–Kaine yard sign. We bought blue star helium balloons that we put on our yard sign and outside our house. We bought champagne. I was ready for the glass ceiling to be shattered.

Oregon votes by mail, so we had voted several weeks earlier. However, I was already hearing stories about early voting in other states where people were being either turned away at the polls or felt intimidated. That little voice of fear spoke to me again, but I was naively optimistic. We had this in the bag! I mean, there was no way Trump would get voted in. No way!

*   *   *

Like many others, I walked around in a daze following the election. A dear Jewish friend told me several of her Jewish friends thought they might need to leave the country. A dear Muslim friend said she was afraid to leave her house in her hijab. My experience was not like theirs. The only thing that makes me a target of this hate is my gender. But I still felt despair. I felt

---

35 U.S. Department of Health and Human Services, "The Hatch Act: Political Activity and the Federal Employee," U.S Food & Drug Administration website (August 2015): http://www.fda.gov.

desperation. I felt anxious. And I kept thinking, *How did this happen?!*

When the CIA confirmed that Russia helped manipulate our election and that Republican Members of Congress serving on the Senate Intelligence Committee knew about this, fury filled my soul. The entire democratic process was betrayed. The United States had been played, and the citizens, especially those who are marginalized, would be the ones to suffer.

With all of the information that has come out—with Trump's beyond-controversial actions, including sending social media posts of lies that plummeted the stocks of American companies and of lies about a private citizen that led to death threats for a union leader and his family, communicating with foreign leaders without security briefings, and communicating with "leaders" who are not recognized by the United States—it is shocking there hasn't been outcry from the Senate, Congress, and leaders of both parties. We have been betrayed. Trump's actions have serious and dangerous implications. And yet, the Republican Party is still behind him despite his committing acts that many consider treasonous. With that, my only thought is *God help us all.*

It is now up to the citizens to ensure we protect one another. We uphold civil rights. We stand up. We fight! We love! We support! We are on the right side of history, and we need to leave a legacy our future generations can be proud of. Together, we make a difference.

Hillary Strobel, age 39
Publisher / professional storyteller
Los Angeles, California

The Day We Almost Won

W E *WIN*. THOSE are the words I kept telling my daughter in the time leading up to the 2016 election. I'd look at her enormous golden eyes, the innocent eyes of a two-year-old, and I'd say, "In three weeks, we win." . . . "In two weeks, we win." . . . "Next week, we win."

By "win," I meant progressives in general, and women, of course. But I mostly meant our family will win, our little two-person family.

I am a single mother. My daughter's father has never participated, never believed he was actually biologically responsible in any way. My daughter is probably my only chance to have children, as I'm nearly forty and have had miscarriages before. I feel like she's my one major gift from the universe in that way. It's us, and we are the two-woman team sprinting to the finish line.

* * *

We win.

I was half desperate for those words to be true. I'd never really felt the direct sting of the single motherhood stigma—the shaking heads, the excommunication from family, the judgmental looks at the store—but I've also never been without the sting of being a woman in a man's world.

It's actually not entirely true to say that no one ever looked at us sideways. My daughter is biracial, and without her father present, I've been asked by complete strangers and even our pediatrician if she's actually my daughter.

"Is she yours?" they ask.

I swallow my soul a little and respond, "Of course."

They always seem a little sheepish after and rush to explain what they really meant. "We get lots of foster moms in here; that's why I asked," says the pediatrician.

Thus opens another layer in our saga. "Lots of foster moms in here" means severely broken-beyond-repair families, a sure and certain sign of poverty.

Yes, I, a single mother, who works hard and plays by all of the middle-class rules of my upbringing, have experienced crushing poverty.

It turns out that a great many single mothers also experience poverty, because we are as women already earning less than men and respected less than men and we have fewer opportunities without a man running the show. There are double-whammy booby traps everywhere. In California, for example, single mothers on welfare are required by law to turn over their child support payments to the state rather than use it for their children, because the state needs to recoup its financial investment in the mother. There are also cases like mine: I don't get any form of child support at all.

Single mothers face all kinds of social stigmas. We are obliged in many cases to put our children in day care in order to be the sole breadwinner but are raked over the coals by people like Mike Pence, who write op-eds claiming we are destroying our children's lives by doing so. The thing that bothers me even more about that is the derision by partnered mothers who have opted out of daycare because they can, who can "sympathize" with Pence's point of view because "it's so much better to raise your own kids yourself, and who could argue with that?"

A single mom can. But very few people listen.

There's that famous saying about working twice as hard as a woman to receive half the credit a man gets. I work twice as hard as a parent too, because I have to be both. I am the one fixing the leaky kitchen sink with my own set of tools so that I can turn right around and wash all of the dishes in it, in the hours that I'm not working at my more-than-full-time job. I work four times as hard so that I can be told by the Republican Party that under their unified leadership, I will be paying four times as much in taxes as my "blameless" ex-partner.

And so I wanted to vote for a woman who understood my efforts and respected me for them. I wanted her to win twenty years ago when she said my rights are human rights, end of discussion. I wanted my daughter to truly believe that not only could the biracial child of a single parent be president but a woman could too.

So I kept looking my child square in the eyes and saying, "Tomorrow, we win."

* * *

It isn't only about losing this election. I feel that I've lost some abstract quality as a mother. No, not that I can't explain this loss or work hard to overcome it—it's something more nebulous.

We are mothers. We are raising the world's future. And we kill each other to do it better, faster, in cuter pairs of shoes, with wider smiles on our faces. We are supposed to be resilient, because we do the real work, but our sisterhood feels utterly broken from over here.

I feel very let down by my sisters, my privileged partnered-up sisters, who threw me and my daughter under the bus for a bigger piece of a pie that was never intended for any of us in the first place. So rather than wake up to a morning in which we had won, I woke up to the realization that I will spend the rest of my life fighting. Of course, I will be fighting four times as hard. I must push back against the men who hate me for existing while secretly (or not so secretly) lusting after my body, which they cannot have. I must push back against a social agenda that hates me for raising my child alone while it lets her father off the hook. And I must wake up my sisters who would support the dangerous agenda of the Republican Party: undue taxation of single mothers, repealing affordable health care, and impeding basic necessities like paid leave and child care.

My whole life, the one that I had prayed would be a victory, is a fight for my daughter's future.

Single mothers face huge obstacles that many people may not be aware of: we are evicted from our homes more often, we need more social services, we are abused in greater numbers, and we are generally treated as abject social failures. My daughter, according to all the "statistics," is more likely to commit a crime and fail in school.

But where is the public outcry? Where is the army of concerned citizens who want to band together and believe something could be different if only we treated mothers, and specifically single mothers, with the economic and political dignity that they deserve?

My fight, catalyzed by this election, is in building that army of concerned citizens. I want the world not only to see my reality for what it is but also to see their own reality in it. Single moms, no matter their race or class, experience similar hardships and universal truths, and everyone could benefit from a little bit of empathy with us. My collaborators and I are building an innovation lab to address the social, economic, and political empowerment of single mothers, and thanks to this election, there is no shortage of people who want to take the risk with us.

It's written into quite a few spiritual traditions that the way we treat the most vulnerable among us is a reflection of the overall strength of all of us. Up until now, we have not treated single mothers with respect and care. Rather, we have vilified and denigrated them. I believe that when single mothers, an incredibly vulnerable group of people, can be seen in the full light of their dignity, strength, power, and sheer force of will, we will all shine brighter for it. On that day, true enough, we will win.

Kami Balmforth, age 37
Licensed clinical social worker
Salt Lake City, Utah

Faith

I GREW UP IN a conservative Mormon community in a town just fifteen minutes north of Salt Lake City, Utah, a member of the Church of Latter Day Saints.

At twelve years old, I remember asking my Sunday School teacher why God tempted Eve with the fruit from the tree of life. His answer? It was part of God's plan. I thought, *Okay, but why? Why didn't anyone have a good explanation for this?* I would later also wonder why people continue to use the fact that Eve partook of the fruit first as a reason to subjugate women.

I was given the same answers to all of my questions: *Pray. Ask in faith. You will get an answer.* What they meant was, I would get the *right* answer. If my answer challenged the Church's teachings, then I wasn't asking with enough faith.

My questions didn't stop me from wanting what they told me to want. As a daughter of God, I wanted what was coming to me. I never doubted the intentions of my leaders. In fact, I don't believe any of them had bad intentions at all. But looking back, I think *Man, that's really screwed up.*

My questions didn't go away, no matter how hard I looked for answers. Every time I felt something was wrong, I prayed. I prayed for knowledge, for more faith. I reminded myself that living a Christ-like life wasn't easy, but that it would be worth it in the end. Any dissenting thoughts were put aside. Who was I to question my leaders? Who was I to question God?

At the same, I was being taught that it was my divine calling to marry a church-worthy man and have a large family. It was as much a cultural assumption as it was a doctrine. I spent my adolescent years and most of my twenties attending every wedding shower, every baby shower, and every wedding reception in the hopes that one day, everyone would be attending mine.

My friends and I spent hours learning how to put makeup on and writing letters to our future husbands. When we were thirteen, we went to a bridal shop to try on dresses. My friends quickly found their dream dresses, but I couldn't find one the right size. All I could do was hold one up in front of me and have someone take a picture.

I kept the picture in my scripture case so I could remember what it was like to hold that dress. That drop-waist, taffeta, puffy sleeved nightmare was my dream come true. I knew it was going to happen for me, because I would do what God asked of me. I would find my eternal companion and we would raise a family together.

But that didn't happen.

I went to college and learned there was a whole other world outside of the way I lived. I began questioning my membership in the church around the time I moved to Baltimore, MD to complete graduate school. I hoped that whatever I was missing would be revealed to me there, away from the culture that had always surrounded me.

Over a period of about three years, I finally came to the

conclusion that I didn't believe in the doctrine. As a defender of the church, I'd always stated that this was the only good reason to leave. I stopped going soon after.

* * *

During my time as a therapist, I met a lot of women who were sexually assaulted and told they were to blame for their assaults. At Brigham Young University, all incoming students are expected to adhere to the school's honor code; one requirement was that unmarried people should remain chaste and sexually pure. I was horrified to learn that victims of sexual assault were told that they were in violation of this part of the honor code.[36]

Additionally, clergy act as counselors and instruct their parishioners to stay with their abusers. Some bishops will "handle" sexual abuse in families without reporting the abuse to law enforcement. Women are told they should be grateful for any attention they receive. They are told that being groped isn't as bad as being raped, and they should be grateful it wasn't worse. They are realizing they were abused by their family members, only to be called liars and attention seekers.

On the day Donald Trump's *Access Hollywood* tape leaked I thought about the women I had counseled, and knew his presidency would cause the re-visiting of trauma for many of my patients. I had hoped his misogynistic statements would be enough to disqualify him for any sort of public office, but I was unsure. There were a few people in my immediate circle who were disgusted, but for the most part the state of Utah— *my* state—stood behind him. They backed this Republican

---

36 Healy, Jack. "At Brigham Young, a Cost in Reporting a Rape." NYtimes. April 26, 2016. Accessed February 4, 2017. https://www.nytimes. com/2016/04/27/us/rape-victims-brigham-young-university-honor-code-suspensions.html?_r=1.

nominee. I thought if my state was willing to back him, it was clear other states would as well.

*   *   *

I didn't get excited about the prospect of having our first woman president until a few days before the election. Her gender didn't factor into my decision when I voted in the primaries. She was the better choice, in every conceivable way. It wasn't until I heard the stories from the women also enthusiastically anticipating electing the country's first female president that I became excited myself. America was about to make history, and it was about time! I felt hopeful. This was going to be big.

And it was big—just not in the way anyone had expected.

I can't help but think as a woman, people voted against me. People voted against my many of my friends and loved ones. It makes me angry, but my hope is that we can work together to educate those ignorant of the damage of which this man is capable. Get involved in a local activist group. Call and write your representatives when you disagree with what's happening. Support, and find empathy and understanding, for those his policies will affect. Cultivate love, have faith and show kindness for those who are different from you.

I'm happy to be on the right side of history.

Jennifer Nicholson, age 39
Veterans Administration caregiver
West Sacramento, California

Doing All I Can, Everywhere, All the Time

I WAS SUCH A weird kid. I liken myself to Alex P. Keaton on *Family Ties*. To say that I was obsessed with politics would be an understatement. The part that always shocked everyone though—including especially my grandparents—was that I was a Democrat in a family of Republicans. By the time I finally turned eighteen and could actually vote, Bill Clinton was in the middle of his first presidential term, and I lived in the heart of Bible Belt, Missouri. Saying that you were a Democrat there was as good as saying a swear word, but I told everyone who would listen how fabulous I thought the Clintons were, especially Hillary. I truly loved the compassion she had for people. I instantly recognized her as a role model: I even wrote in my senior memory book that someday I wanted to be the first woman American president.

So much of my life has changed since high school. I'm now the mom of four beautiful girls and the wife and caregiver to a wounded veteran. Life took me on many rides but, sadly, never took me to the White House.

Around five years ago, my oldest daughter came out to me on the ride home from the grocery store. I couldn't have been more proud of her in that moment. She knew exactly who she was and what she wanted from life—something I had never quite been able to figure out for myself. But I knew in my heart she could never be her authentic self if we stayed in Missouri. We picked up and left a place I'd lived my entire life—for almost thirty-five years—and moved to California, over two thousand miles away. It was the scariest and most exciting thing I'd ever done.

I'm happy to say that my daughter has thrived here, but to this day, almost no one in my family knows she's gay and probably never will. I doubt they will ever even read these words, because I'm a liberal and their Christian views don't allow for thoughts and actions like mine.

I have always encouraged my daughters to be independent freethinkers who would never allow anyone to tell them they were not capable of achieving their dreams. I also have taught them to love and extend a hand of friendship to all who need it.

* * *

Eighteen months ago, when Hillary Clinton decided to run again for president, I was thrilled. This election was exciting for me; I could finally be out and proud as a Democrat! I wore blue everywhere, and I talked about her with strangers on the street and in the grocery store. Sadly, though, I still couldn't post much about my political views on social media (except to my mom and one brother) because all my friends and family were voting for Trump.

November 8, 2016, was my younger sister's birthday, and we'd gotten up early to call her. I was so excited for the day's events that I had barely been able to sleep the night before. While I was getting my girls ready for school, all we could talk about was how historic this day was and that by this time tomorrow, Hillary would be our new president-elect. (Even now, writing the term, I still can't believe it's not true.) The rest of the day, I was on cloud nine.

That evening, I watched for early results. I had gone to the store and bought champagne and snacks; I was that confident she would win. As the night progressed and the results rolled in, a sick feeling came over me. By 10:00 p.m., I shut off the TV and cried. I felt, and still feel, like I was punched in the gut. I knew I would have to face the bragging of all of my family and friends the next day, which made the pain and nausea even worse.

The next morning, I woke up feeling as though I'd failed my daughters and given them hope when there now was none. Then I remembered a quote Hillary had recited in one of her speeches: "Do all the good you can, by all the means you can, in all the ways you can, in all the places you can, at all the times you can, to all the people you can, as long as ever you can."[37]

I knew in that moment, as tears streamed down my face, that just because Hillary didn't win, didn't mean I couldn't do more—a lot more. I felt inspired. I made a choice to become active again, in as many ways as I could.

Since the election I have joined multiple groups, such as American Civil Liberties Union (ACLU) and MoveOn. org, and in the past month since the election, I have become more vocal on social media than I'd ever been before. I have reeducated myself on the Constitution so that I can make sure

---

37 Staff, POLITICO, John A. Farrell, Politico Magazine, Zack Stanton and Alex Guillén, and Sam Kriss. "Full text: Hillary Clinton's DNC speech." POLITICO. Accessed February 04, 2017. http://www.politico. com/story/2016/07/full-text-hillary-clintons-dnc-speech-226410.

that my rights, and those of my daughters and others, will not be impeded. I have signed multiple petitions, sent letters, and made phone calls to senators and representatives.

Susan B. Anthony once said, "The older I get, the greater power I seem to have to help the world; I am like a snowball— the further I am rolled, the more I gain."[38]

I will do all I can, as long as I ever can, for all the people I can.

---

38 Ida Husted Harper, The Life and Work of Susan B. Anthony: Including Public Addresses, Her Own Letters and Many from Her Contemporaries During Fifty Years, Volume 2 (January 1, 1898), Indianapolis: Bowen-Merrill, 1898.

Catherine Wilson, age 43
Behavior analyst
Hanalei, Hawaii

No Woman Is an Island

November 8, 2016, Early morning
I joined a secret women's group online, and I feel special, as if I was handpicked to step into the inner circle of this election. As I laid out my clothes, I thought about the photos of women wearing pantsuits in support of Hillary. I'd found white slacks and a light blue jacket. It wasn't a matching suit like the ones I'd seen, but it was the best I had. People don't dress up much in Hawaii, not even professionals. I remember thinking, *This is going to be one hell of a day,* starting with a volunteer shift to tell people where their voting booths where. It was the first time I had participated in an election other than by voting.

November 8, 2016, 9:00 p.m.
My eleven-year-old daughter, who is with her dad tonight, texted me for the second time, *Trump is winning!* I reply, *It's okay, baby. Sometimes bad things have to happen before good can win. What I mean, Kaya, is Trump is going to win, but for you, there will be no changes in anything. Okay? We'll still live*

here. You'll still go to your same school with your friends and everything will be fine.

Then I realized why she was so fearful. Earlier in the year I made the mistake of telling my daughter that I would leave the country if Trump won—I joked about moving to Canada. She believed what I'd said. When she saw Trump winning, she became anxious we might leave the next day. I felt like the worst mother ever. I know my anxiety is nothing compared to what others were feeling around the United States. We are so removed. So protected. So white. I wondered what other mothers were telling their little girls.

November 12, 2016 (group post)

Today an old friend of mine, a Trump supporter, replied to my Election Day post. Tom asked me, *How did your celebration go?*

My pointed response was, *The day was very sad. I didn't vote for Hillary to be elected just for me. I won't need an abortion or birth control. My tubes are tied. My daughter goes to a private school. My taxes will likely go down under Trump. I did not vote for Hillary because she would improve my life; I voted for her for you and all the women in your life—your mom, your sister, and your wife. Your reply to my post made me angry at first, as I'm sure it was intended to do. I've spent a lot of time between devastation and anger. You want to know how I celebrated? I want to ask you how the KKK celebration went; I hear it was well attended.*

Then I realized your comment was only a glimpse of what people have been feeling all over the country this week. The woman who went outside to find her car spray painted N@@@@@ Bitch. The man who yelled at a woman in passing: "You should be raped before being thrown over the wall!" There are many of these incidents that have been reported, many much worse. I'm afraid,

Tom. I'm very afraid where this country is heading. Your reply hurt me.

I live in Hawaii, a blue state. My friends are all liberals. I've come to realize that my knowledge stays the same when surrounded by like-minded people. By isolating myself from differing perspectives, I miss the chance to understand their views and to explain mine.

I tested the waters a few days later. A friend of my daughter had a birthday party. The girls at the party texted another classmate who was not invited, mocking her. Deeply disappointed at how cruel twelve-year-olds can be, I decided to talk to one of the other moms about the situation. I stated that the current political atmosphere made it even more important than ever that we teach our girls to not bully and to take action if they witness it. I turned to my daughter and said, "You know how upset Mommy is that Trump is elected president. If we can't stop bullying in our own backyard, how are we going to stop it across the United States?"

The woman replied she voted for Trump. I was shocked and wanted to ask why, but chose to just let her talk. She told me that bullying has always happened. She said, "My husband and I did not want Hillary to win because one of Hillary's top advisors is a Muslim. Muslims follow Islam, which says to kill all Christians."

I now had two things to work with: One was the fallacy that if something has been happening for a long time, it will always happen and nothing can be done about it. The other was fear, caused by her misconception that her family might have been killed by Muslims if Hillary had been elected. On the next playdate exchange, I told her we could do something about the bullying, not only in our neighborhood but also out in the world. I reminded her how far we've come as women and how we had to protect our rights. She didn't have much to say, appeared ill at ease, and pointedly changed the subject.

The next time I saw her, she again appeared uncomfortable but was polite. I no longer brought up politics, and eventually the awkwardness faded. I never knew if my words did anything, but I like to think she considered them, at least for a short moment. If we can string these moments together for Trump supporters, perhaps people will see that their logic was flawed.

*   *   *

December 4, 2016 (group post)

I've narrowed down the source of my anger about why Trump's winning the presidency hit me like a fucking Mack truck. For me, the issue wasn't that millions of people had voted for Trump; it was as if millions of people had voted against me. I am a feminist. I've dedicated my life to children with disabilities. I believe in equality for all races and religions. This is who I am. So when Trump won, I felt totally and completely defeated, as if the Trump voters were all against what I believe in and even who I am. It didn't feel like we had lost the presidency; it felt like we had lost humanity.

In the election's aftermath, one other thing occurred to me: we had become too comfortable. With President Obama in office, many of us, including myself, were satisfied with slow progress. When the anti-Trump marches began immediately after the election, I couldn't believe how many people admitted to the press that they didn't vote. Angered by them and, honestly, by the Bernie supporters, I thought, *They did this to us. It wasn't just them. Honestly, we all did it.*

*   *   *

December 30, 2016 (group post)

Before 2016 ends, I have something positive to say. I added around one thousand new people to my online life from different physical places, different cultural places, and different racial places—people different from me. That's what I needed in this time of turmoil. I now have friends who are in interracial marriages, who are Muslims, who have disabilities, who are gay, and the list goes on.

I live in a small place in the middle of the ocean: Kauai, Hawaii. My exposure to the rest of our country is limited. After the election, one of my struggles was being so removed from the fight. Through social media, people have come to me. I see their beautiful families; I send words of encouragement to those who are struggling. Sometimes my gesture is as simple as liking posts when they share their successes or adding an angry face when someone is mad and frustrated. While I really have no idea who the hell you are, I LOVE YOU ALL.

I'm more politically involved now. Most days I make calls, sign petitions, or send emails. I've opened up a Twitter account. I've changed since the election. I'm softer and more open. I don't get worked up over small stuff, because I see with a bigger perspective; I conserve my energy for the right fights. With my expanded circle of friends, I see that people are funny—I mean *really* funny. A profound sense of humor travels with many people. It helps them step through the door of fear and catch their breath before the tears of sadness come. Humor holds back the anger just long enough to allow reason to slip in. There is still so much joy in the world. People go on job interviews, get engaged, buy homes, and have babies—a whirlwind of life. This whirlwind shows that good, happiness, and hope still exist. I see how strong we are. People hold their heads high while going through internal agony and smile for the camera after chemo treatments; they share stories and words of encouragement. We stand together, and it's working. Employees who discriminate against customers on the basis of race are fired because of the outpour of anger from customers. Kids who have lost a parent are walked to school by dozens of other adults. People pay for others' groceries. Beautiful things happen every day. Many more beautiful things are about to happen.

Reina Mystique, age 33
Singer
San Diego, California

Deeper Than Hair:
A Collective Call to Action

I WAS EXCITED THE first time I voted, but the excitement for this election was particularly electrifying. In some way, my voice felt stronger with this vote, stronger than in previous elections. I will never forget when I heard the results. I was in the car. The radio was on. I was more pumped than I had ever been for pretty much anything, ever. The date was November 4, 2008. Were you an active part of history? Did you let your voice be heard? Or did you sit on the sidelines passively waiting for the results? Offering your unwarranted opinions like the nonvoting driver of the car I was in. Muttering phrases like "Things won't change" and "He's just like the rest of them."

Here I was a black woman, or more precisely, a mixed-race woman, whose very existence was frowned upon by her grandfather for the color of her skin. A woman who had been called a *nigger* by her own uncle. A mixed woman whom some believed shouldn't exist based on the notion that my mother and father should not have procreated. After years of trying to figure out who I was going to be, years of figuring out my place in American society, change was happening. For the first time in my life, the American people had used their collective voice to create visible change.

I was twenty-five in 2008. Society had yet to define my role in the country. I was fortunate enough to have two strong women in my life who told me I could be whatever I wanted. More than ever, in 2008 their words resonated. I believed them. In the four years between President Obama's first and second term, I came into my own. I grew as a woman, as a musician, and as a voice to inspire others. I'm not saying that President Obama had any direct causation of my personal growth and development, but having a prominent leader of color during my formative twenties definitely had its moments of inspiration.

While we know the outcome of the 2012 presidential election, it's important to acknowledge the outcome of the voter turnout as well. Many of you answered yes to my opening question. Regardless of how you voted, you proudly voiced your thoughts and offered your opinions, and just like me, you excitedly awaited the results of the 2008 election. Then suddenly, as if stricken with illness, many of you decided your voices didn't matter anymore. One victory and suddenly the fight was over. Mothers and fathers were openly teaching their children to not care about the future of the nation they call home. Many of you joined, or rejoined, the group of passive Americans who no longer fought. They complain and offer opinions, but do nothing more to make changes happen.

In an era when everyone gets a trophy and everyone can be a star in their own reality, people are less passionate, more savage. Our generation has created an era when over half of the voting population believes their voice doesn't matter, that doing the work is pointless.

The social ramifications of something as small as choosing not to vote go deeper than the roots of my natural hair. They extend into the fiber of my being. It connects each of us to one another. It is our job, our charge, our responsibility to raise passionate youths. To raise a nation of leaders and freethinkers. How dare we, as the adults of our nation, sit by silently and inattentively let the savage inherit the land. If you are unwilling to do the work, let me say to you: We have four years to completely undo our lackadaisical way of thinking. Four years to undo generations of self-hate and self-oppression. How do we un-mute the voices of all of those who feel silenced? How do we empower the self-appointed powerless? How do we give the people their voice? My people. Your people. Black people. Brown people. White people. Everyone stuck in the middle. American people.

In a democratic society, where love is the winning affection, we have let hate prevail. By believing your voice won't make a difference, you have taught our youth that their voices will not matter. We are unwilling to do the work, and I fear our youth don't even know what the work is. Vote because your voice is strong. Vote because you can. Be heard because you are already being watched. Now is the time for growth. Now is the time for change. Now is the time to not give up!

Paula Bixel, age 56
Business Owner
Portland, Oregon

Mothers

Chicago, Illinois; 1945

BLOOD. IT NEVER occurred to her there would be so much blood. Blood on her thighs, running down her legs. Blood on her belly and on her back, blood on the newspaper beneath her body, and blood on the wood floors beneath the newspaper and on the dirt and debris beneath everything.

The old doctor seemed unconcerned. He patted her leg with a folded newspaper. "We're done," he said, his voice raspy. She could smell the rye whiskey on his breath. He moved away and out of the corner of her eye, she could see him packing away his tools—shiny metallic medieval-looking gadgets with sharp ends. The sight of them made her body remember, and it shuddered with a ripple of pain.

But what about the blood? she thought.

The old man (*Doc*; that's what her mother called him) leaned over her again. "I'll get your mother," he said.

The girl tried to nod as another wave of pain rippled through her. She could hear boat horns in the distance and the wheeling caw of the gulls—then the light footsteps of her mother, arriving from a nearby stoop.

Her mother helped her stand. The girl wobbled to her feet, the sweet stench of chloroform lingering over her like a cloud. Salty tears trickled from her eyes and ran down the soft corridors of her cheeks.

Her mother pushed the girl's clothes into her hands. "You'll be fine," she assured her daughter. "Hurry up. You can cry later. We need to get home now."

The girl followed her mother to the car, pausing only long enough to take one last look at the shattered building from which she came. This moment was at once the beginning and the end. The life she had created, she had destroyed here, in this place. A rotting, abandoned warehouse drenched in blood was her baby's tomb.

*   *   *

It took my mother decades to understand the decision she made, and a lifetime to accept.

As a child, I watched my mother struggle with depression. She never talked about it, but I knew she suffered from a deep, hidden pain. When she came home from her waitress jobs (she usually had three at a time), I'd rub her back and tell her it would be okay, not really understanding what "it" was or that some things would never be okay.

I always knew when the time was approaching for one of my mother's "little rests" at what the adults referred to as the *quiet place*. She would come home drunk from her shift as a cocktail waitress at the officers club on the base at Camp Pendleton. My sisters and I would lead her into the bathroom and help her out of her clothes that stunk of brandy alexanders. We'd take off her red beehive wiglet and place it in its special box before dragging the rest of my mother to bed. The next day, my mother would apologize, but her guilt never lasted long. Her behavior became more erratic with each passing day, until she could no longer cope with even the smallest of life's nuisances; a lost shoe or tardy slip from school would send her into a swirling panic, ending with her on the floor, collapsed in tears. On the days that finally broke her, a taxi would appear.

My mother would be gone for a week or two at a time. I remember the one occasion my father took me to see her. He and I walked hand in hand down the hospital hallway with linoleum floors polished to shine like a mirror, the surrounding white walls closing in on us like a tunnel. Women in white cotton nightgowns and slippered feet walked past us like ghosts; my six-year-old mind wondered if they were really walking or merely hovering above the shiny floor.

My father jerked my arm. "We're here," he said. "You must be very quiet so you don't upset her." We entered my mother's room to find her sitting on the bed. Her empty green eyes opened wide with new life when she saw me. She patted the space beside her. I moved over toward her and sat down, folding my small freckled hands into my lap. My mother reached over and touched my auburn hair, her touch so gentle that I thought we'd both break.

My mother told me later about the electric shock treatments and pills, how broken she felt, how she couldn't stop crying, how they tried everything to fix her, but nothing worked.

* * *

I spent my sixteenth birthday at Planned Parenthood, rotating from the waiting room to the exam room before landing in the consultation area. A nurse walked in and advised me on the dangers of premarital sex before handing me three purple rectangular flat containers held together by rubber bands.

Butterflies adorned the plastic purple sleeve over the pill container.

I didn't have a boyfriend, but I decided to be prepared for when I did. During that time, my mother and I were hardly speaking. My teenage rebellion was in full throttle; going on the pill seemed like the next big move.

I came home and showed my mother the purple containers. She turned to me, her green eyes staring quietly into mine for a hard second. "Good," she said. "I'm glad you did it."

You could have knocked me over with a feather. *This* was her reaction?

"I don't want you to get pregnant," my mother continued, "and go through what I had to go through."

And that's when my mother told me about Jack and my grandmother and the warehouse in Chicago.

* * *

Jack's blond hair and blue eyes made him the most handsome boy in school. My mother couldn't believe it when he asked her to the movies on Saturday, and the Saturday after that, and so on.

"Why me?" she asked.

"Your eyes," Jack said. My mother didn't need further explanation. Her eyes were beautiful and she knew it. They were large and olive green with yellow flecks and drooping corners, framed by long sweeps of ink-black lashes. (The "family eyes," we call them. The eyes she would one day pass down to me.)

Jack's father owned a successful business in town and didn't approve of his son's dating a girl from the wrong side of the tracks. Jack didn't care. He continued dating my mother throughout their junior year of high school. He told her he loved her and they would be together forever.

Forever ended the day my mother disclosed her secret to Jack: he was going to be a father. Jack didn't want to be a father—and my mother's eyes, as beautiful as they were, weren't enough to tie him down to responsibilities he hadn't asked for.

Jack never spoke to my mother again. His own father showed up at my mother's house a few days later, banging on the front door. My grandmother invited him in, and they walked back to the sitting room and closed the door behind them. The end result: Jack's father would pay for the abortion. My grandmother would arrange it.

My mother spent the weeks after her abortion mostly bedridden, sick with guilt and depression, hot with fever to the point of near death.

* * *

My mom followed Roe v. Wade closely. When given the chance, she always spoke up about women's rights and how important it was for girls to have control over their own bodies. But I never knew why it was so important to her, until that day in 1976, when she told me her story.

As I grew older, my mother and I grew closer, and we spoke more frequently. Often our conversations would turn to women's choices and how far we had come. She expressed her gratitude knowing her daughters and granddaughter would not have to risk their lives the way she had—that we had a choice. No one could force us to do anything. She would say all this with a smile, green eyes shining.

* * *

According to the website Our Bodies Ourselves, the number of illegal abortions that occurred in the United States during the 1950s and 1960s are estimated to be between 200,000 and

1.2 million per year.[39] The fact that the estimate is so broad is a testament to the shame and secrecy ascribed to the choice to end a pregnancy. Prior to Roe v. Wade, "as many as 5,000 American women died" each year "as a direct result of unsafe abortions."[40]

Today abortion is one of the safest clinical procedures performed in the United States, with the death rate at 0.6 per 100,000 procedures—less than 1%—according to the World Health Organization (WHO).[41] Yet, also according to the WHO, "nearly half of all abortions worldwide are unsafe, and nearly all unsafe abortions (98%) occur in developing countries. In countries where abortion remains unsafe, it is a leading cause of maternal mortality."[42]

My mother was one of the lucky ones. She survived her ordeal, but in some ways, she didn't. I can't help but wonder, *What if she had been given the rights to a safe and legal abortion? Autonomy where her own body was concerned? Would she have had a normal life—one free from shock treatments and pills? one with less fear?*

My mother died twenty-nine days after my first granddaughter, Ellie, was born. When I looked into Ellie's green eyes for the first time, I made the same wish for her that my mother had once made for me: the right to live the life she chooses and to live it well.

---

39 OBOS abortion contributors, "The Impact of Illegal Abortion," Our Bodies Ourselves (website), March 23, 2014, http://www.ourbodiesourselves.org/health-info/impact-of-illegal-abortion.

40 IBID

41 IBID

42 IBID

JP Mulvereen, age 58
Business Owner
Chesterfield, Utah

The Truth About Everything

I USED TO LIVE an almost completely reclusive life. People with Developmental Topographical Disorientation (DTD) often do. We have no internal map. We can't go anywhere without planning it out.

I wasn't diagnosed with DTD until 2008. I was lying on a couch in a psychiatrist's office, spilling my guts about my unusual life. I came to the part where, on a family vacation coming home from Vermont in the back of a station wagon in the middle of the night, I was mistakenly left in an Indiana truck stop by my parents, who didn't think to make sure all five kids were in the car before driving off. I was eight.

I told my shrink that getting home wasn't the problem because I had laid out my markers all the way back to our house in Chicago.

A year before, I had devised a way to use images I placed along roads and sidewalks as markers (imaginary breadcrumbs, if you will). If I was walking on a nature trail, I'd place a jewel-embellished unicorn next to a tree. If I was in my dad's car on

I-80I, I knew he would turn off at mile marker 231, because that's where I had previously imagined parking a Schwinn˙ Sting-Ray bike with a pink and white polka-dot shiny plastic seat, plastic tassel hand grips, and a chrome spoiler. I had imaginary treasure scattered all over the roads, trails, and parking lots around my family home. (I still use the Sting-Ray in parking lots, but these days I get around with my car's GPS—prior to that, I hired people to drive my car for me).

The big issue that night at the truck stop was hitching a ride to get home. I must have waited hours in the shadows of the Mobile˙ station until a highway patrolmen pulled in for coffee. The troopers tracked my parents down in Gary, Indiana. My mother was so tired, she told them she had all her children and drove off without me again.

I told the shrink that this was probably the incident that made me realize I had to become fiercely independent. When she didn't say anything, I looked up from the couch and saw her leaning back in her chair, hands clenching her stomach. "Your story makes me ill," she said.

I never got to the part about moving to Utah at fifteen, and how the Utah valleys had mountains, canyons, aspen groves, and numbered roads in a grid where I could find my way even easier than before. The doctor was suddenly talking over me, jabbering on about a diagnosis she had learned about at a conference. She said she could cure me.

Alas, there was no cure. Just support groups and guesswork.

My disability hasn't kept me from enjoying everything. I run two separate businesses from home. I surround myself with my dogs and tend a few of the neighbor's dogs too. For the last three years, I've had a housemate, a real person who allows me more freedom. Sometimes, I'll go on a spontaneous trip. Recently, I flew to San Juan, Puerto Rico to paint pictures of an old convent I found on Google˙ maps. I'm a lot braver now.

*   *   *

I bought a turquoise pantsuit to wear for early voting. It was an eye-stopping costume: the suit, the "nasty woman" white tank, the Hillary hairstyle, the vivid blue contacts. I was excited about Hillary Clinton. I saw her as brave and bold. Maybe she had a reputation for being a bitch, but who's perfect? Donald Trump was a chump and a sex offender. He had no public service in his background, he'd established a bogus university, he had bad hair, and his mouth was like a sphincter with idiotic words spilling out.

On the night of the election, I grabbed a bottle of cabernet and walked two doors down to a friend's house. We took our positions on the couch, the bottle of wine between us. A straggler friend stopped by and joined us. Among the three of us, I knew the most about politics. (I was in the Continental Congress during junior high, so naturally I'm the expert.) I asked the straggler friend if she had voted. She said she was a felon and wasn't allowed to vote. She had served two years for embezzlement, which became the focus of my curiosity for a while as I tried to imagine this camera-ready, runway-thin model type doing two years at Club-Fed. I asked her if she went native and ate the pussy. She said she ate pussy long before she was caught, then took a swig of her beer.

Our conversation died down when the results began trickling in.

*   *   *

The shock of hearing the election results was a punch to my soul. The world upended, and in that exact moment, I felt a catastrophic shift in a way I am only now comprehending. It dawned on me that too many white cisgendered women voted against our own rights. And as a country, we were racist, misogynistic, egomaniacal, xenophobic, ignorant, and who knows what else. Each reason I thought of for this failure was a huge rabbit hole I didn't understand how to navigate. The room was spinning; I couldn't see any directions.

Then the Donald took the stage to accept the victory. He seemed almost humane. He said he wanted to be president of all of the people, and there wasn't the glibness about his consonance that had permeated his campaign.

I felt lighter for a moment, but it was only a moment. *He's a stone cold liar*, I thought. He's a sexual predator and a ruthless soul.

And he's going to be president.

*   *   *

The next morning, I ran into my housemate in the kitchen. Sometimes we don't speak to each other for days. But that morning we looked at each other for a moment, then stepped in for a big bear hug (Me hugging—that's something I don't do). My housemate had been an army medic, a veteran of Desert Storm. As a child, his father had raised him to be a mountain man and live off the land. He assured me that we would be fine; we could live in the mountains indefinitely if we had to. I envisioned eating twigs and moss and placing my imaginary Sting-Ray bike against a tree to mark it as my new home.

*   *   *

Until five years ago, I had been living alone in a 4,500-square-foot villa in a gated community near the Snowbird ski area (the Utah zip code equivalent to 90210). I loved living there until one day a man straight from the fiery depths of hell moved in next door. My new neighbor made things awkward right off the bat when he suggested we "bumper fuck"—whatever that was.

Other times, he'd suggest we should be neighbors with benefits. I said, "Um, I don't see any benefit for me."

My neighbor never touched me, but his dog was a German-trained German Shepherd. Although I have a German Shepherd as well, I wasn't too pleased when my new neighbor let his dog loose on my dog and me, creating a war whenever we tried to enjoy a peaceful walk. I called the police after his third strike, and that's when the verbal threats started.

I conveyed all of this to a friend, who was a real estate attorney in California. I mentioned I might be putting the villa on the market. My friend immediately said he wished to buy it. He flew in, and we finalized the sale over glasses of wine. Talk about lock, stock, and barrel—I sold everything, including the last dish in the sink. I had thirty days to leave.

I contacted another friend who had a home in Park City that I wanted to rent. He said he had already rented it, but we agreed I would stay at his place in the valley until I found other accommodations.

To say it was a step down would be an adequate description. The house had been my friend's childhood home, and although he owned and managed more expensive properties, due to his happy childhood memories, he was always the most comfortable in that house.

I, on the other hand, needed time to adjust.

I'm an Anglican, and I have always believed Christians should walk like Jesus, but until I moved to this home, I was a donating Christian, not a living Christian. Sure, you could count on me for money and volunteer work. But until I lived among the less fortunate, I could not truly call myself a Christian. Three years later in my new neighborhood, I'm definitely living out my values. I've become of great use to aging neighbors and folks who don't speak English. When people need money for gas or animal care, they usually get it from me. If they need a generator, I have one; if they need a refrigerator, I happen to know a guy who has a spare.

* * *

Sometime after the awkward hug kitchen incident, I was sitting on my couch, somewhat in a daze. I wasn't crying; I do cry at will and don't ever hold back when I need a cry. But at that moment, the pain bruising my soul hadn't hit my tear ducts. Right then, I was more angry than sad. I kept thinking about the women and children who would probably face deportation because of Trump's win. The Latter-Day Saints (LDS) Church brought over a lot of converts to Utah from other third-world countries, and even their fear was pouring out at the news of the new administration. Would the LDS Church protect them? *Hell no,* I thought, remembering the quorum of old white male faces who ran the church. The converts were doomed.

I stood up, flew out my front door, and ran across the lawn to my neighbor's house to give them the good news—that they were safe with me.

Some seemed grateful; some did not understand what I was talking about. I explained, "You know, the election. . . . Donald Trump. . . ." They still looked confused. One of my neighbors, Maria, even confessed she voted for Trump, because she was a Mexican American with her legal documents and believed Trump would deport the Mexican thugs living in the apartments behind our block.

* * *

Days after the election, I began digesting books on laws and government. I read the Constitution, looking for loopholes, anything I could find.

I went online and joined an all-female Utah activist group on social media. After a while, I realized most of the members were white renegade Mormons.

Now here's an interesting fact about Mormons I learned after years of living among them: nothing short of the Third Reich is more organized and unstoppable than a bunch of Mormon women on a mission. In the 80's, the Salt Lake Valley flooded, and over three feet of water came running down Main Street. The Mormon churches, so numerous that there's one on every block, teamed up with volunteers who were bagging and stanching the flood with the help of FEMA and other state and federal agencies. The damage was minimized in hours.

I had high hopes about our activist group.

After a week or two of posting crap online, our well-trained organizers flew into action. There were numbers to call and committee meetings to attend. I accepted an invitation to the Women's March on Washington. I even asked my roommate to come with me. He's a good guy, and although he's a little sexist, he says he's working on it (I'll take my allies where I can find them). He wouldn't go because the "marchers would get blown up." A machine gun drone will mow us down into a bloody paste on the Mall. Suicide vests and runaway semi-trucks of eighteen wheels of death coming for us all.

* * *

The first official meeting of our activist group was scheduled two days before Thanksgiving. Hundreds of us had signed up to attend. They had selected a location downtown, which turned out to be a real test for me. I circled block after block trying to find parking. The streets were not equipped to handle parking for such an event and someone had written a sign saying we could park behind the Vision Clinic.

GPS would not save me at night in the back alleys of Salt Lake City. My anxiety heightened, and I thought maybe I wouldn't be an asset if I had to negotiate directions. Finally, I found my way behind the Vision Clinic, to an old cracking black top parking area, sleek and shiny from rain. Without street lamps, the glow from the spaces between buildings was my only source of light.

I pulled up the hood of my jacket and looked around, placing my invisible treasures around my car. Light pole: Sting-Ray would be right beneath it. I looked right and saw a chainlink fence with dead vines and a latched gate. I placed Benedict Cumberbatch leaning against the fence (yes, I've advanced to sexy, imaginary men to keep me focused on points of reference—grow up, girls). I strolled down the wet concrete blocks between buildings and stepped out on a street sidewalk, but before I exited, I added Lawrence O'Donnell between the buildings (I know Lawrence isn't sexy, but he makes me feel safe and would lead me the right way. Okay, I think Lawrence O'Donnell is sexy—there I said it, smart men are sexy as fuck).

The light from a nearby lamppost revealed a line of women entering the building. My apprehension fell away. I'd made it! I could do this. I could almost hear the calliope music.

I walked into the room and took my place among the hundreds of women gathered.

The meeting got off to a quick start. We talked about outrageous ideas and infiltrating the GOP. We talked about civil disobedience to the point of going to jail.

I smiled. A resistance was on the rise. It gave me the encouragement I needed to stand up and walk to the podium. I adjusted the microphone, and before I knew it, words began tumbling out of my mouth, straight into the ears of the like-minded women among me. I talked about the protection of marriage equality, the environment, and stopping the stormtrooper tactics of "stop and frisk." Heads nodded and hands clapped. Many women came up to me after the meeting, and we exchanged names, phone numbers, and promises to meet up soon.

The next morning, I jumped on the computer and discovered the video of me giving my spiel the night before had gone viral. My hands clasped over my mouth. *Damn*, I thought, *I'm a fat ass!* Then I thought, *Good. Trump hates fat women.* Still . . . *damn!*

I calmed down later in the afternoon, after reconciling that my appearance didn't matter. The resistance did, and it was spreading.

*   *   *

A few weeks later, the neighbors called me over for a get-together. When the lady of the house asked me why she hadn't seen me around, I told her I'd been busy.

"We know," she said. "We saw your protest online. Why are you doing this? Protests won't change anything. They promote violence! We need to come together right now."

I think, I'm in the home of the collaborators in occupied France. I'm the resistance and my neighbor will turn me over to the stormtroopers for sure.

"Protests are the only way things really change," I said. "Think about Martin Luther King Jr. marching on the Mall in the 60's."

"That's different," my neighbor said, shaking her head. "We don't need that march. It's ridiculous. I would have marched with Martin Luther King."

"No, you wouldn't have," I argued. "You wouldn't have seen the value back then, any more than you see it now."

"You're probably right," she said, standing up. "But I don't have time for the things you do." She beamed and walked over to offer me a hug.

Sometimes we fight for those who won't fight for themselves.

*   *   *

My activist group has been on a mission to identify Republican members of Congress who could be swayed to vote with us. We made charts, called, and left messages all over the country. (Did you know there are over five hundred assholes controlling our country? Did you know your state is filled with fat bastards who gerrymander the fuck out of your right to a fair election? With a few exceptions, did you know those same fat bastards affect your life more than the federal government? Well, that's a story for another time.)

Trump behaves like a fast-moving cancer with every appointment and Tweet, but my sisters and I are doing what we can. We have written, called, protested, funded, and supported the resistance against our president-elect and his rhetoric of hate. We now see that if we will get any action out of our elected Utah officials, it will have to be from a public confrontation when they least expect us. Mike Lee blew us off and left us talking to a staffer who was pretty rude about our views. Jason Chaffetz and Mia Love have gone into hiding, and Orrin Hatch is always in Washington, as far as I can tell. But we will find them on a golf course or a restaurant and ask the hard questions. We're hitting the town-hall-style meetings here in force just as the motherfucking paid Tea Party members did back in 2008.

I believe the experiment known as "America" is over, and now it's time that women run the show. My activist group and I have chosen women who will run for office in 2018 and I'm one of them. I'm targeting Mia Love's Congress seat, which is up for play in 2018. If you'd like to learn more, come and meet me. You can find me in Utah, living in the bad part of town, where the wine has screw tops and comes in boxes.

Acknowledgements

THANK YOU TO the authors who had the courage to share their stories with the world.

Special thanks to the following people for their talent and dedication: Suzi "Group Momma" Varga, April Padilla, Amanda Kreklau, Amy Erickson, Meredith Womer, Melissa Bellante, Susan E. Stutz, Lacey Carroll, Afro Bo Peep, Aimee Cook, Rachel Goldstein, Ashley Hultman, Andrea Hultman, Chris Kelly, Shannon Broocks Evans, Jennifer Evans, Melissa Lang, Becky Shampay, Amy Ketchum, Raenette Palmer, Barbara Parsons, Ashley Brincefield, Christy M. Rehm, Sabrina Holley-Williams, Valerie Fulton, Elisheva Offenbacher, Ladan Kadkhoda, Dimi Mestier, Eleanor Trickett, Phoebe Meeton, Erin Brown, Sita Wilson Stukes, Caryn West, Elizabeth Tambascio, Tamica Sears, Katherine "Mom" Phillips, Melissa Lirtsman, and Amy Darabos Curry, Rachel G., Jocelyn R., Logan Perkes, and Takako Price.

Thank you to everyone who has provided moral support to others, and helped guide us through the tougher times.

Thank you to Secretary Hillary Clinton and other public figures who stand up for the rights of all Americans. You are our inspiration.

Thank you to Doug, my love, my LB; Ben and Jeanette P. for allowing me to squirrel away in their home for five days;

my kids, for all the memories we missed because mommy was working (I'll make it up to you); and my co-workers: Gurjeet, Neha, Bhumika, and Kristin (for making every post-election day not so terrible).

And finally, thank you to Cecile Richards and Planned Parenthood for your dedication in providing a wide range of affordable, comprehensive health care services for women across America.